MEN

THE PLAYS A

D0006008

MENANDER, the greatest writer of Attic New Comedy, was born
c.341 BC. He was a pupil of the philosopher Theophrastus and
a companion in military service to another philosopher, Epicurus.
He was also a friend and fellow-pupil of Demetrius of Phalerum,
the anti-democratic governor of Athens from 317 to 307. He wrote
over one hundred plays, which were lost in the seventh and eighth
centuries AD, but numerous fragments and one complete play (*The
Bad-Tempered Man*) were discovered on papyri during the twentieth
century. Largely unsuccessful in competition, Menander enjoyed
more fame after his death than in his lifetime. Frequently quoted by
ancient authors, his plays are set in contemporary Greece, usually
Athens or the surrounding countryside, and his characters became
stock figures in comedy for centuries to come. Through the adaptations of the Roman comic writers Plautus and Terence, Menander
deeply influenced the development of European comedy, notably
Molière, the Restoration dramatists, and Sheridan. Menander died
c.290 BC, reputedly by drowning in the harbour of Piraeus.

MAURICE BALME is the author of several books including the
Oxford Latin Course. He was Head of Classics at Harrow School
for ten years.

PETER BROWN is a Fellow of Trinity College, Oxford and has
published extensively on Greek and Roman comedy.

OXFORD WORLD'S CLASSICS

*For over 100 years Oxford World's Classics have brought
readers closer to the world's great literature. Now with over 700
titles—from the 4,000-year-old myths of Mesopotamia to the
twentieth century's greatest novels—the series makes available
lesser-known as well as celebrated writing.*

*The pocket-sized hardbacks of the early years contained
introductions by Virginia Woolf, T. S. Eliot, Graham Greene,
and other literary figures which enriched the experience of reading.
Today the series is recognized for its fine scholarship and
reliability in texts that span world literature, drama and poetry,
religion, philosophy and politics. Each edition includes perceptive
commentary and essential background information to meet the
changing needs of readers.*

OXFORD WORLD'S CLASSICS

====

MENANDER

The Plays and Fragments

====

Translated with Notes by
MAURICE BALME

With an Introduction by
PETER BROWN

OXFORD
UNIVERSITY PRESS

OXFORD

UNIVERSITY PRESS

Great Clarendon Street, Oxford OX2 6DP

Oxford University Press is a department of the University of Oxford.
It furthers the University's objective of excellence in research, scholarship,
and education by publishing worldwide in

Oxford New York

Auckland Cape Town Dar es Salaam Hong Kong Karachi
Kuala Lumpur Madrid Melbourne Mexico City Nairobi
New Delhi Shanghai Taipei Toronto

With offices in

Argentina Austria Brazil Chile Czech Republic France Greece
Guatemala Hungary Italy Japan Poland Portugal Singapore
South Korea Switzerland Thailand Turkey Ukraine Vietnam

Oxford is a registered trade mark of Oxford University Press
in the UK and in certain other countries

Published in the United States
by Oxford University Press Inc., New York

British Library Cataloguing in Publication Data

Data available

Library of Congress Cataloging in Publication Data
Menander, of Athens.
[Works. English. 2001]
The plays and fragments / Menander; translated with explanatory
notes by Maurice Balme; with an introduction by Peter Brown.
p. cm.
Includes bibliographical references and index.
1. Menander, of Athens—Translations into English. 2. Greek drama
(Comedy)—Translation into English. I. Balme, M. G. II. Title.
PA4246.E4 2001 882'01—dc21 00–050425

ISBN 978–0–19–954073–0

11

Printed and bound in Great Britain by
Clays Ltd, Elcograf S.p.A.

To
The President and Fellows
of
Trinity College Oxford

Contents

Introduction

MENANDER was the founding father of European comedy. From *Ralph Roister Doister* to *What the Butler Saw*, from Fielding to Wodehouse, the stock motifs and characters can be traced back to Menander. For the most part, his influence has been indirect, since texts of his plays ceased to circulate in the seventh or eighth century AD; after that, the Latin adaptations by Plautus and Terence were widely read, but Menander himself appeared to have been lost for ever. He was rediscovered in the twentieth century, in texts written on papyrus and preserved by the climate of Egypt, and almost everything contained in this volume was unknown 100 years ago. Even now, it has been calculated that we have perhaps 8 per cent of Menander's total output. But we have one complete play, and substantial portions of several others, and are thus able to form some impression of the skills for which he was famous in antiquity. Like a true comic heroine, Comedy herself has finally been reunited with her father, after some twelve centuries of separation.

Menander lived and worked in Athens at the end of the fourth and beginning of the third century BC; almost certainly, he was born in 342/341 and died at the age of 52 in 291/290. His first play was produced in 321, and in the next thirty years he wrote perhaps 108 plays—an astonishing rate of productivity, but not unparalleled for a Greek comic poet. The one surviving play that is securely dated is the most complete, *Dyskolos* (316), rediscovered in the late 1950s. We are told that Menander's style matured noticeably in the course of his career,[1] but we can only make our own judgement about the relative maturity of the other texts that we possess; some contain references that have been taken to provide a clue to their date, but there are no firm indications. In this volume no attempt has been made to arrange the plays in

---

[1] Plutarch, *Mor.* 853f (in his *Comparison between Aristophanes and Menander*).

chronological order; instead they are printed in descending order
of completeness of what has survived. As it happens, this means
that the first in the book is one of the earliest that Menander
wrote.

Plays at Athens were performed in the Theatre of Dionysos, on
the south slope of the Acropolis, at two great annual dramatic
festivals, the Lenaia in January and the Dionysia in March. Since
a comic playwright competed at each festival with one play only, a
substantial proportion of Menander's output must have been first
performed in theatres elsewhere in Attica, perhaps even in other
parts of the Greek world altogether. It has been guessed that plays
set somewhere other than Athens (such as *Perikeiromene*, set in
Corinth) may have been written for performance in the place
where they are set. But there was no necessary link between
setting and place of performance: *Dyskolos*, set at Phyle in a remote
part of Attica, was put on in Athens, where indeed it won first
prize at the Lenaia. Menander won the first prize at Athens only
eight times, and later it became something of a commonplace that
posterity appreciated him more than his contemporaries had
done. But it was not usual for playwrights to do much better than
this, and he does at least seem to have been acknowledged as one
of the leading playwrights of his day. A statue of him by two sons
of Praxiteles was set up in the Theatre of Dionysos shortly after his
death; this was copied in a large number of busts and other forms
of representation that have survived in various parts of the Greek
world.[2] His plays continued to be acted, and their texts to be read,
for about 1,000 years. For a long time, as far as we can tell, he was
more popular than Aristophanes. But something happened to
change this preference, and it was Aristophanes whose plays (or
some of them) survived the 'Dark Ages' and acquired a medieval
manuscript tradition. A number of reasons have been suggested
for this decline in Menander's popularity: although his plays
(unlike those of Aristophanes) contain barely any obscenity, they
may have been judged more deeply corrupting because their
plots include stories of rape, seduction and prostitution; or
Aristophanes may have been preferred because he was thought to

---

[2] See G. M. A. Richter, *The Portraits of the Greeks* (London, 1965), 224–36, with figs.
1514–1643; P. Zanker, *The Mask of Socrates* (California, 1995), 77–83.

preserve the Attic Greek dialect at a purer stage of its development, or else because his plays contain more topical references that needed to be explained to later readers, thus giving scholars a chance to show off. Any one of these factors may have played a part.

Athens by the time of Menander had ceased to be a major power; like the rest of the Greek world, she became a pawn in the struggle for supremacy between the generals of Alexander the Great after Alexander's death in 323, though her fortunes were also affected by her own internal struggles and rivalries, with an alternation of democratic and oligarchic constitutions, and a succession of rulers who were more or less tyrannical in practice, whatever the nature of the constitution over which they presided. Many of the details are obscure, but it is clear that there were several bloody upheavals in the course of Menander's lifetime. The two key figures were both called Demetrios: the Athenian Demetrios of Phaleron, who presided over an oligarchic constitution from 317 to 307, with Macedonian backing; and the Macedonian Demetrios nicknamed Poliorketes ('Besieger of Cities'), who was welcomed with open arms as the restorer of democracy in 307 and controlled the city until 301 and again (though more consistently at a distance, and less consistently as a democracy) from 295 to 287. This Demetrios had himself and his father Antigonos proclaimed kings of Athens, and he displayed many of the vices traditionally associated with autocratic rule. But it is from the first period of his control that we have a few fragments of comedy referring openly (and sometimes scathingly) to political events and personalities—a great rarity in what survives of the comedies written while Menander was active, and a sign that Demetrios' restoration of democracy did something to restore briefly the democratic spirit that had been manifest in the comedy of earlier generations.[3]

Although not active politically, Menander could not be unaffected. Among other things, he and Demetrios of Phaleron had studied philosophy together and remained on friendly terms; when Demetrios was expelled in 307, Menander was lucky not to

---

[3] For this paragraph, see C. Habicht, *Athens from Alexander to Antony* (Harvard, 1997), chs. 2 and 3.

suffer the same fate. But his plays reflect practically nothing of the violent events that he and his audience witnessed. Act 4 of *Sikyonios* opens with a furious argument between a democrat and an oligarch, but as far as we can judge it is conducted in terms that do not tie it to any particular events outside the play. Demeas and Nikeratos on their return home in Act 1 of *Samia* express affectionate pride in Athens, apparently at 101–4 combined with a certain anxiety; if there was a topical point, its sharpness is somewhat blunted by its combination with traditional comic abuse of a sluggish attendant and jokes at the expense of Byzantium and the Black Sea region. Some have heard an echo of recent events in Knemon's claim at *Dyskolos* 743–5: 'if all men behaved like me, | Law-courts would exist no longer, men would no more haul each other | Off to prison' (since a notorious treason trial had taken place in the theatre itself only two years previously), but the reference is general, and the echo is faint. Like much great literature, the plays focus on the personal relationships of fictional individuals. Citizenship is important to them, above all for its connection with legitimate marriage and the continuation of the citizen stock; the exercise of political rights seems not to interest them.

One sphere in which Athens remained supreme was drama, and perhaps comedy above all. Playwrights and actors came to Athens from all over the Greek-speaking world, and Athenian comedies were exported to every corner of that world. By no means all plays were written for first production there, as we have seen, but all comedy aspired to be Athenian comedy; if there were local differences of style, we are in no position to detect them. The social stratifications appear to be the same wherever the play is set, and citizenship seems to be important in just the same ways whether the characters are Athenian or Corinthian. Inevitably, we interpret Menander as an Athenian dramatist writing for an Athenian audience; he surely aimed to please them first and foremost with the majority of his plays, and to win prizes at their festivals. But he had an international audience as well, and it is not hard to see why his comedies had (and have) such universal appeal: whatever the specific details of their setting, the presentation of characters, situations, and relationships is true to universal elements of human experience.

Of course Menander did not create his style of comedy from nothing. When he began writing, comedies had been performed at the Dionysia at Athens for well over 150 years, and at the Lenaia for some 120 years. Probably five comedies were produced each year at each festival, a total of 1,400 or so before Menander's first. Of these, the only complete plays we possess are eleven by Aristophanes written between 425 and 388 (*Dyskolos* is the only other complete Greek comedy that we possess at all). It is conventional to divide Greek comedy into three periods, the Old Comedy of the time of Aristophanes, the New Comedy of Menander's generation, and the Middle Comedy that came between these two. Like all such classifications, this division doubtless obscures almost as much as it illuminates, but it was probably first proposed soon after Menander's lifetime in acknowledgement of the fact that he and his contemporaries had developed a distinctively new style. There are elements of continuity as well (such as the door-knocking scene in Act 3 of *Dyskolos*, which can be traced back to *Acharnians*, Aristophanes' first surviving play), but we can certainly see differences between the comic styles of Menander and Aristophanes, even if the intervening period is less clear to us.

Aristophanes, unlike Menander, regularly does refer to contemporary politicians and political events; indeed, he sometimes makes them central to his plays. But his treatment of them is fantastic and unrealistic, and he writes in an exuberant and varied style; there is also a large musical element, and a prominent part for a chorus. In Menander, some sections (such as the closing scene of *Dyskolos*) had instrumental accompaniment, but there is much less music altogether, and the chorus has been reduced to performing a song-and-dance routine between the acts (also, comedy has acquired a standard five-act structure which it did not previously possess). His style is less exuberant, and his plots are more elegantly constructed, with more attention to consistency of characterization. Two of the greatest differences from Aristophanes are that love (always heterosexual) is a central ingredient, and comic irony a central type of humour: his characters are constantly at cross-purposes, or in despair, for reasons that the audience can see to be based on ignorance and misunderstanding.

(Love is by no means the only ingredient—Menander excels at the sympathetic portrayal of many kinds of relationship—but it is normally at least part of the plot to show love triumphing over obstacles of one kind or another.) Menander's plays include a number of stock characters such as the boastful soldier and toadying parasite (both in *Kolax*), and a number of stock situations such as the rediscovery of a daughter who had been abandoned or kidnapped in childhood (for instance in *Perikeiromene*). This type of story-pattern clearly has universal appeal, and it has exercised a strong hold on the imagination of subsequent generations. It was Greek New Comedy that put it on the map.

As well as being heir to a long-standing comic tradition, Menander was much influenced by Athenian tragedy, particularly the plays of Euripides. Indeed, stories of rape, abandonment of babies, and subsequent recognition had tragic prototypes, as is drawn to our attention by Syros in Act 2 of *Epitrepontes*, and Euripides was famous for having developed such plots.[4] The influence is most obvious in the highly stylized recognition-scene in Act 4 of *Perikeiromene*, or in the lengthy messenger-speech in Act 4 of *Sikyonios*, which we can see to be modelled on a similar speech in Euripides' *Orestes* (though the style of Menander's speech is for the most part not high-flown). But tragedy is explicitly quoted or referred to at a number of other points, for example in Onesimos' teasing of Smikrines in Act 5 of *Epitrepontes*, or in Demeas' attempt to calm Nikeratos down at the end of Act 4 of *Samia*. The arbitration-scene in *Epitrepontes* is a particularly interesting example: not only does Syros at 325 ff. explicitly refer to tragedy as providing relevant parallels to the situation the characters are in, but the entire context and structure of this particular scene were apparently modelled on a scene in Euripides' *Alope* (now lost); there too the man arbitrating a dispute over some jewellery that had been found together with an exposed baby was (though neither he nor the disputants realized it) the grandfather of the baby itself. We do not know of any verbal echoes of that play in Menander's scene, and we cannot tell whether he took for granted that his audience would see the

---

[4] Satyros, *Life of Euripides*, fr. 39 VII (probably 3rd cent. BC): 'These things form the subject matter of New Comedy, and Euripides brought them to perfection.'

similarity, or reckoned that it did not matter if they missed it. Altogether, Menander's use of tragic models is one of his more enigmatic features. Is it simply ludicrous that a slave like Syros appeals to tragic plots, or does it invite us to take the scene more seriously? What are we to make of the recognition-scene in *Perikeiromene*, where father and daughter (on being reunited after many years of separation) address one another in the manner of tragedy for over thirty lines of text? Does the tragic manner make the dialogue more intense and moving, or is Menander mocking the conventions of what had become a hackneyed type of scene? Should we be close to tears at this point, or helpless with laughter? That will depend on the performers, just as it depends on them whether we are amused, moved, or outraged by *Così fan Tutte*. There cannot be one correct interpretation, and this point applies also to scenes without such clear tragic colouring (and to other operas by Mozart): where irony is the prevailing mode, we never know how to strike the balance between sympathy and laughter.

Sometimes the comic effect of tragic allusions is more obvious, above all in the farcical scene at the beginning of Act 3 of *Aspis* where Daos declaims in tragic style, quotes relevant lines from tragedy, and comments on how good they are—a ludicrous way to persuade Smikrines that his brother has been struck down by an illness and appears to be dying. We are inevitably reminded that we are watching an actor in a play, and that the part he is playing is that of someone putting on an act. In general, when we laugh at a comic situation, we are aware that it has been set up for us by the dramatist, and by his actors. Reference to its sister genre is one way in which comedy can entertain us by drawing attention to this fact.

The plays were written for performance in the open air by an all-male company of masked actors; they must have been virtuoso performers, not only taking female parts as required, but capable of imitating a succession of different voices in set-piece mono-logues such as that of Demeas in Act 3 of *Samia* or of Eleusinios in Act 4 of *Sikyonios*. They also had to command the attention of a very large audience: the Theatre of Dionysos at Athens could hold as many as 17,000, and even the smaller theatres elsewhere often had a capacity of well over 1,000. By today's standards, this was not intimate theatre, however much Menander's texts might seem to suggest otherwise. The wearing of masks was traditional on the Greek stage, and this too must have affected the style of presentation. The texts refer to facial expressions which may sometimes have been shown in the masks but must more often have been conveyed by voice, gesture and body-movement; in large open-air theatres the gestures may have been quite grand.

We have some idea what the masks looked like, since a large number of terracotta statuettes and imitation masks has been discovered, most notably in excavations on the island of Lipari (north of Sicily) in the second half of the twentieth century.[5] A great deal of the material found there (several hundred items) must date from the first half of the third century BC, immediately after Menander's lifetime; there is even a portrait-mask of Menander, based on the statue erected at Athens. Similar material, mostly of later date, has been found in many areas that had been colonized by Greeks; and this material forms a large part of our evidence for the widespread popularity of Athenian comedy. Some of the terracottas correspond closely with the descriptions in the list of 44 'masks of New Comedy' by Julius Pollux (second century AD),[6] and there clearly came to be a more or less standard repertoire of masks. It has even been suggested that particular masks were attached to particular names and that in some sense the same character was seen to appear in play after play with the same name and mask. On the whole, the evidence of the texts does not support this: the various slaves called Daos, for instance, seem to have very little in common beyond their name and status.

The audience was seated in a raked semicircle or horseshoe round an area known as the *orchestra* ('dancing-floor'), where by tradition the chorus sang and danced. In the fifth century the chorus had been an active participant in the drama; by Menander's time, as noted above, its sole function was to perform

---

[5] See L. B. Brea, *Menandro e il teatro greco nelle terracotte liparesi* (Genoa, 1981, sumptuously illustrated); and, for a detailed survey of the entire range of relevant artefacts, including mosaics and wall-paintings that illustrate scenes from some of Menander's plays, T. B. L. Webster, *Monuments Illustrating New Comedy*, 3rd edn. revised and enlarged by J. R. Green and A. Seeberg (London, 1995).

[6] *Onom.* 4. 143–54.

in the interludes between acts. The arrival of the chorus is regularly announced at the end of the first act, when a character remarks that it is advisable to get out of the way as a drunken group is approaching (a reminder that Dionysos, the patron god of the Athenian theatre, was also the god of wine); at the other three act-breaks there is no reference to the chorus in the text of the play, only the word 'Chorus' written between the acts in the papyrus texts. We have no idea what the chorus performed in these interludes, but there is no reason to think that it had any connection with the events of the play. Nor do we know whether the chorus stayed (somehow unobtrusive) in the *orchestra* during the subsequent acts or left and returned. If it was still there during the final act, it may have taken part in some kind of procession at the end.

At Athens, the diameter of the *orchestra* was about twenty metres. Beyond it, the spectators saw the wall of a building of the same width or more, with doorways in it representing (normally) the doors of houses. The setting of New Comedy is regularly the space in front of two houses; the area directly in front of the wall can be imagined as the street on to which the houses face. Characters come and go through the doors of the houses, or along the street, which is represented as leading off left and right towards whatever off-stage location the text invites us to imagine (typically, the harbour, or the main square, or the countryside). Characters entering from the side can be seen approaching from a distance. (*Dyskolos* is unusual in showing the entrance to the shrine of Pan and the Nymphs as well as the houses of Knemon and Gorgias. There was such a shrine at Phyle, where it was in fact a cave in a steep rock face in the side of a gorge, 'a holy place exceedingly well known', as Pan says at the beginning of the prologue. But Menander has relocated this well-known shrine, placing it between two houses, with a road running in front of it. Doubtless in the theatre the entrance to the shrine was decorated in some way to show that it was a cave and not a house, but we do not know how elaborate such decoration is likely to have been.)

The setting stays the same throughout each play; conversations that might have been expected to take place indoors in fact take place in the street in front of the house, or they are reported to the audience by a character who has overheard them indoors. Similarly, important events which have taken place off-stage are reported to the audience or to other characters on-stage. (Conventions such as these are found throughout ancient drama.) Some characters establish a particularly close relationship with the audience, informing them what they plan to do next as they leave the stage, and bringing them up to date with their progress on their return; sometimes they address the audience explicitly, not so much breaking the dramatic illusion as drawing the audience into their world.

It has been widely assumed that the area representing the street was the performing area for the actors (other than the chorus), with the *orchestra* between them and those spectators who sat most directly in front of them. In the fifth and fourth centuries this area may even have been covered by a platform or stage raised slightly above the level of the *orchestra* (though this, like almost everything to do with the Athenian theatre, is much debated). From the late fourth century onwards it became normal in Greek theatres for the actors to perform on a stage raised significantly above ground level, with the result that fewer spectators looked down on them from above. Some scholars think that the Theatre of Dionysos at Athens had been rebuilt in this way shortly before Menander began writing, and that he wrote his plays for performance on a stage three to four metres deep, twenty metres wide, raised some four metres above the ground. But this would be a cramped area for a play with as much lively action as *Dyskolos*; those who argue for this tend to represent Menander's comedies as being far more static than they in fact are. It seems more likely that the Theatre of Dionysos was not remodelled until later.

The theatre was dedicated to Dionysos, and the dramatic festivals were religious festivals held in his honour. Menander's plays often contain a traditional religious element, namely a prologue spoken by a deity who controls the action, but this does not make them profound explorations of the human condition. The prologues of *Perikeiromene* and *Aspis* are put in the mouths of Misapprehension and Chance respectively. These two goddesses can be seen as the controlling forces of Greek New Comedy altogether: misunderstandings bring characters close to disaster, or plans conceived in ignorance of the full truth lead them into ever deeper water, but Chance comes to their aid just in time; or Chance herself creates confusion and complication in their lives but then steers events towards a happy conclusion.[7] The function of the prologues is partly to explain the true facts to the audience, partly to reassure them that all will turn out well; they do not by any means give away the whole plot in advance, but they enable the audience to savour the irony of many situations by providing information that is not available to the characters themselves. The contrast between appearance and reality is a central theme of Menander's plays, and the prologues play a part in helping the audience to appreciate it. They also help to give shape to what might otherwise seem a series of unlikely coincidences, leading us to feel that there is a force controlling the events of the play and steering them in a particular direction. To some extent, these prologue-speakers can be seen as a metaphor for the playwright himself. Admittedly, they are represented as goddesses. There was a long tradition of deifying abstract forces in Greek religion, and Chance was worshipped as a goddess in Menander's lifetime, just as Pan (who speaks the prologue of *Dyskolos*) was worshipped as a god. Pan's control of events in *Dyskolos* is very similar to that of Chance in *Aspis*, and the characters themselves worship at his shrine; indeed his shrine is constantly before our eyes, and his control of events is symbolized by the fact that we see character after character go into it—by the end of the play, that is where almost every one of them is to be found. But Pan was not a solemn god, and we should not be solemn about what this element contributes to the plays. The divine forces function as agents of poetic justice; they are there to reassure the audience that all will turn out as it should. We cannot always name the god or goddess who spoke the prologue of other plays, but it is sometimes certain and often probable that there was one; *Samia* is so far the only play by Menander that we know not to have had a divine prologue-speaker. But the actions of the characters remain entirely explicable in human terms. The prologue to *Perikeiromene* might seem to imply an unusual degree of divine intervention when it says (164–5) 'He's not like this by nature but I led | Him on, to start the

---

[7] Cf. p. 274, the third fragment from *Hypobolimaios*.

revelations'; but this too is a reassuring hint for the spectator, and we have no difficulty in taking it to mean that Polemon acted with uncharacteristic violence because he was ignorant of the true situation.

Typically, Menander delays the divine prologue to follow the opening scene; *Dyskolos* is so far the one certain exception to this. Menander is a master of the attention-grabbing opening that intrigues his audience before offering an explanation. Thus, for instance, *Epitrepontes* opens with a question that throws us right into the middle of an unexpected situation: Charisios married only recently, but he has now started relations with a prostitute. *Aspis* opens with the arrival of a number of foreign captives and a considerable amount of booty, together with a slave carrying a battered shield and lamenting the death of its owner—a strange way for a comedy to start. *Perikeiromene* may well have begun with Glykera rushing on to the stage immediately after her hair had been cut off. (On *Misoumenos*, see below.)

These opening scenes introduce us to an aspect of Menander's comedy that has not always been appreciated: it is often very *lively*, both verbally and in terms of the action presented. *Dyskolos* in particular is full of comic action, and it contains much coming and going, often at some speed. Knemon is presented in the first part of the play as a monstrously antisocial recluse whose instinctive reaction to his fellow creatures is to shout at them, throw things at them, and even bite them. Sostratos' passion for Knemon's daughter makes him quite restless and impatient: there is no risk that he would lose her if he took more time, but he is determined to allow no delay. Before the play begins, he has sent his slave Pyrrhias to make contact with her father; one of the first things we see in Act I is Pyrrhias fleeing from this encounter, running at top speed on to the stage to escape from Knemon, who began by throwing things at him but now follows at some distance behind. This makes a wonderful build-up for Knemon's entry, and his opening words do not disappoint, as he expresses the wish that he could be like Perseus: if he had wings he could fly in the air and avoid all contact with humans, and if he had the Gorgon's head he could turn those who annoyed him into stone. ('I wish I had that gift! Then there would be | No shortage of stone statues

everywhere!') As the play progresses, we come to see that there
are reasons for Knemon's strange behaviour; but the explanation
is delayed. This both serves to intrigue us, making us wonder what
reasons there could possibly be, and enables us to enjoy his
extreme presentation in an uncomplicated way—for instance in
Act 3, where first a slave and then a cook knock at his door and
ask to borrow a stewing pot, each in turn being driven violently
away. Menander gives considerable space to this traditional
comic scene exactly at the mid-point of the play, making it central
to his presentation of his main character. The point is underlined
when the slave and the cook treat us to a repeat performance in
Act 5; now it is part of their punishment of Knemon for his anti-
social behaviour, but this time it is they who exaggerate in
demanding the loan of a ludicrous series of items: several pans
and trays, seven tripods, twelve tables, nine rugs, 'eastern linen
curtains | One hundred feet in length', and a large bronze bowl
for mixing the wine. By this stage of the play, Knemon has had a
chance to explain himself to the audience; but Menander makes
the play end on a note of riotous entertainment. Julius Caesar
complained that Terence's Latin adaptations of Menander lacked
'force' (*vis*);[8] we can see why he found this to be characteristic of
Menander, even if some may be surprised that he thought it
absent from Terence.

Another type of humour prominent in *Dyskolos* is the comedy to
be extracted from a series of apparent failures, and, linked to
this, the setting up of expectations that are defeated. Pyrrhias'
encounter with Knemon is a total failure. On learning of it,
Chaireas, the next person Sostratos has turned to for help, beats a
hasty retreat. Sostratos himself is so terrified on meeting Knemon
in Act 1 that he pretends he just happens to have arranged to meet
someone in the area—although in fact it is Sostratos' one aim to
make contact with him and ask to marry his daughter. Sostratos'
next thought is to turn for help to another slave, Getas: he goes
home to consult him, only to find that Getas is not there. He then
goes to work in the fields, in the hope that Knemon will see him
and be impressed; but Knemon is detained at home and never

---

[8] See the epigram quoted by Suetonius, *Life of Terence* 7 (in E. Courtney, *The Fragmentary Latin Poets* (Oxford, 1993), p. 153).

sees him at work. Finally, he is presented a golden opportunity when Knemon falls down the well in his courtyard and Sostratos has a chance to share in his rescue—but he is so excited to find himself standing next to the girl he loves that he is quite unable to concentrate on the matter in hand: several times he lets go of the rope on which he ought to be pulling Knemon to safety, thereby all but killing the very man he most needs to impress. The natural conclusion to the play is that he should get his girl, and the obvious obstacle for him to overcome is Knemon's misanthropy; but it seems that everything he tries is doomed to failure, mainly through a combination of his own feebleness and Knemon's unapproachability. In this way the audience is kept guessing how the happy ending is ever to be achieved. The ultimate outcome is predictable—it is unthinkable that Sostratos will not finally marry Knemon's daughter, and also unthinkable that Knemon will not in some way be forced to come to terms with society; Menander's skill lies in making it impossible to see how these things are to happen, and in giving the impression that Sostratos has made no progress in three and a half acts. There is an obvious analogy with detective stories: we expect the murderer to be identified by the end, but this is more satisfying if we feel we are getting no nearer to the truth until very shortly before the end. We can see Menander playing this kind of sophisticated game with his audience already at this early stage of his career.

Expectations were also set up for the audience by their knowledge of comic traditions. Professional cooks appeared in many comedies; they were hired to supply and prepare the food for special occasions, and they tended traditionally to boast at length of their culinary skills and inventiveness. It was thus an effect to show Sikon on his first entry in *Dyskolos* (towards the end of Act 2) not boasting but admitting that he is unable to control the sheep he is bringing to be cooked for dinner. (Unfortunately we do not know how the sheep was portrayed.) Similarly, our first view of the cook in *Aspis* shows him leaving the house that had hired him, complaining that something always happens to make his employers cancel their contracts with him. Perhaps Menander's most striking use of this technique is in his presentation of soldiers, another traditionally boastful stock type. Fragments 2–4 of *Kolax* show us what the audience probably expected, and they also show that Menander did not always disdain to give it to them. But in three of the plays in this volume (*Misoumenos*, *Perikeiromeme*, *Sikyonios*) the soldier is sympathetically portrayed as the young lover who ends up marrying his girl. The opening scene of *Misoumenos* must have been particularly effective: it was probably clear at first sight that the character on stage was a mercenary soldier; all the more surprising, then, that he presents himself at some length in the words of the text as a man unhappy in love who declines to force himself on the woman he loves although he bought her as a prisoner of war sold into slavery. This is one of those delicate effects on which Menander's reputation has chiefly rested.

There is nothing so delicate in the portrayal of the cook in *Dyskolos*, nor does that play include a soldier. But it is tempting to think that Menander is playing yet further with his audience's expectations towards the end of Act i when he makes Sostratos say 'Getas, my father's slave, | Suppose I go to him? By heaven, I shall. | Yes, he's a ball of fire, experienced | In every kind of thing. He'll drive away | All the old man's bad temper, I'm quite sure.' Particularly in the Latin adaptations of Plautus and Terence, the plot is sometimes dominated by the clever slave who comes up with schemes to help his young master's love life (the ancestor of a long line of loyal servants culminating in Jeeves, who plays on the tradition by exercising much ingenuity in helping his young master to remain unattached); but Plautus in particular has clearly enhanced and enlarged the presentation of this character, and it has been debated whether the slaves are likely to have played so prominent a part in the Greek originals he was adapting (which we still do not possess, for the most part). However, Sostratos' remark here would be all the more effective if Menander's audience had already come to expect a household slave to be 'a ball of fire, experienced | In every kind of thing', and the natural ally of the boy in love; that would sharpen their surprise on learning that the boy did not even find the slave at home. Furthermore, other plays by Menander show the slave as a schemer, even if we cannot date them relative to *Dyskolos*. In *Aspis* it is Daos' scheme that drives the action in the central section of the play. Even from the scanty remains of *Perinthia*, it is clear that Daos' boast that he could easily trick his elderly master was a significant element in that play. Finally, in the one case where we can compare Plautus' text with the Greek original that he was adapting, we cannot doubt that *Dis Exapaton* (the model for Plautus' *Bacchides*) is named after the exploits of the slave Syros, who succeeds in tricking his elderly master a second time in one day, even after his first deception has been betrayed to his master; he tricks him out of some money to help his master's son conduct an affair with a prostitute. Details in the papyrus remains of *Dis Exapaton* show that his trick in the first part of the play was to tell his master exactly the same story as Plautus makes him tell in *Bacchides*, and that this trick was betrayed to his master in exactly the same way. Plautus may well have made the slave's trickery even more the focus of attention than it had been in Menander's play, but it must have been a major element of the Greek play as well. We cannot tell how much of a pioneer Menander was in this, but we can at least see that Greek comedy gave the lead to Plautus and Terence.

In the plays that survive best, however, the overall effect of the slave's presentation is quite different from that of Plautus' more outrageous and unscrupulous slaves. Daos in *Aspis* has remained astonishingly loyal to the Athenian household in which he serves. Finding himself in Rhodes in sole possession of a considerable amount of war booty, and believing his Athenian master to have been killed on the battlefield, he has not taken the opportunity to abscond with the loot and return home to Phrygia, but has brought everything back to Athens. The strangeness of this is even drawn to his and our attention by the Waiter at 239–41: 'All this gold you had | And slaves, and yet you've come and brought them back | For master? And you didn't run away? From where | Do you come then?' But Daos is not unique: Menander's slaves have often absorbed the values of their masters, as we see for instance in the complaints of another Daos at the end of Act 1 of *Dyskolos*, when he criticizes Knemon for failing to protect his daughter as he should; and at the end of *Dyskolos* it is the slave Getas, together with the cook Sikon, who forces Knemon to be less antisocial in his behaviour. The slave on p. 279 who says

'Often a slave who has | An honest character is wiser than | His master. And if Fortune has enslaved | His body, yet his mind still remains free' is not complaining about his station in life but underlining his loyalty and his eagerness to help his master. It is interesting to speculate why the slave came to be so prominent in this type of comedy. Part of the answer probably lies in his link with plots of deception: even in a noble cause such as the deception of Smikrines in *Aspis*, it would perhaps have seemed beneath the dignity of an Athenian citizen to be seen to take the initiative in devising such a scheme as Daos comes up with in Act 2; and similarly in Act 2 of *Dyskolos* it is Daos at 366 ff. who suggests that Sostratos should work in the fields and thus lead Knemon to think that he is a farmer without means. In *Epitrepontes* it may be a new twist that the effective schemer is not the male slave Onesimos but the slave prostitute Habrotonon, who at 468–70 expresses her outrage at the idea that a child entitled to Athenian citizenship might be brought up as a slave.

This portrayal of slaves clearly has the potential to raise some awkward questions in the minds of the audience (which consisted overwhelmingly, and perhaps exclusively, of male citizens). Daos in *Aspis* not only takes the initiative in scheming against Smikrines, but he organizes some perfectly respectable Athenian citizens to take part in the deception, and his quick-wittedness and resolve are contrasted with their slowness and hopelessness. This might seem provocative, on a grand civic occasion. Similarly, the treatment of Chrysis in *Samia* (who is a free woman but a foreigner) has the potential to set the audience thinking about the vulnerability of those on the fringes of its society, since Demeas can throw her out of his house without a word of explanation; and Moschion's moralizing about legitimacy and character at *Samia* 140–2 could provoke thoughts about another of society's barriers, however much we may smile at his deviousness in arguing this case in this context. In *Dyskolos*, it is the barriers between rich and poor that might seem to be called into question. It would indeed be a complacent spectator who had no such thoughts on seeing these plays, but Menander seems to be appealing to a common humanity, not aiming to inflame revolutionary passions. Far from pleading for radical social or political reform, the plays end by accepting the status quo. Habrotonon probably secured her freedom at the end of *Epitrepontes*; but emancipation was always possible within the system, and in her case it was a reward for helping a citizen family—there is no suggestion that it was wrong to enslave her in the first place. Chrysis helps two citizen households in *Samia*, at considerable risk to her own position; but in the final act her return to Demeas' home is simply accepted without comment, and the play ends as it began with the focus on the citizen father and son. Charisios in Act 4 of *Epitrepontes* acknowledges that he has applied double standards in his treatment of his wife, in a monologue which may well have been his first appearance in the play—a master-stroke of presentation, if so, since the state of his marriage has been the main focus of attention since the play's opening words. But he evidently thinks his own action in raping a woman was no worse than hers in being raped: he speaks of 'My wife who'd had the same | Misfortune', and he imagines a divine power addressing him and saying 'I'll show you that | You've stumbled just the way she did'—simply by being the parent of an illegitimate child, presumably. Menander's all-male audience would probably not have been surprised: they would have accepted that drunkenness and lust were irresistible impulses, and if they thought at all about the degree of force involved they probably regarded it more as reflecting well on Pamphile than badly on Charisios.[9] They may also have accepted it without qualms as a standard element of a dramatic plot, on a par with exposure at birth and kidnapping in childhood: these things all happened in real life, but perhaps not quite as often as comedy seems to suggest. Their function in the plays is to create complications that we know will be resolved, and the audience is glad to see Charisios and Pamphile happily reunited at the end of the play. Modern readers are bound to be disappointed that Charisios'

---

[9] See K. F. Pierce, 'The Portrayal of Rape in New Comedy', in S. Deacy and K. F. Pierce (eds.), *Rape in Antiquity* (London, 1997), 163–84, at p. 166: 'For the purposes of New Comedy it is apparently preferable that a "respectable" woman should be raped rather than seduced. Physically her honour may have been defiled but mentally she remained pure. To portray an Athenian girl being seduced would perhaps have reduced her respectability in the eyes of the audience. Paradoxically we find that the force of rape, as is so often illustrated by the torn clothing of the victim, emphasises the respectability of the woman raped.'

insight is so limited, and some are disappointed altogether by Menander's lack of radicalism. But mild irony can often be a more effective stimulus to thought than passionate preaching.

Menander's plays would never have become so popular if they were simply clever entertainments. A century after his death, Menander was declared by the great scholar Aristophanes of Byzantium to rank second only to Homer as a poet; in particular, Aristophanes found Menander's character portrayal so true to life that he was moved to ask 'Menander and life, which of you imitated which?' This should not lead us to think that he simply holds a mirror up to life; his plays also reflect and refract dramatic traditions that had built up over 150 years, as the above pages have tried to show. But they are rooted in the realities of everyday life, and they provide invaluable evidence for social, legal, and religious practices and attitudes, and even for everyday patterns of speech (though they are written in verse, like all ancient drama with any literary pretension).[10] They also reflect habits of philosophical thought that were current in Menander's day; Menander had studied under Aristotle's successor Theophrastos, and it is tempting to see the influence of Aristotle in many of his character studies—though it does not follow that he uses his plays to advocate the doctrines of a particular philosophical school.[11] By today's standards, Menander's presentation of characters may sometimes not seem very profound: the plays are short, and there is little exploration of the influences that have made the characters what they are. But this does not prevent the audience from finding them subtle and convincing, and above all (perhaps) from feeling that they react to situations in a believable way.

Samia is particularly successful in combining lively humour with psychological insight. Demeas comes to think that Chrysis has seduced his son Moschion and had a baby by him while Demeas was abroad on a long trip. The suspicion is entirely false, but Demeas has good reasons to believe it—indeed, on the evidence before him, it is inevitable that he will believe it. He decides to

---

[10] Two recent studies that have used Menander to excellent effect are A. C. Scafuro, *The Forensic Stage: Settling Disputes in Graeco-Roman New Comedy* (Cambridge, 1997), and E. Dickey, *Greek Forms of Address* (Oxford, 1996).

[11] For some judicious remarks on this vexed question, see R. L. Hunter, *The New Comedy of Greece and Rome* (Cambridge, 1985), 147–51.

throw Chrysis out of his house, but he persuades himself that it would be better not to explain why he is doing so. In two great monologues in Act 3, at the centre of the play, we see him coming to terms with what he has seen and heard, drawing the inevitable conclusion, and deciding to expel Chrysis. For him, this is a dreadful situation: he loves Chrysis, and he also loves his son; he tries to weigh up the evidence calmly and rationally, but his brooding drives him to a frenzy. As we watch him, we are bound to feel a certain detached superiority, because we know that he is wrong, and we know we are watching a comedy—the situation is sure to be resolved happily in the end. On the other hand, we can see all too clearly how and why he has gone astray; any one of us in his situation would have come to the same conclusion. It is for his son's sake that he decides to keep his reasons to himself. It is also for the sake of the plot, of course, because the play would end too soon if the truth were explained to him at this stage; but his behaviour flows naturally from his character, and from the sort of relationship he has with Moschion.

Samia does not have any particular moral, beyond the obvious moral that it is better to tell people straight out if you suspect them of something. The relationship between Demeas and Moschion is subtly portrayed, but it is not held up as a model. The events of the play give us something to think about, simply by showing people reacting to each other in certain ways; family relationships concern nearly all of us, so we cannot help being interested. However, there is also much scope for laughter, particularly in Act 4, when Demeas finds himself forced (or so he thinks) to explain his suspicions to his next-door neighbour Nikeratos. Nikeratos had taken Chrysis into his own house at the end of Act 3, when Demeas had thrown her out; he now decides that he himself should expel her, goes indoors to do so, but finds—horror of horrors!—that his own daughter is breast-feeding the baby that Chrysis has brought with her (because, of course, it was Nikeratos' daughter who had given birth to the baby, not Chrysis at all). The fun becomes fast and furious, as Nikeratos runs in and out of his house, coming out to report what he has seen to Demeas and then rushing back in again. Finally, we see Chrysis running out of the house, clutching the baby, with Nikeratos in hot pursuit. Demeas has to struggle with Nikeratos to restrain him, while he tells Chrysis to run back into his house. The sight of Chrysis and the baby is a strong visual element, a visible reminder of the way Demeas drove her out of his house in the previous act; now she is seen running from the house next door, once again the victim of an angry Athenian citizen, and Demeas lets her back in because in the meantime he has learnt the truth. We could reflect at this point on the vulnerability of Chrysis, and we could also think about the effects of anger. But we do not really have time to think at all, because the action moves so quickly and we are too busy laughing. Everything still flows from the essentially believable reactions of the characters to the situation they find themselves in; but Menander would surely have agreed with Woody Allen: 'Primarily I want the audience to laugh. If they laugh and don't think, then I'm successful; if they laugh and think, then I'm very successful. If they think and don't laugh, then I've had it.'[12]

---

[12] Quoted in the *Independent* (London), 13 May 1995.

Select Bibliography

W. G. ARNOTT, *Menander*, Loeb Classical Library, vol. 1 (1979), vol. 2
(1996), vol. 3 (2000).
D. M. BAIN, *Menander, Samia* (Aris and Phillips, 1983).
A. W. GOMME and F. H. SANDBACH, *Menander, A Commentary*
(Oxford, 1973).
E. W. HANDLEY, *The Dyskolos of Menander* (Methuen, 1965; repr.
Bristol, 1992).
STANLEY IRELAND, *Menander, The Bad-tempered Man* (Aris and
Phillips, 1995).
—— *Menander, Dyskolos, Samia and other Plays, A Companion to the Penguin
Translation* (Bristol Classical Press, 1992).
NORMA MILLER, *Menander, Plays and Fragments* (Penguin, 1987).
F. H. SANDBACH, *Menandri Reliquiae Selectae* (Oxford Classical Text,
revised edition, 1990).

K. B. FROST, *Exits and Entrances in Menander* (Oxford, 1988).
S. M. GOLDBERG, *The Making of Menander's Comedy* (London, 1980).
E. W. HANDLEY, *'Comedy'*, in Cambridge History of Classical
Literature, vol. i (Cambridge, 1985).
R. L. HUNTER, *The New Comedy of Greece and Rome* (Cambridge, 1985).
D. KONSTAN, *Greek Comedy and Ideology* (Oxford, 1995).
D. WILES, *The Masks of Menander* (Cambridge, 1991).
N. ZAGAGI, *The Comedy of Menander* (Duckworth, 1994).

Translator's Note

UNTIL the beginning of the twentieth century Menander's plays were known only from numerous short quotations by ancient authors and the Latin adaptations of some of his plays by Plautus and Terence. He was clearly one of the most popular of all ancient authors, but by the eighth century AD all else was lost. Then in 1907 the Cairo Codex was published, part of a papyrus book of the fifth century AD, which contained large parts of *The Girl from Samos*, *The Girl with the Shaven Head*, and *The Arbitration*. In 1959 *The Bad-Tempered Man* was published, almost complete, from the Bodmer papyrus (the third century AD); in 1969, from the same papyrus book, more of *The Girl from Samos* and about half of *The Shield* appeared. Since then most years have seen the recovery of more papyrus fragments of Menander from the sands of Egypt, most recently large portions of *The Arbitration* (the Michigan papyrus, not yet fully published).

The principal difficulty in writing a translation of Menander intended for the general reader lies in the mutilated state of the papyri on which we rely almost exclusively for our knowledge of the text. Scholarly editions, such as the Oxford Classical Text or Arnott's Loeb text, show exactly what is missing and where supplements are made. A translation following this principle would not be at all easy for the general reader to use. The Penguin translation of Norma Miller cuts the Gordian knot by translating only passages which are more or less complete. In my version I make a compromise which I hope will be acceptable to the general reader and not too repugnant to the scholar. Where the Oxford Classical Text or Arnott's Loeb text have proposed supplements which are generally accepted, I have given no indication that the text is damaged. Where there are lacunae the content of which may be reasonably guessed, I have sometimes written supplements which are printed in italics, so as to produce a continuous text. Where there are lacunae and damaged passages which are beyond conjecture, I have indicated what is missing in brackets, e.g. [lacuna of 3 lines, 4 lines mutilated, supplements speculative].

I have translated into verse since it seemed to me that a prose translation was likely to lose much of Menander's variety in tone and pace. Menander uses the metre called iambic trimeters for most of his dialogue; this is the metre of nearly all the dialogue of Greek tragedy and most of the dialogue of Old Comedy; Aristotle describes it as 'closest to ordinary speech'. For this I have used English blank verse. In most of the plays of which much survives Menander has scenes written in trochaics, usually in passages of heightened excitement; I have translated these passages into English trochaics. The principles of Greek and English versification are quite different; Greek verse is quantitative, English accentual. And so the verse translations are metrically a remote reflection of the original; and the English trochaics risk becoming monotonous, since they do not admit of the variations possible in quantitative verse.

The diction of Menander is generally, as far as one can judge, that of ordinary educated conversation, neither excessively colloquial in tone nor elevated. But of course it varies. When slaves or cooks are speaking, it is sometimes more colloquial. In the frequent moralizing passages it rises to an elevated style. There are passages which verge on the poetic or the mock-poetic. Menander makes his characters speak in a manner appropriate to the dramatic situation. My translations follow the Greek closely except in one respect. The characters in Menander's plays are continually appealing to the gods—Zeus, Apollo, Poseidon, Athene, etc.; the overtones of these appeals differ according to the god named, but these shades of meaning would mean little to an English reader, and so I have preferred to use a generalized 'by god' etc unless there was some special reason for naming the deity concerned. In the spelling of proper names I have not attempted to achieve consistency; I have usually transliterated the Greek form, e.g. 'Nikeratos' (rather than the Latinized form 'Niceratus'), but I have retained the English spelling of names commonly found in English, e.g. Arcadia, Aeschylus.

Ancient dramatic texts (with a very few exceptions) do not include stage directions. Both the setting of the plays and the movements of the characters must be deduced from the context given by the words of the speakers, which usually make it clear what is happening. The papyrus texts indicate changes of speaker but seldom name the speakers, and so in some fragments we cannot be certain who the speakers are.

Judging from the number of Menandrean papyri, Menander was the most popular author in the ancient world except for Homer and he is very often quoted by ancient authors. To name a few of these, by far the greatest number of quotations come from Stobaeus (fifth century AD), who wrote an anthology for his son. Athenaeus (floruit AD 200) gives a good many in his *Deipnosophistai* (*The Learned Banqueters*), an immense dialogue (originally thirty books), in which the guests at a dinner party discuss an endless variety of topics. Plutarch, biographer, philosopher, antiquarian (floruit 100 AD) contributes a fair number. A number of quotations come from the *Suda*, a lexicon compiled in the tenth century AD, which often quotes entire lines to illustrate the meaning of a word.

I have followed the Oxford Classical Text (Sandbach, revised 1990) closely except in a few cases where I have accepted supplements and conjectures different from those in that text; I have not drawn attention to these differences. Of the quotations from ancient authors which supplement our knowledge of fragmentary plays, I have omitted a few, usually quotations from grammarians explaining the meaning of single words, but for ease of reference I have kept the Oxford text numbering.

I have tried to keep up to date with papyri recently published. And so the reader will find a number of passages not in the Oxford text. The line numbers given in the margin of the translations are usually those of the Oxford text, so that readers who wish to do so may more easily refer to the original; where new fragments necessitate renumbering, I have used those of Arnott's Loeb text.

It is not surprising that the plays of so popular an author were illustrated in ancient times in wall-paintings and mosaics; where such works throw light on the plots when our texts are deficient, we have referred to them in the text.

I owe an immense debt to the unstinting help given me by leading scholars of Menander; Professor Geoffrey Arnott and Professor Colin Austin have been my guides and mentors throughout, reading all that I have written and helping me both on points of principle and detail. Professor Eric Handley has assisted me over some difficult passages. Peter Brown has not only written the Introduction but has also meticulously revised the whole, correcting my errors and supplementing my ignorance with unfailing good nature. Without their generous assistance I could never have brought this project to completion. Any errors which remain are entirely my responsibility.

Arnott's third volume of the Loeb edition came out when my translations were already in proof and so regrettably I have not been able to incorporate changes which I would have made after reading it.

In references in the notes I use the following abbreviations:

OCT	Oxford Classical Text, *Menandri Reliquiae Selectae*, F. H. Sandbach (revised 1990)
Sandbach	A. W. Gomme and F. H. Sandbach, *Menander, A Commentary* (Oxford 1973)
Arnott	W. G. Arnott, Loeb Classical Library, *Menander* (vol. i, 1976; vol. ii, 1996; vol. iii, 2000)
K–A	R. Kassel and C. Austin, *Poetae Comici Graeci*, (vols. vi. 2, 1998; and viii, 1995; Berlin, New York) (vol. vi. 1 forthcoming).

The Plays and Fragments of Menander

The Bad-Tempered Man (Dyskolos)

The papyrus codex of the *Dyskolos* was published in 1958, the first complete play of Menander to have been discovered in the sands of Egypt (see Introduction). It is damaged in places; there are several lacunae of four or more lines where the papyrus is torn and many gaps where half-lines, whole words, or a few letters are missing or illegible.

Characters

PAN (Prologue)
CHAIREAS, a toady
SOSTRATOS, a rich young man
PYRRHIAS, Sostratos' slave
KNEMON, an old misanthrope
THE GIRL, his daughter
DAOS, the old slave of Gorgias
CHORUS of worshippers of Pan
GORGIAS, Knemon's son by a previous marriage
SIKON, a cook
GETAS, a slave of Gorgias' father
SOSTRATOS' MOTHER
SIMICHE, Knemon's old servant
KALLIPPIDES, Sostratos' father

Silent characters:

PLANGON, Sostratos' sister
PARTHENIS, a pipe player
MYRRHINE, Gorgias' mother
DONAX and SYROS, slaves

The scene is set in Phyle, a mountainous district in central Attica. In the middle of the stage is the shrine of Pan and the Nymphs, to the right the house of the old misanthrope Knemon, to the left that of his son Gorgias.

Prologue

The god PAN *enters from his shrine and addresses the audience.*

PAN. You must imagine we're in Attica;
    Phyle's the place; the shrine* from which I come
    Belongs to Phyle's people and the men
    Who farm these rocky heights as best they can,
    A holy place exceedingly well known.
    This farm here on the right is Knemon's home,
    An utter misanthrope, cross-grained to all;
    He hates the crowd—he hates the crowd, I say?
    He's getting on, yet never in his life
    Has spoken willingly to anyone   10
    Or greeted anyone except me, Pan,
    His neighbour, as he must when passing by,
    And then he's promptly sorry that he spoke,
    I'm sure of that. And yet despite his ways
    He wed a widow whose first husband had
    Just died, leaving a son, a baby then.
    He fought with her not only in the day
    But most of every night—a wretched life.
    He had a daughter by her. Things got worse.
    But when her troubles were beyond repair,   20
    Her life laborious and harsh, the wife
    Went off back to the son she'd borne before.
    He had a little plot not far from here,
    Where now in hardship he supports himself,
    His mother, and one loyal family slave.
    The boy by now's become a lad with sense
    Beyond his years—experience brings men on.
    The old man with his daughter lives alone   30
    And has but one old servant; so he digs

And carries wood; it's work, work, work for him,
Hating his neighbours most, and wife, and then
The whole world to Cholargos* far below.
The girl, brought up in total innocence,
Remains unchanged. She cultivates the nymphs
Who live with me with careful reverence;
So she's persuaded us to have some care
For her; I've made a youth, a city boy,
Whose father's rich and farms a great estate   40
Not far from here, go hunting with a friend
And happen to come near her home; I've made
Him fall head over heels in love with her.
These are the main points; and the rest you'll see,
If you are willing; and willing you must be!
But look! I think I see this lover now
Draw near, together with his huntsman friend;
They're deep in talk about the whole affair.

[*Exit into shrine*

ACT I

Enter SOSTRATOS *and* CHAIREAS *from the right, deep in conversation.*

CHAIREAS. What's that you say? You saw a freeborn girl   50
    Give garlands to the Nymphs* here and you went
    Away in love, at once?
SOSTRATOS.   At once.
CHAIREAS.   That's quick!
    Had you decided as you left your home
    To fall in love with someone?
SOSTRATOS.   Chaireas,
    You're laughing at me. I'm in a bad way.
CHAIREAS. I believe you.
SOSTRATOS.   That is why I've come with you
    To help me, since I think you are my friend
    And very competent.
CHAIREAS.   Well, Sostratos,

In cases of this sort, this is my policy:
One of my friends falls for a courtesan
And calls me in: I seize the girl at once
And bring her; I get drunk, burn down the door,*   60
Reject all sense! We don't know who she is
But he must have her now. For slowness feeds
Such love; quick action brings a quick relief.
But someone speaks of marriage, a free girl,
I am another man then; I inquire about
Her family, finances, character;
For now I leave my friend all I arrange
In this affair to be a record for
All time.

SOSTRATOS. Yes, very good. [*Aside*] But not quite what I want.

CHAIREAS. And now we must hear all the facts.   70

SOSTRATOS. I sent my fellow-huntsman, Pyrrhias,
From home at dawn today.

CHAIREAS.   To whom?

SOSTRATOS.   To meet
The father of the girl or master of
The house, whoever he may be.

CHAIREAS.   Good god!
What are you saying?

SOSTRATOS.   I was wrong. Perhaps
This sort of thing was not a servant's job.
But it's not easy for a man to see
What's best when he's in love. But I'm surprised
At his delay. I told him to return
At once when he had learnt the set-up here.   80

Enter PYRRHIAS *from the left, running and breathless.*

PYRRHIAS. Let me through! Look out! All of you, out of the way!
A raving loony's after me.

SOSTRATOS.   What, boy?

PYRRHIAS. Run! Run!

SOSTRATOS.   What's up?

PYRRHIAS.   He's pelting me
With clods and stones. I'm done for.

SOSTRATOS.   Pelting you?
    Where are you going, fool?
PYRRHIAS [*stopping*].   Perhaps he's not
    Still chasing me.
SOSTRATOS.   He's not.
PYRRHIAS [*looking round*]. I thought he was.
SOSTRATOS. What do you mean?
PYRRHIAS.   I beg you, let's get out.
SOSTRATOS. Where to?
PYRRHIAS.   As far as may be from that door.
    Some child of Woe, or else a man possessed
    Or melancholy-mad, lives in the house here,   90
    The man you sent me to—what agony!
    I've stubbed and broken nearly all my toes.
SOSTRATOS. Good god! What's he been up to on his way?
    Some drunken trick?
CHAIREAS.   He's clearly off his head.
PYRRHIAS. No, Sostratos, by god, may I be damned
    And blasted, if I am. Be on your guard!
    But I can't speak. My breath is choking me.

                                    [*He pauses for breath*

    I knocked at that door there and said that I
    Was looking for the master of the house;
    A miserable old woman answered me;
    From where I'm standing now she pointed out   100
    The fellow on the hill there wandering round
    Unhappily and collecting pears, a load
    Of trouble for himself.
CHAIREAS [*aside*].   How cross he is!
    What next, my friend?
PYRRHIAS.   I set foot on his plot
    And walked towards him, and from some way off—
    I wished to seem a friendly, tactful sort
    Of man—I said, 'Father, I've come to see
    You on a matter that's for your own good.'
    Immediately he says, 'You're on my land;
    You villain, what's your game?', takes up a clod   110
    And hurls it at my face.

CHAIREAS.   To hell with him!

PYRRHIAS. I shut my eyes and said, 'God blast you!', then
    He took a stick this time and beat me up,
    Saying, 'What business have you and I
    Together? Don't you know the public road?'
    Shouting with all his might.

CHAIREAS.   The farmer is
    Quite mad from what you say.

PYRRHIAS.   But hear the rest:
    I fled; he chased me for about two miles,
    First round the hill, then down below into
    This thicket, pelting me with clods and stones   120
    And pears when he had nothing else, a wild
    And savage beast, a barbarous old sod.
    Please, please, get out!

SOSTRATOS.   No, that's the coward's way.

PYRRHIAS. But you don't know how dangerous things are.
    He'll eat us all.

CHAIREAS.   Perhaps he is a bit
    Upset just now. And so I think we should
    Put off approaching him; for, Sostratos,
    You know, in everything success depends
    On finding the right time.

PYRRHIAS.   That's sensible.

CHAIREAS. Poor farmers are sharp-tempered folk; he's not   130
    The only one, they're nearly all like this.
    At dawn tomorrow I'll go to him alone—
    I know the house; now you go home and wait.
    That will be best.   [*Exit* CHAIREAS *to the right*

PYRRHIAS.   Let's do just as he says.

SOSTRATOS. He's gladly taken an excuse to go.
    It's clear he didn't want to come with me
    At all, and didn't like my marriage plans.
    [*To* PYRRHIAS] But you, may all the gods annihilate
    You utterly as you deserve, you rogue.

PYRRHIAS. But, Sostratos, please, what have I done wrong?   140

SOSTRATOS. You did some damage to his land, that's clear;
    You stole something.

PYRRHIAS.   I stole?
SOSTRATOS.   Did someone beat
   You up when you were doing nothing wrong?

Enter KNEMON *from afar left.*

PYRRHIAS. Yes—here he is himself. I'm off, my friend,
   And *you* can talk to him.   [*Exit* PYRRHIAS *right*
SOSTRATOS.   I can't. In talk
   I never can convince a soul. [*Looking at* KNEMON *approaching*]
     What should
   One say about this man? He does not seem
   To have a very friendly look. God, no!
   And what a rush he's in! I think I'll get
   Back from the door. That's better. And, what's more,
   He's shouting though he walks alone! He seems
   To me to be unwell. But I'm afraid   150
   Of him. By god, I am. And that's the truth.

Enter KNEMON *from the left, talking to himself.*

KNEMON. Now Perseus,* wasn't he a lucky man
   In two respects? He could take wings on high
   And never meet the men who walked on earth.
   And then he had this gift with which he turned
   All people who annoyed him into stone.
   I wish I had that gift! Then there would be
   No shortage of stone statues everywhere!
   But now life's not worth living. No, it's not.   160
   Men trespass on my land and chat to me.
   [*Ironically*] I usually waste my time of course beside
   The very road! Why, I don't even work
   That part of my estate. I've left that bit
   To avoid the passers-by. But now they chase
   Me into the hills above. What swarming crowds!
   But help! Here's someone else standing beside
   My door!
SOSTRATOS [*aside*]. Does he intend to beat me up?
KNEMON. You can't find solitude, not anywhere,
   Not even if you want to hang yourself.   170

SOSTRATOS [*coming forward*]. Is it me you're angry with? I'm
    waiting here
For someone, father, as I had arranged.
KNEMON. Just what I said! Do you take this for a park
    Or public meeting place?* [*With heavy irony*] Well, if you want
    To see someone, arrange to meet him here
    Beside my doors; go on, by all means; yes,
    Erect a bench, if that is what you want,
    Or better still a council-room. [*As he enters his house*] Oh dear!
    Malicious interference is the cause
    Of all this trouble so it seems to me.

            [*Exit into his house.* SOSTRATOS *is left alone on the stage*
SOSTRATOS. This business requires, it seems to me,
    No common effort, something more serious.   180
    That's obvious. [*He reflects*] Getas, my father's slave,
    Suppose I go to him? By heaven, I shall.
    Yes, he's a ball of fire, experienced
    In every kind of thing. He'll drive away
    All the old man's bad temper, I'm quite sure.
    For I refuse to tolerate delay.
    Why, lots of things may happen in one day.
    But someone's rattled on his door.

                  [SOSTRATOS *withdraws*

    The GIRL *comes out of* KNEMON's *door, carrying a water pot.*

GIRL.   Alas!
    More trouble still! Oh, what shall I do now?
    My nurse has dropped the bucket in the well.   190
SOSTRATOS [*aside*]. O father Zeus, Phoebus, and heavenly Twins,*
    What beauty irresistible!
GIRL.   And Dad
    Told me to get the water hot as he
    Went out to work.
SOSTRATOS [*to the spectators*]. Friends, what am I to do?
GIRL. But if he learns of this, he'll beat her up
    And kill her for her crime. It's not the time
    For idle talk. O dearest Nymphs, I must
    Take water now from you. I am ashamed,

If anyone is making offerings inside,
To bother you—
SOSTRATOS [*comes forward*]. But if you give the pot
To me, I'll fill it from the spring at once   200
And bring it back to you.
GIRL.   O thank you. Please
Be quick.
SOSTRATOS [*aside, as he goes into the shrine*]. A country girl she is, but how
Unlike a bumpkin. Gods above! what power
Can save me now?   [*A door rattles*
GIRL.   But help! Who made that noise?
Is father coming back? Then I shall get
A hiding, if he catches me outside.

> [*The girl retires to* KNEMON'*s door. But it is the door of* GORGIAS' *house that opens*
>
> *Out comes* DAOS, *the old slave, talking to* GORGIAS' *mother who is inside; he does not see the* GIRL.

DAOS. I've spent a long time working here for you,
While master digs alone. Now I must go
To him. [*As he moves off*] O damn you, cursed Poverty,
Why have we found you such a crushing weight?
Why do you settle down so long inside
Our house and make your home with us for good?   210
SOSTRATOS [*coming out of the shrine*]. Here, take the pot.
GIRL.   Please bring it here.
DAOS [*aside*].   What does
This fellow want?
SOSTRATOS.   Goodbye to you, and take
Good care of father.

> [*Exit* GIRL *into* KNEMON'*s house.* SOSTRATOS *soliloquizes, while* DAOS *watches him*

             Hell! Oh, misery!
Stop moaning, Sostratos! It'll be all right.
DAOS [*aside*]. What does he mean 'all right'?
SOSTRATOS.   Don't be afraid.
Tell Getas clearly, as you planned to do

Just now, about the whole affair and then
Come back with him.   [*Exit right*
DAOS.   Whatever's going on?
  I don't like this at all. A youngster here
  Is helping out the girl—that's really bad!   220
  May all the gods destroy you horribly,
  You horror, Knemon! Leave a virtuous girl
  Alone, abandoned in a lonely place
  And not give her protection, as you should!
  Perhaps this fellow knew this and stole here,
  Thinking his luck was in. But anyway
  I'd best inform her brother with all haste
  So we can take the girl into our care.
  I think I'd better go and do so now.
  For I can see some worshippers of Pan   230
  Approaching here, a bit the worse for drink;
  It's not the time to bother them, I think.   [*Exit to the left*

CHORAL INTERLUDE

> *A* CHORUS *of worshippers sings and dances outside the shrine.*

ACT 2

> *Enter* GORGIAS *and* DAOS *from the left.*

GORGIAS. You mean to say you treated the affair
  So casually and feebly?
DAOS.   What do you mean?
GORGIAS. Good god! You should have seen the man at once
  Who chatted up the girl, no matter who,
  And told him to be sure that no one should
  See him behave like this ever again.
  But as it is, you backed away as though
  You weren't involved. But, Daos, I suppose
  We can't escape the duty owed our kin.   240

I still care for my sister. Father wants
To be a stranger to us, but don't let us
Be like him in misanthropy. For if
My sister fell into disgrace, I too must feel
The shame. Outsiders never care who was
To blame but only know the actual facts.
Come on, let's knock.

DAOS. Sir, Gorgias, I'm scared
Of the old man. If he discovers me
Approaching near his door, he'll string me up
At once.

GORGIAS. He's rather difficult, it's true,
And quarrelsome; there's no way anyone   250
Could force him to reform, or change his mind
By good advice such as a friend might give.
He has the law behind him to prevent
Us using force; his character prevents
Persuasion—

DAOS. Stop a bit! We've not come here
For nothing; as I thought, he's coming back.

GORGIAS. You mean the man there in that splendid cloak?

DAOS. That's him.

Enter SOSTRATOS *from the right.*

GORGIAS. His looks at once show he's a rogue.

[DAOS *and* GORGIAS *withdraw*

SOSTRATOS. I did not find Getas within at home;
Mother, all set to make a sacrifice   260
To appease some god—I don't know which—she does
This every day and round and round the whole
District she goes, making her sacrifices—
Had sent him out to hire a cook. I wished
Her offerings luck and back I've come to deal
With matters here. I'll stop this roundabout,
I think, and speak out for myself. I'll knock,
So that I can no longer hesitate.

GORGIAS [*comes forward*]. Young man, would you be willing to
attend

To something rather serious I want to say?
SOSTRATOS. Yes, very gladly. So say on.   270
GORGIAS.   I believe
  For every man, both rich and poor, there is
  A limit to their fortune which brings change.
  The wealthy man's success in life remains
  Unbroken only for so long as he
  Can bear his luck without committing wrong.
  But when he comes to that, led on by his
  Prosperity, he suffers then a change for worse.
  The poor, as long as they do nothing wrong   280
  In their distress but bear their cruel fate
  With honour, still may come in time to win
  Some credit* and expect a better lot.
  What do I mean? Though you are very rich,
  Don't put your trust in that and don't
  Despise us poor men; prove yourself to all
  Who see you worthy of good luck that lasts.
SOSTRATOS. But do you think I'm acting wrongly now?
GORGIAS. You seem to me to have planned a wicked crime,
  Intending to seduce a freeborn girl   290
  Or watching for a chance to do a deed
  Deserving death twice over.
SOSTRATOS.   Gods above!
GORGIAS. It's certainly not right your idleness
  Should upset us who never can be idle.
  You surely know, a poor man, when he's wronged,
  Is hardest of all men to tamper with.
  First, he rouses pity,* then he treats
  All that he's suffered not as simply wrong
  But as an outrage.
SOSTRATOS.   Friend, as you may hope
  To have some luck, please hear a word from me.
DAOS. Master, well said! May you be blessed for this!   300
            [DAOS *is applauding* GORGIAS' *words, disregarding*
                                SOSTRATOS' *interruption*
SOSTRATOS. You too, who speak before you know the facts.
  I saw a girl here and I fell in love.

If that's the wrong you mean, perhaps I did
Do wrong. For what else can I say? Except
I don't come here to her but want to see
Her father. I'm freeborn, well-heeled enough,
And ready to accept her with no dowry,
And guarantee to cherish her for life.
But if I came here with some wrong intent
Or wanting to plot ill behind your backs,   310
May Pan here and the Nymphs now strike me dumb,
Right here, beside the house. Believe me, I'm most
Upset I seem to you that kind of man.

GORGIAS. Well, if I spoke more hotly than I should,
    Don't let that go on worrying you. For you've
    Convinced me now and have me as your friend.
    And I'm concerned in this, as I'm the girl's
    Half-brother, let me tell you that, good friend.

SOSTRATOS. Good god, then you can help me with the rest.   320

GORGIAS. Help? How?

SOSTRATOS.   I see you have a noble heart—

GORGIAS. I don't intend to pack you off with vain
    Excuses; I will tell the simple truth.
    There's never been a human in the past
    Or in our own time like the father of
    This girl.

SOSTRATOS.   That old curmudgeon? Yes,
    I think I know.

GORGIAS. He's bad as bad can be.
    He has this farm that must be worth a cool
    Two talents;* yet he goes on farming it
    Alone; he has no man to work with him,
    No servant of his own, no labourer hired   330
    From the vicinity, no neighbour even,
    But just himself, alone. He'd be best pleased
    If he saw no one, but he usually takes
    His daughter with him when he goes to work
    And only talks to her. Apart from her
    He'd hate to speak to anyone. He says
    He'll marry her to someone when he finds

At last a bridegroom something like himself.
SOSTRATOS. That must mean never.
GORGIAS.   So don't bother, friend;
    You'll waste your labour. Leave his family
    To bear the burden fortune's given us.   340
SOSTRATOS. Good god, man, have you never been in love
    With anyone?
GORGIAS.   Impossible, my friend.
SOSTRATOS.   Why's that?
    What is to hinder you?
GORGIAS.   Thinking about
    My present troubles never gives me time.
SOSTRATOS. I don't suppose you have; at least you talk
    Like one with no experience in love.
    You tell me to back off. The god* alone
    Can stop me; it's no longer up to me.
GORGIAS. Well then, you're doing us no wrong, but you
    Are suffering pointlessly.
SOSTRATOS.   Not, if I win
    The girl.
GORGIAS.   You'll never win her, *as you'll see*,
    If you will come with me *and stand by him*;   350
    He's working in that valley just near us.
SOSTRATOS. Well then?
GORGIAS.   I'll make some chance remark about
    Her marrying; for I myself would love to see
    This happen. Straightaway he'll have it in
    For everyone, and shout abuse at how
    Men lead their lives. And if he sees you there,
    Idle and proud, he won't endure the sight.
SOSTRATOS. Is he there now?
GORGIAS.   He's not, but very soon
    He'll come out by his usual way.
SOSTRATOS.   My friend,
    Do you think he'll bring the girl with him?
GORGIAS.   He may,
    Or maybe not.   360
SOSTRATOS.   I'm ready then to go

Where you propose. But, please, give me support.
GORGIAS: How?
SOSTRATOS.   How, you ask? Come, let's push on.
DAOS [*intervenes*].   Well, then?
  Are you to stand beside us while we work
  Wearing that cloak?
SOSTRATOS.   This cloak? Why ever not?
DAOS. Because he'll pelt you straightaway with clods,
  And then abuse you as an idle pest.
  No, you must dig with us. For seeing this,
  He might perhaps endure a word from you,
  Supposing you a farmer, poor like us.
SOSTRATOS. I'm ready to obey your every word.   370
              [*He takes off his cloak and leaves it in the shrine*
  Lead on!
GORGIAS.   Why force yourself to suffer so?
DAOS [*aside*]. I'd like us all to work flat out today
  And him to wrench his back and then to stop
  Annoying us by coming here.
SOSTRATOS.   Bring out a fork!
DAOS. Come and take mine. I'll mend the wall a while,
  For that needs doing too.
SOSTRATOS.   Then give it here.
  [*To* GORGIAS] You've saved my life—
DAOS.   I'm off, young master, then.
  You follow on!   [*Exit* DAOS *left*
SOSTRATOS.   For this is how I stand—
  I die today or marry her and live.
GORGIAS. If you are really saying what you feel,   380
  Then all good luck to you.   [*Exit to the left*
SOSTRATOS. O honoured gods above!
  You thought you'd put me off by what you said
  Just now, but no, you've made me doubly keen
  To win her hand. For if the girl has not
  Been brought up amongst women and has learnt
  Nothing about life's evils from the tales
  Some aunt or nanny tells to terrify,
  But schooled by her own father liberally,

Who may be rough but hates all wickedness,
Surely he must be blessed who wins this girl.

[*He shoulders the mattock*

This mattock weighs a ton. It'll be the death   390
Of me. But still I must not now go soft,
When I have just begun to sweat it out.   [*Exit to the left*

Enter SIKON, *the cook, from the right, carrying a sheep;* GETAS
follows, well behind.

SIKON. A fine sheep I've got here, remarkable!
O, go to hell! If I lift him off the ground
And carry him, he gets hold of a fig branch
In his mouth and eats the leaves and pulls like mad.
But if I put him on the ground, he won't
Budge on. Our roles are topsy turvy; I,
The cook, am cut to pieces by the sheep,
As I haul him along the road just like a ship.*
But here with any luck must be the shrine   400
Where we will sacrifice. So greetings, Pan!
Hey! Getas, are you left so far behind?

GETAS *emerges, carrying a mass of rugs and other clobber.*

GETAS. Yes, for those blasted women tied a load
Four asses could not carry on my back.
SIKON. It looks as if a fairish crowd is due.
What stacks of rugs you're carrying!
GETAS.   What should I
Do now?
SIKON.   Well, stick them here.
GETAS.   Then there you are.
You see, if she should have a dream and see
Pan of Paiania,* we'll be off for sure
To him at once, to make a sacrifice.
SIKON. Who saw a dream?
GETAS.   Don't wear me out, man.
SIKON.   Still,
Do tell me, Getas, who was it saw the dream?   410
GETAS. My mistress.

SIKON.   Tell me what she dreamt she saw.

GETAS. You'll do for me. She thought that the god Pan—

SIKON. This Pan?

GETAS.   Yes, this—

SIKON.   Was doing what?

GETAS. Took hold of my young master, Sostratos,

SIKON. A nice young man—

GETAS.   And fastened fetters on
   His legs—

SIKON.   Good god!

GETAS.   Then gave him a rough coat
   And fork and ordered him to dig the plot
   Near by.

SIKON.   How weird!

GETAS.   And that is why we have
   To sacrifice, so that this fearful dream
   May turn out for the best.

SIKON.   I understand.
   Lift up this stuff and carry all inside.
   Let's make some pretty beds of straw in there   420
   And get all else prepared. Nothing must stop
   The sacrifice when they at last arrive,
   May all go well! Stop frowning, you poor chap!
   I'll fatten you up properly to-day.   [*Exit* SIKON *into the shrine*

GETAS. Well, I have always praised you and your skill,
   But all the same I don't trust you an inch.

                              [*Exit into the shrine*

CHORAL INTERLUDE

ACT 3

KNEMON *comes out of his house, speaking to* SIMICHE *over his shoulder.*

KNEMON. Now lock the door, old woman; open up
   To none till I return again, and that
   Will be when it's completely dark I think.

The party of worshippers appears from the right, led by SOSTRATOS'
MOTHER, *who is followed by her daughter,* PLANGON, *the piper,*
and slaves. KNEMON *watches from his door.*

SOSTRATOS' MOTHER. Plangon, come on, speed up; we should
    have made   430
The sacrifice by now.
KNEMON.   What's this to-do?
    A mob of people! oh, to hell with them.
MOTHER. Come, Parthenis, and play your pipe for Pan.
    They say that one should not approach this god
    In silence.

Enter GETAS *from the shrine.*

GETAS.   Lord! You're safely here at last.
KNEMON [*aside*]. Good god, how odious!
GETAS.   We've hung around
    For ages waiting.
MOTHER.   But is everything
    All ready for us?
GETAS.   Yes, it is. At least
    The sheep is ready—almost dead.
MOTHER.   Poor thing!
    It will not wait for you to take your time.
    Go in and get the basket* ready and   440
    The holy water and the sacred grain.
    [*To* KNEMON] What are you gaping at, you half-wit, you?
           [*Exit with the sacrificial procession into the shrine*
KNEMON. O, go to hell the lot of you! They stop
    Me working. For I can't desert the house
    And leave it empty. But the Nymphs next door
    Are a perpetual plague; I think I'll have
    To move again—knock down the house and go.
    The sacrifices that these devils make!
    They bring their picnic hampers and their jars
    Of wine not for the gods but for themselves.
    A pinch of incense and a holy cake
    Are offerings of true piety; they're burnt   450
    And god receives them all. But they put on

The altar for the gods only the tail
And gall bladder, the parts they cannot eat,
And guzzle down the rest themselves.* Old hag,
Open the door at once. For I suppose
I must get on with jobs inside the house.   [*Exit into his house*

Enter GETAS *from the shrine, talking to someone inside.*

GETAS. Forgot the stewing pot, you say? You must
  Be sleeping off an orgy. So now what
  Are we to do? Pester Pan's neighbours, I
  Suppose.   [*He crosses to* KNEMON'*s door and calls*
        Hey, boy! [*He waits*] By god, I do not think
  There are more useless servants anywhere.   460
  Boys! Sex is the only thing they know about—
  Hey, lovely boys—and telling slanderous lies,
  If someone sees them at it. Come on, BOY!
  What is the matter? BOYS! No one at home?
  Hallo! there's someone running to the door,
  I think.
                    [KNEMON *flings open the door in a rage*
KNEMON.   Why are you pounding on my door,
  You miserable man, just tell me that?
GETAS. Don't bite my head off.
KNEMON.   Yes, I shall, by god,
  And swallow you alive.
GETAS.   God, don't do that.
KNEMON. Have you and I some contract, godless swine?
GETAS. No contract. No, I've not come here to ask   470
  Repayment of a debt—I've brought with me
  No witnesses—but just to ask you for
  A stewing pot.
KNEMON.   A stewing pot?
GETAS.   That's right.
KNEMON. You rogue, do you think I'd sacrifice an ox
  And act the way you do?
GETAS [*aside*].   I don't suppose
  You'd sacrifice a snail! [*To* KNEMON] Goodbye, my friend.
  The women told me to knock at your door

And ask you; so I did just that. You have
No pot. Then I'll go back and tell them so.

> [*He starts off back towards the shrine*

Great gods, a grizzled viper, that he is.   480

> [*Exit into the shrine*

KNEMON. They're murdering animals. They come straight up
And knock, as though I was a friend of theirs.
If I see one of them come near our door,
If I don't make him an example for
The neighbourhood, consider me a mere
Nonentity. This man, goodness knows who,
Has got away with it—I can't think how.

> [*Exit* KNEMON *into his house*

SIKON *comes out of the shrine shouting back to* GETAS.

SIKON. Well, damn you! He abused you, did he? Perhaps
You asked him like a shit. [*To the audience*] Some folk have no
Idea how they should do such jobs. I've learnt
Some skill in this. For in the city I do work   490
For thousands, and I pester those next-door
And borrow pots from all. One has to use
A little flattery when making a request
For something. So, if it's an older man
Answers the door, at once I call him 'Dad'
Or 'Father'; older women I call 'Ma',
If middle aged, I greet her 'Madam dear';
If a young servant answers, say, 'Good friend';
But you deserve to hang! What ignorance!
'Boy! slaves!', you say. I'll show you how it's done.

> [*He goes to* KNEMON'*s door and knocks*

Come out, dad, come, I want to speak to you.

> [KNEMON *bursts out of the door*

KNEMON. What, you again!
SIKON.   My word, what's this?
KNEMON.   Provoke   500
Me purposely, will you? Did I not tell
You 'Don't come near my door'? Give me the whip,
Old woman.   [*He seizes hold of* SIKON

SIKON.   No, stop that and let me go!

KNEMON. I let you go?

SIKON.   I beg you, please, kind sir.

[*He wriggles out of* KNEMON'*s gras*p

KNEMON. Come back!

SIKON.   God blast you!

KNEMON.   You still blathering?

SIKON. I came to ask you for a pot-bucket

KNEMON. I haven't got a bucket or an axe,
   Or salt or vinegar or anything.
   I've told my neighbours straight they're not to come
   Near me.

SIKON.   You've not told me.

KNEMON.   Well then, I tell
   You now.

SIKON.   Yes, and worse luck for you. Could you   510
   Not even say where I could go and get one?

KNEMON. I warned you. Will you still keep nattering
   At me?

SIKON.   Good day, sir.

KNEMON.   I don't want 'good day'
   From any of you.

SIKON.   Then, bad day to you.

KNEMON. This is intolerable!   [*Exit into his house*

SIKON.   He's pretty well
   Chopped me to pieces. What a thing it is
   To make a polite request! It really makes
   A difference! Should one try the other door?
   But that's not easy, if they're all round here
   So quick to put on gloves* and beat you up.
   Perhaps it's best for me to bake the meat?
   I think it is. I've got a roasting dish.
   Goodbye to the Phylasians! I'll use   520
   The things I've got to hand.   [*Exit into the shrine*

   Enter SOSTRATOS *from the left, rubbing his back and limping.*

SOSTRATOS.   If anyone
   Is short of troubles, let him come to hunt

In Phyle! Agony! Oh, what a state I'm in—
My back, my chest, my neck, the whole of me!
For I fell to at once like a young fool;
Swinging my mattock right up high, just like
A navvy, I dug deep and went at it
Much too industriously, but not for long.
Soon I kept turning round a bit to see
When the old man would turn up with the girl.   530
Then, heavens! I began, first furtively,
To feel my spine; and when an age had passed,
I started straightening out, but I was now
Becoming stiff as wood. And no one came.
The sun was scorching. Gorgias looked round
And saw me bobbing up and bobbing down,
With my whole body, like a pumping beam.*
'I don't think he'll come now, young man', he said.
At once I answered, 'What are we to do?
Shall we watch for him tomorrow? but today   540
Let's give it up.' And Daos then appeared
To take my mattock over. So that's how
My first attempt turned out. I've come back here;
By god, I can't say why, but of its own
Accord the situation draws me here.

Enter GETAS *from the shrine in a cloud of smoke; he shouts at* SIKON,
who is inside the shrine.

GETAS. What *is* this? Do you think I've sixty hands?
It's I blow up the charcoal, fly around
And bring the offal, wash and cut it up,
And make the cakes, and carry round *the pots*,
Although I'm blinded by the smoke. They think   550
I'm just the donkey at the festival.*
SOSTRATOS. Hey, Getas!
GETAS.   Who's that calling me?
SOSTRATOS.   It's me.
GETAS. And who are you?   [*Rubbing the smoke from his eyes*
SOSTRATOS.   Can you not see?
GETAS.   I see;

My master.

SOSTRATOS. Tell me what you're doing here?

GETAS. We've just this moment made the sacrifice
  And now we're getting ready lunch for you.

SOSTRATOS. Is mother here?

GETAS.   She's been here ages.

SOSTRATOS.   And father?

GETAS. We're still expecting him. So in you go.

SOSTRATOS. I will, when I have done a little job.

                                        [*He turns to the audience*

  This sacrifice has proved quite opportune.
  I'll go in as I am,* and I'll invite
  This young man and his servant to the lunch.   560
  For when they've shared our offerings, they'll be
  More useful allies in my marriage plan.

GETAS [*grumbling to himself*]. What's that you say? You're going to invite
  Some friends to lunch? As far as I'm concerned
  Ask thousands; for I've always known I should
  Not get a taste. How could I? Bring them all
  Along. You've made a splendid sacrifice,
  Well worth a look. But would the womenfolk,
  Delightful ladies, give a share to me?
  God, no, not even just a lick of salt.

SOSTRATOS. Getas, it'll be all right today. O Pan,   570
  I'll make this prophecy myself; but still,
  I'll always make a prayer to you when I
  Pass by your shrine and I'll be generous *

                        [*Exit to left to find* GORGIAS *and* DAOS

            Enter SIMICHE *from* KNEMON'S *house.*

SIMICHE. O misery, and misery again!

GETAS. O hell and blast! Some woman of the old
  Man's now appeared.

SIMICHE.   O, what will be my fate?
  Wanting to save the bucket from the well
  Myself, without the master knowing, if
  I could, I tied the mattock to a weak

And rotten piece of rope, and then it broke—   580
GETAS [*aside*]. Ah, good!
SIMICHE.   And so I've dropped the mattock too
    Into the well to join the bucket. Oh!
GETAS [*aside*]. It's only left for you to throw yourself
    In too.
SIMICHE.   And master—what bad luck!—decides
    To move some dung that's lying in the yard;
    He's running round and looking for the fork
    And shouting; now he's banging on the door.
GETAS [*aside*]. You poor old woman, run—he'll murder you—
    Get out, or better still defend yourself!
KNEMON [*bursting out of his door*]. Where is the thief?
SIMICHE.   Master, I did not mean
    To drop it in.
KNEMON.   Go on, inside!
SIMICHE.   What do
    You mean to do?   590
KNEMON.   Do? Tie you up and let
    You down the well.
SIMICHE.   No, no, not that! alas!
KNEMON. I shall, and with the selfsame rope, by god.
GETAS [*aside*]. That's fine, if it is rotten through and through.
SIMICHE. Shall I call Daos from next door?
KNEMON.   Shall you
    Call Daos, wicked hag? you've ruined me.
    Do you hear me? Quickly, get inside! [*Exit* SIMICHE *into the house*
                      Ah me!
    Unhappy in my isolation now,
    Of all men most unhappy. I'll go down
    Into the well. What else is left to do?
GETAS. Then we'll provide a hook and rope for you.
KNEMON [*notices* GETAS]. May all the gods blast you to bloody
    hell,   600
    You villain, if you say a word to me.   [*Exit into house*
GETAS. That's fair enough. He's burst back in again.
    What an unhappy man! What a life he leads!
    The Attic farmer in his purest form!

Battling with rocks which bear nothing but sage
And thyme, he reaps a crop of pain and gets
No good from it. But I must say no more—
The master's here, bringing his guests with him.
They're local labourers. How very odd!
Why is he bringing them here now? How did
He get to know them?

      Enter SOSTRATOS, GORGIAS *and* DAOS *from the left.*

SOSTRATOS.   I will not allow
  You to say no. 'We're all right thanks.' Good god!
  Would anyone on earth refuse to come
  To luncheon with a friend who's sacrificed?
  For I have been your friend, you know, since long
  Before I met you.   [SOSTRATOS *hands* DAOS GORGIAS' *tools*
                  Daos, take these things inside
  And then come back.
GORGIAS [*to* DAOS].   Don't leave mother alone
  But see to all her needs. I'll join you soon.
        [*Exeunt,* DAOS *into* GORGIAS' *house,* SOSTRATOS *and* GORGIAS
                                   into the shrine.

CHORAL INTERLUDE

ACT 4

          SIMICHE *runs out of* KNEMON'*s house, shrieking.*

SIMICHE. Won't someone help? O misery! Help! Help!   620
         SIKON *comes out of the shrine, grumbling.*

SIKON. Good lord! by all the gods and spirits, please
  Let us get on with making our libations.*
  You wail, abuse us, beat us up! A most
  Extraordinary house!
SIMICHE.   My master's down
  The well!

SIKON.   How's that?

SIMICHE.   How? He was climbing down
   To get the fork and bucket out, when at
   The top he slipped; and so he's fallen in.

SIKON. You mean that difficult old sod? Good lord,
   He has done well! My dear old woman, now
   It's up to you.   630

SIMICHE.   What do you mean?

SIKON.   Why, get
   A mortar or a rock or some such thing
   And drop it on him from above.

SIMICHE.   Dear friend,
   Go down the well.

SIKON.   My god, to suffer what
   The man did in the story, fight the dog
   In the well!* No Thanks.

SIMICHE [*shouts*].   Where are you, Gorgias?
                  Enter GORGIAS *from the shrine.*

GORGIAS. I'm here. What is the matter, Simiche?

SIMICHE. You ask me what? I tell you once again,
   My master's in the well.

GORGIAS.   Here, Sostratos,
   Come out.

                  Enter SOSTRATOS *from the shrine.*

            Lead on and quickly go inside.
                  [*Exeunt* GORGIAS, SOSTRATOS *and* SIMICHE *into*
                     KNEMON's *house.* SIKON *is left alone on the stage*

SIKON. The gods exist, by Dionysos! Yes.
   You don't give us a stewing pot when we
   Are sacrificing; you're too mean for that,
   You wicked rogue? Then fall into the well   640
   And drink it dry, so you can't give a drop
   To anyone. The Nymphs have punished him
   For me, as he deserved. No one can wrong
   A cook and get away scot-free. Our art
   Is somehow sacred. But waiters you can treat
   Just as you like. [*Cries off-stage*] What? Surely he's not dead?

Some girl is weeping and bewailing her
Beloved dad.
[Lacuna of four lines; then three deficient; supplements speculative.]
     That's no *concern of mine* *[More cries off-stag*e
He must be still alive. Someone perhaps
Has gone right down the well to rescue him;   650
They'll tie him to a piece of rope and so
They'll haul him up, that's obvious. Oh, what
A sight! What do you think he'll look like then,
Soaked to the skin and trembling? What a joke!
I'd love to see him, friends, by god, I would.
       [He shouts to the women inside the shrine
But, women, pour libations for their sake   660
And pray the old man's rescue—may go wrong
And leave him lamed and crippled. For that way
He'll be a harmless neighbour to Pan here
And to the folk who come to sacrifice.
That's my concern too, if I'm hired to cook
        [Exit SIKON *into the shrine*

Enter SOSTRATOS *from* KNEMON'*s house and addresses the audience.*

SOSTRATOS. Friends, by Demeter, by Asklepios,
By all the gods, I never in my life
Have seen a man so nearly drowned, and so
Conveniently! What fun it was to watch!
For Gorgias, the moment we went in,   670
Leapt down into the well; the girl and I
On top did nothing; what were we to do?
Except she tore her hair and wept and beat
Her breast like mad. And I, the fool I was,
Stood by her, like her nurse, and begged and prayed
Her not to, gazing at that priceless work
Of art. But I cared less than nothing for
The casualty below, except I had to keep
On pulling him—that really was a bore.   680
And, god, I nearly sent him to his death
Three times at least; as I was gazing at
The girl, I let the rope go. Gorgias

However proved a true Atlas, held firm,
And finally has hauled him up. When he
Emerged, I came out here, because I could
Control myself no longer but almost
Dashed up and kissed the girl; I am in love
So desperately. I'm getting ready now—
They're rattling at the door!

The door opens and KNEMON *is wheeled out on a couch by* GORGIAS
and the GIRL.

God help me, what   690
An extraordinary sight!
GORGIAS.   Knemon,
Say if there's anything you want?
KNEMON.   What should
I say? I'm not too good.
GORGIAS.   Oh, do cheer up!
KNEMON. I have cheered up. For Knemon now will cease
To give you trouble for all time to come.
GORGIAS. This is the evil consequence, you know,
Of isolation. Do you see? Just now
You were within a hair's breadth of your death.
From now on, then, at your age, you must live
With someone to look after you.
KNEMON.   I know,
I'm not so well. Call me your mother, Gorgias,
And say it's urgent. Troubles alone, it seems,   700
Can teach us.   [*Exit* GORGIAS *to his house to fetch his mother;*
                      KNEMON *appeals to his daughter*
Daughter dear, please hold me tight
And help me up.
       [SOSTRATROS, *seeing the girl putting her arms round*
          KNEMON, *is madly jealous and comes forward*
SOSTRATROS.   O, lucky man!
KNEMON   Why are
You standing there beside me, wretched man?
          [SOSTRATROS *retires to the back of the stage*

GORGIAS *and his* MOTHER *enter while* KNEMON *stands to make
his harangue, supported by his* DAUGHTER.

[*Lacuna of five lines, then three line-endings; supplements speculative.*]
KNEMON. *Listen, all of you; stand round me, while I tell you what I want.**
In the past I worked my heart out and I liked to work alone.
Neighbours seldom came to help me, so I managed by myself.
Gradually I came to realize I was better on my own.
Loneliness became habitual; I would rather die than change;
Death is welcome if you cannot live the way you want to do.
Hear then what I have decided. Myrrhine and Gorgias,
You perhaps may not approve of what I've chosen; *all the same,*   710
None of you could ever make me change my mind; you must
  give way.
One mistake perhaps I did make— thought myself alone of all
Self-sufficient, never needing anything from anyone.
Now I see that death may strike one, swift and unpredictable;
So I've found how wrong I was then. Surely one must always
  have
Someone near to help. But, truly—I was quite unbalanced
  then,
When I saw, tho' men's lives differed, profit was their only
  goal—
I imagined no one ever would show kindness to another.   720
This it was that caused my blindness. Now one man, and one
  alone,
Gorgias, has proved my error, showing true nobility.
I'm the man who never let him near my door, who never gave
  him
Help at all, who never greeted, never spoke with courtesy—
All the same it's he has saved me. Any other man, quite fairly,
Might have said, 'You don't let me near. Now I'll not come
  near to you.
You yourself have never helped us, now I'll give no help to
  you.

                          [GORGIAS *shows signs of wanting to intervene*
What's the matter, boy? So whether I am now about to
  die—   730

Which I think is very likely; I seem ill—or I survive,
I adopt you as my son, boy; all I own consider yours;
I entrust my daughter to you; you must find a husband for her.
Even if my health were perfect, I'd not find one; none would
    ever
Satisfy me. As for Knemon, if I live, then let me live
As I wish. All else take over; manage things yourself. You are
Sensible, thank god, and care for your own sister, as you
    should.
Split in two all my possessions; give one half to her as dowry;
With the rest support your mother and myself. So much for
    that.
[*To his* DAUGHTER] Lie me down. I hold that no one should say
    more than he needs must.   740
This, however, you must know, boy; certain things I wish to
    say
Of myself, my way of living: if all men behaved like me,
Law-courts would exist no longer, men would no more haul
    each other
Off to prison; war would cease then; all would live content
    with less.
But perhaps you find more pleasure in your present ways—
    good luck!—
This bad tempered misanthrope will be no longer in your way.
GORGIAS. All of this I gladly welcome. Now we quickly have to
    find,
If you agree, a husband for her.
KNEMON.   Hey, I've told you what I think.
Don't, for heaven's sake, annoy me.   750
GORGIAS.   Someone's here who wants to meet you—
KNEMON. No!
GORGIAS.   He's asking for your daughter.
KNEMON.   That's no longer my concern.
GORGIAS. He's the one who helped to save you.
KNEMON.   Who?
GORGIAS.   He's here.
KNEMON.   Come forward, you!
    [SOSTRATOS *comes forward and* KNEMON *has a good look at him*

Well, he's sunburnt; he's a farmer?

GORGIAS.   Yes indeed, father, he is.

He's no dandy, not the type to saunter idly all the day;

[*Six lines deficient; supplements speculative.*]

KNEMON. *I suppose then we must have him, if his family's all right.*

Gorgias, you give *her to him and* arrange *this whole affair.*

Wheel me in.

GORGIAS.   *Yes, certainly. Simiche,* look after him.

[SIMICHE *wheels* KNEMON *into his house followed by* MYRRHINE
and KNEMON's DAUGHTER. SOSTRATOS *and* GORGIAS *are left
alone on the stage*

SOSTRATOS. Nothing's left for you to do now but betroth your
sister to me.

GORGIAS. You must ask your father's blessing   760

SOSTRATOS.   Father won't oppose the match.

GORGIAS. Then I call the gods to witness that I now betroth the
girl,

Sostratos, to you and give her gladly, as is only right.

For you came to seek her hand with no disguise but
open-hearted;

For this marriage there was nothing you were not prepared to
do.

Spoiled you are, yet took the mattock, dug and laboured with a
will;

This is how a man's true nature is revealed, when though he's
rich

He's prepared himself to lower to the level of the poor.

Such a man will bear with courage all the changes chance may
bring.

Proof you've given of your nature; may you only stay that way.

SOSTRATOS. Why, I hope I get much better. But self-praise
perhaps is vulgar.

KALLIPPIDES *appears on the far right of the stage.*

There, I see my father coming, smack on time.

GORGIAS.   Kallippides!

He's your father?

SOSTRATOS.   Sure, that's father.

GORGIAS.   He's a millionaire, by god;
He certainly deserves his riches; he's a farmer none can beat.
                              [KALLIPPIDES *approaches talking to himself*
KALLIPPIDES. I suppose I've been abandoned; they have eaten all
    the sheep,
Gone away back to the farm now.
GORGIAS.   God, he really does seem famished!
Shall we tell him all this moment?
SOSTRATOS.   Better wait for him to lunch.
He'll be more amenable then.
                              [KALLIPPIDES *suddenly sees* SOSTRATOS
KALLIPPIDES.   Sostratos, what's up? Is lunch
    Finished?
SOSTRATOS.   Yes, but plenty's over. In you go!
KALLIPPIDES.   I'm going now.   780
                              [*Exit into shrine*
GORGIAS. If you like, go to your father; you can talk to him alone.
SOSTRATOS. You will stay inside then, won't you?
GORGIAS.   Yes, I shall not stir from there.
SOSTRATOS. Well, I shall not be a moment. Then I'll call you out
    to us.
    [*Exeunt*—SOSTRATOS *into the shrine,* GORGIAS *into* KNEMON'*s house*

CHORAL INTERLUDE

ACT 5

Enter SOSTRATOS *and* KALLIPPIDES *from the shrine, talking.*

SOSTRATOS. You are not granting, father, all I wished
    Nor all that I expected.
KALLIPPIDES.   Have I not
    Agreed to all? I do want you to have
    The girl you love, indeed, I say you must.
SOSTRATOS. I think not, father.
KALLIPPIDES.   Certainly, I do,

For I know well the marriage is secure
That's made by a young man inspired by love.　　　790
SOSTRATOS. So I'm to have the young man's sister then,
　Considering him good enough for us?
　How can you now say you'll not offer him
　My sister's hand?
KALLIPPIDES.　　　　　That will not do at all.
　I have no wish to take at once a bride
　And bridegroom who are paupers. It's enough
　To have one in the family.
SOSTRATOS.　　　　　　　You talk
　Of wealth, a thing on which you can't rely.
　For if you know that it will stay with you
　For ever, keep it then; don't give a share　　　800
　To anyone. But where you're not the master
　And hold it not by right but by the gift
　Of Fortune, father, don't begrudge a share
　Of this to anyone. For Fortune may
　Take all from you and hand it on perhaps
　To someone less deserving than yourself.
　And so I say that all the time you have
　It, father, you should use it generously,
　To help all men and through your means enrich
　As many as you can. Such deeds will live,
　And if you chance to fall yourself some time,
　You will receive a fair return from them.　　　810
　Far better, father, is a friend you see
　Than hidden treasure buried underground.
KALLIPPIDES. You surely know my nature, Sostratos;
　I shall not carry with me to the grave
　What I have gained. How could I? It is yours.
　You want to make a man your friend for good;
　You've tested him? Then do so, and good luck!.
　Why preach at me? Get on with it; you're right.
　Give, share! I'm totally convinced by you.
SOSTRATOS. And willingly?
KALLIPPIDES.　　　　　Yes, willingly; that need.
　Not worry you.

SOSTRATOS.   Then I'll call Gorgias.   820

Enter GORGIAS *from* KNEMON'*s house.*

GORGIAS. As I was coming out, I overheard
  Beside the door all that you said from start
  To finish. Well then? Sostratos, I think
  You are a loyal friend, and I'm remarkably
  Attached to you. But I don't wish to take
  On what's too much for me, nor, if I wished,
  Could I do so, I swear.
SOSTRATOS.   What do you mean?
GORGIAS. I give my sister to you as your wife;
  But as for marrying yours, I'd like to, but—
SOSTRATOS. Why 'like to but'?
GORGIAS.   No pleasure, in my view,
  Can come from living in the luxury   830
  That's won by others' work; a man must make
  His way himself.
SOSTRATOS.   That's rubbish, Gorgias.
  You're worthy of this marriage, don't you think?
GORGIAS. I consider myself worthy of her, yes,
  But when I have so little, count myself
  Unworthy to receive so much.
KALLIPPIDES.   Almighty god!
  Your sense of honour *makes you go too far*.
GORGIAS. What do you mean?
[The following seven lines are mutilated and their meaning dis-
puted.]
KALLIPPIDES.   You have *no money* yet you want
  To seem *to other people to be rich.*
  You see I've been convinced. *Give way yourself.*

                                              [GORGIAS *reflects*
GORGIAS. You have convinced me by your words. I would
  Be doubly sick, in purse and mind, *if I*   840
  Refused the only man who offered me
  Security.
SOSTRATOS [*to his* FATHER]. *That's splendid.* Now what's left
  For us to do except to give our word?

KALLIPPIDES. My daughter I betroth to you, young man,
  To bear a crop of children in wedlock,
  And I shall give three talents as her dowry.
GORGIAS. And for my sister's dowry I have one.
KALLIPPIDES. You have? Don't give too much.
GORGIAS.   I have the farm.
KALLIPPIDES. But, Gorgias, hang on to all of that.
  Now bring your mother and your sister here
  To meet our womenfolk.
GORGIAS.   All right, I shall.
[Two lines deficient.]
SOSTRATOS. Let's all *stay here* tonight *and celebrate;*   850
  Tomorrow we shall hold the weddings. Gorgias,
  Bring Knemon here; perhaps the old man will
  Be better off with us.
GORGIAS.   He will refuse
  To come, my friend.
SOSTRATOS.   Persuade him.
GORGIAS.   If I can,
  I will.   [*Exit into* KNEMON'*s house*
SOSTRATOS. Now, father, for us men we must
  Lay on a splendid binge; the ladies too
  Must make a night of it.
KALLIPPIDES.   The opposite's
  More likely; they will drink, while we, I'm sure,
  Will not be short of night work. But I'll go
  And get things ready for the party now.
SOSTRATOS.   Do so.
        [*Exit* KALLIPPIDES *into the shrine;* SOSTRATOS *is left alone*
                  No man of sense should ever feel   860
  Complete despair of any plan he makes.
  All things may be achieved by care and work.
  I'm now a living proof of this. One day
  Has seen me win a marriage which no one
  On earth would have thought possible.

  Enter GORGIAS *with his* MOTHER *and* SISTER *from* KNEMON'*s house.*

GORGIAS.   Come on,

Speed up!

SOSTRATOS.   This way. [*To his* MOTHER *in the shrine*] Mother, you
    must receive
These ladies. [*To* GORGIAS] Knemon not yet here?

GORGIAS.   Not here!
    He begged me to bring out the old hag too,
    So he could be completely on his own.

SOSTRATOS. What a type! invincible!

GORGIAS.   That's what he's like.

SOSTRATOS. Goodbye to him then! Let us go inside.   870

GORGIAS. But, Sostratos, I'm shy of being in
    The company of women—

SOSTRATOS.   Nonsense, man!
    Come, in you go! Now we must think we're all
    One family.

                    [*Exeunt* GORGIAS *and* SOSTRATOS *into the shrine*

Enter SIMICHE *from* KNEMON's *house, speaking over her shoulder*
to KNEMON.

SIMICHE.   I'm going too. And you
    Will lie here on your own. Unhappy man!
    What a sad character! When they all wished
    To bring you to the god you still refused.
    A heap of trouble is in store for you,
    By both the goddesses,* much worse than now.

                Enter GETAS, *speaking to someone in the shrine.*

GETAS. I will go in and see how Knemon is.

                                            [*The pipe plays**

GETAS. Why play your pipe at me, you wretch? I have no time for
    that yet.   880
    They've sent me here to see the poor old invalid. So belt up!

SIMICHE. Yes, one of you must go inside and sit yourself beside
    him.
    I'm losing my young mistress, so I want to have a chat first,
    To talk to her, kiss her goodbye.

GETAS.   That's sensible. Go on then.
    I will look after him a while.

                                        [*Exit* SIMICHE *into the shrine*

I made my mind up long since
To take this opportunity, but had to work a plan out.
[Two lines mutilated; supplements speculative.]
Now let me see how Knemon is. If he's awake, I can't yet
Begin what I have planned to do.

[*He peeps in at the door*
Ah good, he's sound asleep. Cook!

Sikon, come out here, come to me and hurry up! Good
heavens,
What splendid fun I think we'll have!

Enter SIKON *from the shrine.*

SIKON.   You calling me?
GETAS.   I am, yes.   890
You want to get your own back now for what you went
through lately?
SIKON. What *I* went through? You bugger off, you and your
bloody nonsense.
GETAS. That difficult old rogue's asleep and all alone.
SIKON.   How *is* he?
GETAS. Not altogether down and out.
SIKON.   Could he stand up and hit us?
GETAS. He could not stand at all, I think.
SIKON.   What lovely news you give me!
I'll go inside and ask for something. He will go quite bonkers!
GETAS. But look! Suppose we drag him out and then we dump
him down here,
Bang at his door, and ask for things, and get him really heated.
I say, there'll be some fun in that!
SIKON.   It's Gorgias I'm feared of—   900
If he should catch us on the job, he'd beat us up and thrash us.
GETAS. There's such a din inside the house; they're drinking; they
won't hear us.
In any case we've got to tame the fellow. We're related;
He's now one of the family; suppose he never changes,
Shall we not have an awful job to tolerate his manners?
SIKON. Then just take care that no one sees you while you hump
him out here.

GETAS. You lead the way!

SIKON.   Please wait a bit. Don't steal away without me.
For heaven's sake don't make a noise.

GETAS.   I'm not, by Earth.

[*They enter the house and carry out the sleeping* KNEMON
Keep right now.

SIKON. There!

GETAS.   Dump him here. Now is the time.   909

SIKON.   I'll lead. All right. You [*to the piper*] keep time.

[SIKON *goes to* KNEMON'*s door and bangs loudly and rhythmically*
Boy! Boys! Hey, lovely boys! boys! Hey!

KNEMON [*waking up and groaning*].   Oh dear, oh dear! I've had it.

SIKON. Hey, lovely boys! Hey, boy! Hey, boys! Come on!

KNEMON.   Oh dear! I've had it.

SIKON [*pretending to see* KNEMON *for the first time*]. Who's this? Do *you*
come from this house?

KNEMON.   Of course. What *are* you after?

SIKON. I want to borrow pans from you and trays.

KNEMON.   Who'll help me stand up?

SIKON. You've got some, surely. And I need seven tripods and
twelve tables.
But boys, inform the staff inside. I'm pushed for time.

KNEMON.   I have none.

SIKON. You've not got one?

KNEMON.   I've told you so a thousand times.

SIKON.   I'm off then.

KNEMON. Oh misery! How've I got here? Whoever was it dumped
me
Before the house?   [GETAS *comes forward to take over*

GETAS [*to* SIKON].   You then be off! It's my turn now.   920

[GETAS *bangs on the door*
Boy! Boys! men! women! porter!

KNEMON.   Man, you're mad. You'll break the door down.

GETAS. Lend us nine rugs.

KNEMON.   Wherever from?

GETAS.   And eastern linen curtains
One hundred feet in length.

KNEMON. I wish I had *a whip* from somewhere.

Old hag! Where *has* the woman gone?

GETAS.   I'll try the other door here?

[GETAS *retires*

KNEMON. Get out! Hag! Simiche! [SIKON *approaches*] May all the
    gods blast you, you scoundrel.

What do you want?

SIKON.   I want to have a big bronze wine bowl from you.

KNEMON [*tries to get up*]. Who'll help me up?

GETAS.   You have the drapes, you really have them, grandad.

KNEMON. I've not by god!

SIKON.   And no wine bowl?   930

KNEMON.   I'll murder that old woman.

SIKON. Sit down, don't make a sound. You flee from crowds; you
    hate the ladies;

And you refuse to let us take you out to join the party

With people making sacrifice. You must endure these tortures;

There's no one here to help you now. So bite your lips and
    listen

[Six lines deficient; supplements speculative.]

To all we did inside the shrine, preparing for the weddings.

First, *when* the ladies from your place *had come along to join us,*

Your wife and daughter were embraced and shook our hands
    in greeting.

They really did enjoy themselves. And I was getting ready,

Not far away, a party for the men here—you listening?

Don't go to sleep.

GETAS.   No, don't.

KNEMON.   Oh dear!

SIKON.   What's that? You want to be there?

Now listen to the rest of it. Libations were all ready.

A couch of straw was being spread upon the ground. The
    tables

I myself was laying out—that was, you see, my duty—

You hear? I am the cook, don't you forget.

GETAS.   He's coming round* now.

        [*as* SIKON *warms to his description, his language becomes elevated
                                                                and poetic*

SIKON. One man was pouring vintage wine into a hollow vessel,

And mixing in the Nymphs' clear stream, he went right round
    and offered
A toast to all the men; meanwhile another pledged the ladies.
You might as well pour water out into the sand!* You get me?
One of the girls, a trifle drunk, whose fair young face was
    shaded,   950
Took up the rhythm of the dance, from shyness hesitating
And trembling, but another girl joined hands with her and
    danced too.
GETAS. You've had a dreadful accident, poor man; now dance,
    now join in.

                          [GETAS *tries to pull* KNEMON *to his feet*
KNEMON. What *do* you want, you wretched men?

                                 [KNEMON *resists*
GETAS.   Try harder; up and join in.
  You are so clumsy.   [*They pull him up*
KNEMON.   Don't, my god, please, don't.
GETAS.   Then do you want us
  To lift you in?
KNEMON.   What shall I do?
GETAS.   Dance, dance!
KNEMON.   Oh, carry me then.
  Perhaps it's better to endure the party there.
GETAS.   That's good sense.
  We've won! Hooray! Donax,*

        Enter DONAX *from the shrine.*

               and you as well,
Sikon, now lift him up and carry him
Inside. [*To* KNEMON] But you, look out! For if we find   960
You stirring things again, you may be sure,
We'll treat you pretty harshly. Someone give
Us garlands, torches!

    [*Garlands and torches are distributed to the actors;* GETAS *throws a*
                                garland to KNEMON
          Here, this one's for you!
[*To the audience*] Well, if you've all enjoyed our victory
Over this tiresome old curmudgeon, then

Boys, youths and men, give us a friendly clap.
And may that noble, laughter-loving maid,
Victory, attend us always as our friend.

The Girl from Samos (Samia)

There are several substantial lacunae in the first two acts but the last three are pretty well complete.

Characters

MOSCHION, adopted son of Demeas, in love with Plangon
CHRYSIS, a courtesan from Samos, Demeas' mistress
PARMENON, a slave of Demeas
DEMEAS, a wealthy Athenian
NIKERATOS, his neighbour and father of Plangon
COOK

Silent characters:

Plangon, Nikeratos' daughter
Plangon's nurse
Nikeratos' wife
Cook's assistants
Various slaves

The Scene is set in a street in Athens, with the houses of Demeas and Nikeratos adjoining.

ACT I

The play opens with a long monologue by Moschion, which takes the place of a prologue; in this Moschion tells the audience the facts they need to know to make the plot intelligible.

The opening of Moschion's monologue is lost; the supplement is based on the assumption that he explains to the audience what they need to know to understand the dramatic situation.

MOSCHION. *I'm in a mess, and utterly depressed.*
  If you will listen, I will tell you why.
  I was adopted as a child by Demeas,
  A wealthy bachelor who had no heir.
  He's been abroad, in Pontos,* with a friend,
  And while he was away I fell in love
  With Plangon, daughter of our neighbour; he's
  The friend with whom my father's gone abroad.
  What's more, I promised I would marry her.
  My father won't, I'm sure, agree to this;
  He'll want me to accept a wealthier bride.
  That's bad enough but things are worse than that;
  I hardly like to tell you all the facts.

For why should I upset myself? *To tell*
The truth is painful; yes, I did do wrong.
I reckon it will hurt me, as I say,
But I may make you understand it more,
If I describe my father's character.
I well remember how he pampered me
Soon after my adoption, when I was
A little child, but I'll not dwell on this;
I was too young to know his kindness then.
When I was entered on the register,*   10
Like all the world, I was 'one of the mob',
As people say; and really *I've become*
More miserable, I swear, because we are
So rich. When I was made choregus,* I
Excelled all men in my munificence;
Horses he used to keep for me and hounds;
I led my tribe* with brilliance; and I
Could give a little help to friends in need.
Through him I was a man indeed. But still,
For this I made a fair return to him;

For I was well behaved. It happened then—
I'll go through all our troubles with you; yes,   20
I've time—he formed a passion for a girl
Who came from Samos*—she's a courtesan—
It's only human nature, I suppose.
He kept it dark, ashamed. I got to know,
Although he did not want me to, and thought,
Unless he got her under his control,
That younger rivals would soon trouble him.   26
He was ashamed to act, because of me
Perhaps. *I told him he should* take the girl
[Lacuna of about twenty-three lines, for which we give a supplement of two lines only.]
Into his house and he eventually
Agreed. So now she's living here with us. . . .
[Four lines mutilated, including the mysterious words 'seeing him bearing', 'I added everywhere', 'to our neighbour', 'smashing the seal'.]
Soon my girl's mother was on friendly terms   35
With father's girl from Samos, and usually
She'd visit them; sometimes they came to us.
One day I ran back from the farm and found
Them, as it happened, gathered at our house   40
With other women there to celebrate
Adonis' festival.* As you'd expect,
The festival involved a lot of fun,
As I was there, I thought I'd stay and watch.
Their rowdiness made sleep impossible;
For they were carrying their gardens up
Onto the roof and dancing; scattered round,
They kept it up all night. I hesitate
To say what followed; perhaps I am ashamed
When shame can do no good; but still, I am.
The girl got pregnant. When I tell you this,
I also tell you what went on before.   50
I did not then deny I was to blame,
But visited the mother of the girl
At once and promised I would marry her

As soon as father had returned to us
With his companion; and I swore an oath.
The child, born recently, I have received
Into our house. And by coincidence
There now occurred stroke of real luck;
Chrysis (that's what we call her) had a child;
[One broken line, then a lacuna of about twenty-nine lines, for
which we give a supplement of eleven lines only.]

But her poor baby died in a few days
And she has gladly taken Plangon's on
And nurses it as though it were her own.
But I must go and look for Parmenon,
Whom I have sent ahead to find out news
About my father, who's due home just now.

[*Exit to the harbour*

Enter CHRYSIS *from* DEMEAS' *house and soliloquizes for some lines,*
until she sees MOSCHION *returning with* PARMENON *from the harbour.*
She withdraws and overhears them.

CHRYSIS. *I hear that Demeas will soon be back.*
I wonder what will happen when he sees
The baby? He will think it's mine and ask
Who is the father. If he learns the truth—
But who's that on the path? It's Moschion.
He's hurrying home *with Parmenon.* I'll wait
And overhear what they are going to say.   60
MOSCHION. Did you see father, Parmenon, yourself?
PARMENON. Did you not hear me? Yes.
MOSCHION.   Our neighbour too?
PARMENON. They're here.
MOSCHION.   That's good.
PARMENON.   Then you must be a man
And straightaway put in a word about
Your marriage.
MOSCHION.   How? I'm nervous now the time
Has come.
PARMENON.   What do you mean?
MOSCHION.   I am ashamed

To tell my father.

PARMENON [*shouts in indignation*]. What about the girl
    You've wronged and the girl's mother?—Why, you wimp,
    You're trembling!

CHRYSIS [*comes forward*]. What are you shouting for, you wretch?

PARMENON. So Chrysis is here too! You want to know   70
    Why I am shouting? That's ridiculous!
    I want the marriage celebrated now
    And him to stop his weeping at the door;
    I want him to remember what he swore—
    That he would go himself to sacrifice,
    Put garlands on his head, cut up the cake;*
    So don't you think I have reasons enough
    For shouting?

MOSCHION.   Well, I'll do it all; no need
    For words.

CHRYSIS.   I'm sure you will.

MOSCHION.   And what about
    The baby? Shall we leave it just as now,
    For her to rear and say that she's its mother?

CHRYSIS. Why not?

MOSCHION.   My father will be cross with you.   80

CHRYSIS. He'll soon get over that. He's hopelessly
    In love, my friend, as badly as you are.
    That makes even the angriest man come round
    Quite soon and make it up. I think I would
    Put up with anything rather than see
    The baby brought up by a nurse in some
    Foul tenement.*

[Lacuna of twenty-three lines, for which we give a supplement of
eleven lines; then seven mutilated.]

              So come on, Parmenon,
   We must go in, if Demeas is on his way,
   And get things ready for him. For perhaps
   He'll be less angry when he hears our news,
   If he arrives to find all spick and span.

           [*Exeunt* CHRYSIS *and* PARMENON *to* DEMEAS' *house;*
                      MOSCHION *soliloquizes*

MOSCHION. *They're nearly here. I must make up my mind*
   What I'm to say to father. How can I
   Persuade him to accept my marriage plan?
   He won't agree to Plangon as my bride
   And he'll be livid if he finds I've had
   A child by her. I want *to bring him round;*
   . . . You might accept . . .
   I might declare that no one in the world's
   Unhappier; 'I'll hang myself at once.'   90
   Only an orator . . . of a friend.
   I am not good enough for this debate.
   I'll go to some deserted spot and train.
   I've really got a testing time ahead.

                        [*Exit* MOSCHION *to the country*

   Enter DEMEAS *and* NIKERATOS *with attendants from the direction of*
                      the harbour.

DEMEAS. Well, don't you see the change of scenery
   And feel the difference from those ghastly spots?
   Pontos! Nothing but fat old men and heaps
   Of fish! And boring business affairs!
   Byzantium! just wormwood,* everything   100
   There bitter! God! But here the poor enjoy
   Pure happiness. Athens, my dearest home,
   May you enjoy all blessings you deserve,
   So we who love our city may become
   The happiest of all men. [*To his attendants*] Get inside.

        [*Exeunt attendants to the houses of* DEMEAS *and* NIKERATOS
   [*To one who lingers*] You half-wit, don't stand staring at me
     there.
NIKERATOS. The thing that most surprised me, Demeas,
   About that place was this: sometimes you could
   Not see the sun for ages. A thick mist,
   It seemed, caused darkness.
DEMEAS.   Yes, there's nothing there
   To see that's wonderful, and so the sun   110
   Allowed them just the minimum of light.
NIKERATOS. How right you are!

DEMEAS.   Let's leave these subtleties
To worry other men. But what d'you mean to do
About the matter we were talking of ?
NIKERATOS. You mean your young man's marriage?
DEMEAS.   Yes, I do.
NIKERATOS. I've never changed my mind. Let's fix a day
And do it, and good luck to them.
DEMEAS.   Are we
Resolved on this?
NIKERATOS.   I am.
DEMEAS.   And so am I
And made my mind up earlier than you.
NIKERATOS. Then call me when you leave the house.
[One broken line, then a lacuna of about fourteen lines.]
DEMEAS.   *I'll stay.*
    There are a few things *I must think about.*

                        [*Exit* NIKERATOS *to his house;* DEMEAS *soliloquizes*
    There goes an honest man; he may be poor
    But I shall be delighted if my son
    Is married to his daughter. I don't think
    The boy is likely to object to this;
    He's always done what I have asked of him.
    I'd better go inside and find him now,
    Since I can see a crowd of drunken youths
    Approaching; I won't stay to clash with them.

                                        [*Exit into his house*

CHORAL INTERLUDE

ACT 2

Enter DEMEAS, *talking to himself, from his house and* MOSCHION *from the
    country.* DEMEAS *withdraws and listens to* MOSCHION *soliloquizing.*

DEMEAS. *I can't find Moschion at home and so*
    I've come out here to look for him and learn

What's happened while I've been away and how
It is that Chrysis has a child. Who can
The father be? I will not keep her here.
Out she'll go and take her child as well.
But there he is. He's talking to himself;
I shall withdraw and listen to his words.

[*He withdraws*

MOSCHION. *I went away to put some practice in*
But now I'm back and still have *not* rehearsed   120
One of the things I had in mind just now.
For when I was outside the town alone,
I started, in my mind, to sacrifice,
Invite my friends to join the wedding feast,
Send off the women for the lustral water,*
Walk round distributing the cake, and hum
The wedding song sometimes. I was an ass.
And when I'd had enough of this— good god!
There's father. Then he's heard me. Hello, dad.
DEMEAS. Hello, my son.
MOSCHION.   Why look so grim?
DEMEAS.   Why grim?
It seems I have a mistress who's a wife,   130
And never knew it.
MOSCHION.   What? A wife? I don't
Know what you mean.
DEMEAS.   It seems I've had a son,
Born secretly. Well, she can go to hell,
Out of the house, and take the baby too.
MOSCHION. Oh, no!
DEMEAS.   'Oh no?' Do you expect I'll rear
A bastard child for someone else in my
Own home? That's shocking, not my way at all.
MOSCHION. For heaven's sake, who is legitimate
Of all of us, who illegitimate,
If he is born a man?
DEMEAS.   You surely must
Be joking.
MOSCHION.   No, I'm deadly serious.

Birth, as I see it, makes no difference. 140
If you look fairly at the situation,
The good man is legitimate, the bad
Man's both a bastard and a slave as well.

[Nine lines mutilated beyond repair, a lacuna of about sixteen lines, then eight more badly mutilated; supplements speculative.]

So don't turn Chrysis out; keep her and keep
Her baby. Think—she may not be to blame,
If she was raped. I'm sure she loves you still.

DEMEAS. *You say she loves me? Well, maybe you're right.*
I'm sure I'm still in love with her. But I'll
Not let her stay and keep the child, by god.
Now, Moschion, there is another thing
I must discuss with you. You're old enough
To marry now; indeed, you should do so,
And I am going to suggest a match
Which would please me and satisfy you too.
What would you say to taking as your bride
Our neighbour's daughter, Plangon?

MOSCHION. *What do you say?*
There's nothing I'd like better in the world.

DEMEAS. *You really mean this? You are serious?*

MOSCHION. I love *the girl and long* to marry her.
So let's be quick; I beg you, don't *put off*
The wedding.

DEMEAS. *Don't you hustle me,* my boy.

MOSCHION. I want *to meet your wishes, father, and*
To seem *in all things an obedient son.*

DEMEAS. That's a god boy.

MOSCHION. Then let's get on with it.

DEMEAS. If they agree, you'll marry her *all right.* 150

MOSCHION. When you've learnt nothing of the affair,
How can you know I'm serious and help?

DEMEAS. 'You're serious'? 'Learnt nothing', do you say?
I understand your meaning, Moschion.
I'll run to him and tell him to begin
The wedding now. We'll play our part.

MOSCHION. Well said.

So I'll go in and have a ritual wash,
Pour a libation, and put incense on
The fire; and then I'll fetch the bride.
DEMEAS.   Don't go
Until I'm sure her father will agree.   160
MOSCHION. He won't oppose you. But it's wrong for me
To stay and be a nuisance here. *I'm off.*

> [*Exit to the city*

DEMEAS. Mere Accident is like a god, it seems,
And brings fulfilment of a lot of things
We cannot see. I did not know my son
Was so in love;
[Lacuna of about twenty-seven lines.]
> *this fits in with my plans,*
For now we can fulfil what we both want.
Let's hope Nikeratos will not object
To hurrying on the wedding, for the boy
Is so distraught with love he cannot wait.
I'd better find Nikeratos and get
Him to agree to hold the wedding now.
I don't imagine he'll be pleased at this,
But still, for my boy's sake, I'll have a go.
I want *to call* him *out.*

> [*He goes over to the door of* NIKERATOS' *house and shouts*

[The rest of the act is badly mutilated; the supplements speculative.]

> *Nikeratos,*

Come out and join me here in front.
NIKERATOS [*he comes out of his house*].   What for?
DEMEAS. I wish you a good day.
NIKERATOS.   *The same to you.*
What is it?
DEMEAS.   You remember that just now   170
We did not fix the wedding day?
NIKERATOS.   I do.
DEMEAS. *Well, what do you think of holding it* today?
You may be sure *the boy wants no delay.*
NIKERATOS. How? When?

DEMEAS.   *He wants the wedding* to take place
  Quickly *and says he'd like it held* today.
NIKERATOS. How *can we do that?*
DEMEAS.   *I can see no snag.*
NIKERATOS. No, it's impossible
DEMEAS.   *It's possible*
  For me and no *less possible* for you.
  We only have to tell your family.
  The preparations need not take too long.
NIKERATOS. Good god, *you really mean this, Demeas?*
  I'm bound to tell you *how it seems to me:*   180
  I'm all for haste but must insist on this:
  We cannot hold the wedding till we've told
  Our friends and seem *to do it properly.*
DEMEAS. Nikeratos, *if you agree to this,*
  My gratitude *to you will know no bounds.*
NIKERATOS. How am I to decide? *I want to fall*
  In with the wishes of a friend. You're set
  On this *then, Demeas? Well, I must not*
  Resist but *give way* and agree with you.
  It's *not the time* to start an argument.
DEMEAS. Now you are talking sense, and you will not
  Regret *what you've decided.*
NIKERATOS.   So you say;
  I hope you're right. We must begin to get
  Things ready.
DEMEAS.   Parmenon, boy, Parmenon!
                    Enter PARMENON *from* DEMEAS' *house.*
  Go and get garlands, get an animal   190
  For sacrifice and seeds of sesame*—
  Buy up the market and then come back here.
PARMENON. Buy everything? I'll do so, Demeas,
  If any's left.
DEMEAS.   Be quick about it; now.
  And bring a cook.
PARMENON.   A cook as well? When I
  Have bought *the lot?*
DEMEAS.   Yes, when you've bought the lot.

PARMENON. I'll get some cash and run.　　　[*Exit into* DEMEAS' *house*

DEMEAS.　　　　　　　　　　　Nikeratos,
　　You've not yet *gone to market?*

NIKERATOS.　　　　　　　　I'll go in
　　And tell my wife to get the house prepared,
　　Then I'll be on the heels of Parmenon.

　　　　　　　　　　　　　　　　　[*Exit into his house*

Enter PARMENON *from* DEMEAS' *house, carrying a basket; he shouts
to someone inside.*

PARMENON. I don't know anything, except what I've
　　Been told to do; I'm rushing off there now.

DEMEAS. Persuading his good wife will be a job.　　　　200
　　But we must not give explanations
　　Or waste our time. [*To* PARMENON] You hanging round, boy?
　　Run!

　　　　　　　　　　　　　　　　　[*Exit* PARMENON *to the city*

Enter NIKERATOS *from his house.*

NIKERATOS. My wife *is nosy, asking me what's up;*
　　She says, 'For god's sake, tell me what's the need
　　For all this haste?' So what? How she goes on!

　　　　　　　　　　　　　　　　　[*Exit* NIKERATOS *to the city*

[*Lacuna of ten lines.*]

DEMEAS. *What next? I'd better go and tell my son*
　　Nikeratos has grudgingly agreed
　　To hold the wedding, as we hoped, today.

　　　　　　　　　　　　　　　　　[*Exit into his house*

CHORAL INTERLUDE

ACT 3

　　　DEMEAS *comes out of his house and launches into a long soliloquy.*

DEMEAS. *Sailors may be enjoying* a fair voyage
　　When suddenly, out of the blue, a storm

Blows up in force; it shatters those who were
Just now running before the wind in calm
And overturns the ship. That's just my case;   210
For there I was, about to organize
The wedding and to make the sacrifice
To god, and everything was working out
Just as I wished—but now I hardly know,
My god, if I am even seeing straight.
I really don't; but I am coming out
To tell you what a knock-out blow I've had.

              [*He goes to the front of the stage to address the spectators*

It's quite incredible. Consider, friends,
Whether I'm sane or mad, and took the facts
All wrong and bring upon myself a great
Misfortune needlessly. As soon as I
Had gone into the house, in haste to get   220
All ready for the wedding, I explained
Things to the servants quite straightforwardly
And told them to get on at once with all
The necessary work—to clean the house,
To bake, to get the ritual basket* out.
They set to willingly enough, of course,
Although the speed they worked at caused a bit
Of chaos, just as you'd expect. The child
Was dumped down on a couch out of the way
And bawled its head off. And the maids were all
Shouting at once: 'Flour, water, olive oil,
Some charcoal, please.' And I myself was there
Passing them this and that and helping them;
I happened to have gone into the store,
From which I was selecting more and stayed   230
Inspecting things, so did not leave at once.
While I was there a woman came downstairs
Into the room in front of the storeroom.
It's where the weaving's done, in fact, through which
You pass to go upstairs or to the stores.
The woman proved to be Moschion's nurse,
Who's getting on; she'd been my slave, but now

She's free. And when she saw the baby there,
Neglected, crying, as she did not know 240
That I was in the house, she thought it safe
Enough to chatter; she went up to it
And said the usual things; 'My darling child,'
She said,'You treasure, where's your mummy then?'
She kissed the child and carried it around.
When it stopped crying, she said to herself,
'Dear me, it's just the other day I nursed
Moschion at this age and cuddled him,
And now he has a baby of his own
[Lacuna of two lines, then three lines mutilated.]
And here it is asleep, safe in my arms.
But why are they neglecting the poor thing?
Just then a servant girl came running in; 251
She said to her, 'The baby needs a bath.
Dear me, what's this? It's father's wedding day
And you're not caring for the little mite?'
At once the girl said, 'Wretch, don't talk so loud!
Himself is here.' 'Oh no!' nurse whispered 'where?'
'He's in the storeroom'; then she raised her voice,
'Mistress is calling, nurse. [*Quietly*] Go on, be quick.
He has not heard a thing, that's luck for us.'
'O what a wagging tongue I have!' she said, 261
And off she went away, I don't know where.
And I walked out exactly as I came
To you just now, quite calm, pretending I'd
Not heard or seen a thing. Outside I saw
The Samian girl alone; she held the child
And it was feeding at her breast. So now
I know it's hers, but who the father is,
Whether it's mine or else—I won't say that
To you, my friends, or even think of it,
But now I simply put the facts to you 270
Of what I heard myself—not angry—yet.
I know the young man through and through as one
Who's always in the past been well behaved,
As dutiful to me as he could be.

But then, when I reflect on this, that she
Who said that had once been Moschion's nurse
And spoke out of my hearing, as she thought,
And yet again when I think of the girl
Who so adores the baby and insists
That we should rear it, though against my will—
I'm absolutely done, out of my mind.

    [*He sees* PARMENON *entering, followed by the* COOK *and his* ASSISTANT
But Parmenon is here—how opportune!—   280
On his way back from market: I must let
Him take the men he brings into the house.

                              [*He withdraws*

    Enter PARMENON *with the* COOK *and* ASSISTANT.

PARMENON. God, cook, I don't know why you carry knives
   With you. You're sharp enough to chop the lot
   Just with your tongue.
COOK.   You wretched ignoramus!
PARMENON. What, me?
COOK.   I really think you are a clot.
   I ask how many tables you will need,
   How many women will be there, what time
   The dinner will begin, whether we need
   To hire an extra waiter, if you have   290
   Sufficient crocks, whether the kitchen's roofed,
   And whether all the rest we need is there—
PARMENON. You're chopping me to pieces, my good friend,
   In case you didn't notice, and do so
   Most skilfully.
COOK.   Oh, go to hell!
PARMENON.   The same
   To you with knobs on! Get along inside!
      [*Exeunt* COOK *and* ASSISTANT *into* DEMEAS' *house, followed by*
             PARMENON. DEMEAS *comes forward and calls him*
DEMEAS. Hey, Parmenon!
PARMENON.   Did someone call me?
DEMEAS.   Yes.
PARMENON. Master, hello.

DEMEAS. Put down the basket first,
  Then come back here.
PARMENON. All right, I will.   [*Exit into* DEMEAS' *house*
DEMEAS.   I'm sure
  There's nothing of this kind that he'd not know;
  There's no such busybody in the world.   300
  But there's the door again; he's coming out.
PARMENON [*speaking over his shoulder to* CHRYSIS *inside*]. Chrysis, you
      give the cook whatever he
  Demands; for heaven's sake, don't let old nurse
  Get near the wine. [*Turning to* DEMEAS] Well, master, what's to
      do?
DEMEAS. You ask me what's to do? Come here, away
  A little from the door; a little more.
PARMENON. There.
DEMEAS.   Listen, Parmenon. I do not want
  To whip you, no, I really don't for lots
  Of reasons.
PARMENON.   Whip me? Why, what have I done?
DEMEAS. You're hiding somethimg from me. That I know.
PARMENON. I am? I swear by Dionysus and
  By our Apollo herc* and Saviour Zeus,   310
  And by Asklepios—
DEMEAS.   Stop! Swear me no oaths!
  I'm not just guessing.
PARMENON.   May I never be—
DEMEAS. You, look at me.
PARMENON.   All right, I'm looking now.
DEMEAS. Whose is the baby?
PARMENON.   Ah!
DEMEAS.   I'm asking you
  Whose is the baby.
PARMENON.   Chrysis'.
DEMEAS.   And who is
  The father?
PARMENON.   You, she says.
DEMEAS.   You've had it now;
  You're lying to me.

PARMENON.	Me?
DEMEAS.	I know it all.

I've learnt that it is Moschion's, that you
Are in the know, and she is bringing up
The brat for him.

PARMENON. Who says so?

DEMEAS. Everyone.

Just answer me one thing: is this the case?

PARMENON. Master, it is; we hoped to keep it dark—   320

DEMEAS. To keep it dark! [*He shouts into the house*] Hey, one of you, give me
A strap to whip this godless rogue.

Enter a SLAVE *with a whip.*

PARMENON. No, don't.

DEMEAS. By god, I'll brand you.

PARMENON. Brand me?

DEMEAS. Straightaway.

PARMENON. I've had it. [*He escapes and runs off*

DEMEAS. Where're you running to, you rogue?
[*To the* SLAVE, *who pursues him*] Catch him! O citadel of Kekrops'
land,*
Encircling Air, O—Shouting, Demeas?
Why shout, you fool? Restrain yourself. Bear up.
For Moschion's not wronging you. [*To the audience*] Perhaps
My words seem wild, my friends, but they are true.
For if he did this of his own freewill,   330
Or else infatuated, or hating me,
He'd still be shameless, still in the same state
Of mind and ready to do battle with me now.
But as it is, he made a full defence
When happily agreeing to the plan
I sprang on him. For he was in hot haste
Not since he was in love, as I thought then,
But eager to escape that Helen* of mine
And get away from her; for she's to blame
For what has happened; she got hold of him
When he'd been drinking, yes, that's obvious,

And lost his self-control. Neat wine and youth 340
Result in many a foolish action, when
They have at hand to help them one who's schemed
To bring him down. I simply cannot believe
That he, so well behaved and self-controlled
Towards all others, would treat me like this,
Not if he were ten times adopted, not
My natural son. No, it's not his birth
I'm thinking of but his good character.
The woman's just a whore, a pestilence.
Why waste my breath on her? She'll not last long.
Now, Demeas, now you must be a man.
Forget you've missed her, finish with your love, 350
And hide the trouble which has come on us
As far as maybe for your dear son's sake,
And throw this wonder-girl from Samos out
Head first, out of the house to feed the crows.
You've got a reason—that she's kept the child.
Give nothing else away. So bite your lip,
Bear up, and bravely see the whole thing through.

Enter the COOK *from* DEMEAS' *house, looking for* PARMENON.

COOK. Surely the fellow's here, before the doors?
    Hey, Parmenon! The man's deserted me,
    And never gave a helping hand at all.
DEMEAS. Out of my way!

              [DEMEAS *rushes into the house to find* CHRYSIS]
COOK.   Heavens above, what's this? 360
    Some lunatic old man's gone tearing in;
    Whatever's up? Oh well, it's no concern
    Of mine.   [*Loud shouts from inside the house*
          Good god, he really must be mad;
    At least he's shouting loud enough. Wow! All
    That crockery I've just set out, suppose
    He breaks the lot to smithereens, that would
    Be a good joke! But there's the door—O, damn
    You, Parmenon, for fetching me here! I'll
    Move back a bit.   [*He retires to the back of the stage*

Enter DEMEAS, *driving* CHRYSIS *before him; she holds the baby
and is followed by the* NURSE.

DEMEAS.   Get out! D'you hear?
CHRYSIS.   Oh dear,
  Wherever to?
DEMEAS.   Oh, go to hell!
CHRYSIS.   Poor me!
DEMEAS [*aside*]. Yes, poor indeed. Her tears do really make   370
  Me pity her. [*To* CHRYSIS] I'll stop you, yes, I will—
CHRYSIS. From doing what?
DEMEAS.   Nothing. You've got the child
  And nurse; get out!
CHRYSIS.   Because I kept the child?
DEMEAS. Because of that and—
CHRYSIS.   'And'?
DEMEAS.   Because of that.
COOK [*aside*]. Ah that's the trouble then; I get it now.
DEMEAS. You did not know how to behave when you
  Enjoyed such luxury.
CHRYSIS.   I didn't know?
  What do you mean?
DEMEAS.   You came here, Chrysis, dressed
  In a simple linen smock—you follow me?
CHRYSIS. So what?
DEMEAS.   Then I was all in all to you,
  When you were badly off.
CHRYSIS.   And now who is?
DEMEAS. Don't bandy words with me. You've got all your   380
  Own things and I will add some servant girls
  And gold. Now go away, out of my house!
COOK [*aside*]. Some nasty temper here. I must go up
  To them.[*He approaches* DEMEAS] Consider, friend—
DEMEAS.   Are you addressing me?
COOK. You needn't bite me.
DEMEAS [*disregarding the* COOK].   Yes, some other girl
  Will be delighted with my gifts, Chrysis,
  And sacrifice in gratitude to god.

COOK [*aside*]. What is he on about?
DEMEAS.   You've borne a son,
   You've all you want.
COOK [*aside*].   Not biting yet! [*To* DEMEAS] But still—
DEMEAS. I'll smash your head in if you speak to me.
COOK. And quite right too. I'm going in now, look!.

                              [*Exit into* DEMEAS' *house*

DEMEAS. A fine figure you'll cut! Yes, you will see   390
   Exactly who you are when you're in town.
   The other girls, not in your style, Chrysis,
   Who only earn ten drachmas, all run off
   To dinner parties and they drink wine neat
   Until they die or, if they don't accept
   Such invitations readily, they starve.
   You'll learn, I'm sure, no less than them
   And realize what you are and what a fool
   You've been. [CHRYSIS *tries to approach him*] Stay there!

              [*Exit* DEMEAS *into his house and bolts the door*

CHRYSIS.   Oh dear, oh, what ill luck!

Enter NIKERATOS *from the city leading a scraggy sheep.*

NIKERATOS. This sheep here will provide all the accustomed
   Offerings* to the gods and goddesses,   400
   When it is sacrificed. It's got some blood,
   And gall bladder enough, some splendid bones,
   A great big spleen; and that's what is required
   For the Olympians. Then, for my friends
   To have a taste, I shall chop up the skin
   And send it them. That's all I shall have left.
   But, god! what's this? Chrysis is standing here
   In tears. It's her all right. [*To* CHRYSIS] What's up?
CHRYSIS. That honest friend of yours has thrown me out,
   That's what it is.
NIKERATOS.   Good god! Who? Demeas?
CHRYSIS. Yes, him.
NIKERATOS.   But why?
CHRYSIS.   Because I kept the child.
NIKERATOS. The women told me you'd taken up the child   410

And that you're keeping it. You idiot!
But he's soft-hearted.

CHRYSIS.　　　　　　　　He was not cross at once,
But later on. Just now he said I was
To get things in the house all ready for
The wedding; but, while I was doing this,
He fell upon me like a lunatic,
And now he's locked me out.

NIKERATOS.　　　　　　　　He must be sick.
The Black Sea's not at all a healthy place.
Come with me to my wife. Cheer up! Don't fret!
He'll cease this madness soon when he reflects
And gives some thought to what he's doing now.　　　　420

　　　[*Exit* NIKERATOS *into his house together with* CHRSYIS, *the baby, the*
　　　　　　　　　　　　　　　　　NURSE, *and the sheep*

CHORAL INTERLUDE

ACT 4

Enter NIKERATOS *from his house, speaking over his shoulder to his wife.*

NIKERATOS. Wife, you'll wear me all to pieces. I'm off now to
　　　tackle him.*　　　　　　　　　　　　[*He soliloquizes*]
　　I would not have had this happen if you'd offered me a
　　　fortune,
　　Heavens, no, I really wouldn't. When the wedding's just
　　　begun,
　　Here's a most untimely omen come on us; a girl's arrived
　　At our house, thrown out by someone, with a baby in her
　　　arms.
　　So there're tears and all the women have completely gone to
　　　pieces.
　　Demeas has proved a shit and, god, I'll make him pay for this.

Enter MOSCHION *from the city; he does not see* NIKERATOS
and soliloquizes

MOSCHION. Will the sun never start setting? What can be the
    explanation?
Has the night forgot its function? What an endless afternoon!
Shall I go and bath a third time? I have nothing else to do.

NIKERATOS [*comes forward*]. Moschion, I'm glad to see you.   430

MOSCHION.   Do we hold the wedding now?
Parmemon told me just lately, when he met me in the town.
Can't I go and fetch your daughter?

NIKERATOS.   Don't you know what's happened here?

MOSCHION. No, I don't. What?

NIKERATOS.   What, you ask me? Something horrible's occurred.

MOSCHION. God! What is it? I know nothing, since I've only just
    got back.

NIKERATOS. Dearest boy, your father's driven Chrysis from his
    house just now.

MOSCHION. That's incredible.

NIKERATOS.   It's happened.

MOSCHION.   Why?

NIKERATOS.   Because she kept the child.

MOSCHION. Where's she now then?

NIKERATOS.   She's with us here.

MOSCHION.   What a shocking piece of news!
How amazing!

NIKERATOS.   If it really seems to you so awful, then—

Enter DEMEAS *from his house, in a rage, shouting back to his servants,
who are in tears.*

DEMEAS. If I get a stick, I'll teach you, knock the tears out of your
    eyes.   440
What's this nonsense? Now get cracking. Give the cook a
    helping hand.
[*Ironically*] Tears are certainly in order, such a treasure's left
    our house!
All the facts tell us this clearly.
        [*He turns to the statue of Apollo which stands before the house*
          Dear Apollo, greetings to you,

Grant, I pray you, that the wedding which we are about to
    hold
May for all of us be lucky. [*To the audience*] I shall hold the
    wedding still,
Friends, and swallow down my anger. [*To Apollo*] Master,
    watch me, see that I
Do not give myself away now; make me sing the wedding
    hymn.
Not that in my present temper, I shall sing it very well.   450
Never mind. She'll not come back here.

> [MOSCHION *and* NIKERATOS, *who have been discussing*
> *what to do, approach* DEMEAS

NIKERATOS.   Moschion, go on, you first.

MOSCHION. Very well.[*To* DEMEAS] Why are you, father, doing
    this?

DEMEAS.   What's that, Moschion?

MOSCHION. Doing what, you ask? Then tell me, Why has Chrysis
    left the house?

DEMEAS [*aside*]. Clearly someone's acting for her as a go-between;
    that's bad.

[*To* MOSCHION] That's no business of yours, boy, it is only my
    concern.

Why this nonsense? [*Aside*] This is awful. He is helping them to
    wrong me.

MOSCHION. What d'you say?

DEMEAS [*still aside*].   That's clear enough now. Why should he
    approach me for her?

He should surely be delighted this has happened.

MOSCHION.   What d'you think
All our friends will say about this, when they learn—

DEMEAS.   My friends, Moschion,
I suppose—leave that to me, boy.

MOSCHION.   I should not be acting rightly,
If I let you carry on so.   460

DEMEAS.   Then you'll stop me?

MOSCHION.   Yes, I shall.

DEMEAS [*aside*]. Look at that! This takes the biscuit! Worse than
    what he said before!

MOSCHION. You should not give way to anger.

NIKERATOS.   Demeas, he is quite right.

MOSCHION. In you go, Nikeratos, and tell the girl to run home
    here.

DEMEAS. Moschion, I tell you, drop it; drop it, Moschion, I say;
    For the third time I repeat it; I know everything.

MOSCHION.   Know what?

DEMEAS. Say no more to me.

MOSCHION.   I have to.

DEMEAS.   Have to? Am I not to be
    Master here?

MOSCHION.   Grant me this favour.

DEMEAS.   Favour! such as asking me,
    'Go away from your own house, please, leave us two here on
        our own.'
    Let me carry on the wedding—let me, if you've any sense.

MOSCHION. Yes, I'll let you, but I'm anxious Chrysis should be
    here with us.

DEMEAS. Chrysis?

MOSCHION.   It's for your sake mostly I insist on having her.

DEMEAS. Now we know; it's clear as daylight. Be my witness,
    Loxias:*
    Someone's plotting with my enemies. Help! I'll burst a blood
        vessel!

MOSCHION. What d'you mean?

DEMEAS.   Am I to tell you?

MOSCHION.   Yes.

DEMEAS [*he leads* MOSCHION *aside*].   Then come this way.

MOSCHION.   Speak on.

DEMEAS. Right. The baby's yours, I'm certain. I have heard from
    Parmenon,
    Who himself was in the secret. Don't you play these games
        with me.

MOSCHION. How is Chrysis wronging you then, if I'm father to this
    child?

DEMEAS. Who is wronging me? It's you, boy—

MOSCHION [*disregarding* DEMEAS' *interruption*]. How is she responsible?

DEMEAS. What d'you say? Have you no conscience?   480

MOSCHION.   Why're you shouting?
DEMEAS.   Why, you scum?
  Why, do you ask? Then tell me whether you take all the blame
      yourself?
  And you dare to say this to me while you look me in the face?
  Have you really so completely turned against me?
MOSCHION.   Turned against you?
  Why do you say that?
DEMEAS.   Why, you ask me? Do you dare to ask me this?
MOSCHION. Yes, it's not an awful scandal; thousands, dad, have
      done the same.
DEMEAS. God, how shameless! Now I ask you, here before this
      audience,
  Who's the mother of your baby? Tell it to Nikeratos,
  If you think there's no great scandal.   490
MOSCHION [*aside*].   That, my god, will cause a scandal,
  If I tell him. He'll be livid when he finds out all the facts.
NIKERATOS [*bursting in on the conversation*]. Oh, you worst of human
      beings! Now at last I start to guess
  What has happened, what an outrage he's committed.
MOSCHION.   That's the end.
DEMEAS. Now, Nikeratos, you see it?
NIKERATOS.   Yes, I do. Most wicked crime!
  O incestuous beds of Tereus, Oedipus, Thyestes,* and
  All the rest we've ever heard of—you have made them seem
      nothing!
MOSCHION. Me?
NIKERATOS.   You really dared to act so, had the bloody nerve
      for this?
  You should take Amyntor's rage on,* Demeas, and blind the
      boy.
DEMEAS [*to* MOSCHION]. You're to blame that all's discovered.
NIKERATOS.   Is there nothing you'd not do?
  Anyone you'd keep your hands off? Then am I to let my girl
  Marry you? I'd rather suffer—absit omen*—Diomnestus
  As my son-in-law, a marriage all would think the bottom end.
DEMEAS [*to* MOSCHION]. Wronged by you, I held myself in.
NIKERATOS.   Demeas, you're just a slave.

If my bed had been defiled, I'd make sure that he would never
Once again abuse another, nor the girl who slept with him.
Come tomorrow, first to get there, I'd be selling off the whore,
And at once renounce my offspring, publicly; no barbers'
    shop, 510
No stoa* empty; all would gather, sitting round from sunrise
    on,
Gossiping about me only, saying that Nikeratos
Had been proved a man, who'd rightly prosecuted you for
    murder.

MOSCHION.   Murder!

NIKERATOS.   Yes, I judge it murder, when a son rebels
    like this.

MOSCHION [*aside*]. God, my throat is dry with terror and I'm
    frozen stiff with fright.

NIKERATOS. And, what's worse, it's I who welcomed in my home
    the very girl
Who was guilty of this outrage.

DEMEAS.   Throw her out, Nikeratos,
Think yourself as wronged as I am; be a proper friend to me.

NIKERATOS. I'll explode if I but see her. [*To* MOSCHION] Can you
    look me in the face,
Savage, yes, and truly Thracian?* Let me pass.

                        [*He rushes past* MOSCHION *into his house*

MOSCHION.   For heaven's sake,
Father, hear me. 520

DEMEAS.   I'll hear nothing.

MOSCHION.   Even if what you suspect
Never happened? I'm beginning now at last to understand.

DEMEAS. Never happened?

MOSCHION.   Chrysis is not mother to the child she tends;
She is doing me a favour, saying it belongs to her.

DEMEAS. What do you say?

MOSCHION.   The simple truth, sir.

DEMEAS.   Why's she doing this for you?

MOSCHION. I don't want to tell the reason, but escape the greater
    charge
And admit only the lesser, if you clearly learn the truth

Of what happened.

DEMEAS.   Hurry up then. Tell me quickly or I'll die.

MOSCHION. I'm the father, and the mother is Nikeratos' daughter.
  But I wished to keep it secret.

DEMEAS.   What do you say?

MOSCHION.   What really happened.

DEMEAS. See you do not try to fool me.

MOSCHION.   Try when you can check the facts?
  What shall I gain now by lying?

DEMEAS.   Nothing—someone's coming out

NIKERATOS *staggers out of his house, lamenting in tragic style.*

NIKERATOS. Misery! What have I seen there! Maddened, I am
  rushing out,
  Struck at heart with pain unlooked for.

DEMEAS [*aside*].   What on earth's he going to say?

NIKERATOS. I've just found inside my daughter feeding the baby at
  her breast.

DEMEAS [*aside*].   So it's true.

MOSCHION.   You hear that, father?

DEMEAS.   Moschion, you did not wrong me,
  I wronged you, by my suspicions.

NIKERATOS [*seeing* DEMEAS *at last*].   Demeas, I come to you.

MOSCHION [*aside*]. I'm away.

DEMEAS.   Keep up your spirits.

MOSCHION.   Seeing him I'm all but dead.
                                              [*Exit to the city*

DEMEAS [*to* NIKERATOS]. What's the matter?

NIKERATOS.   I've just come on my own daughter in the house
  Feeding the baby at her breast there.   540

DEMEAS.   Well, perhaps, it was just play.

NIKERATOS. Certainly she was not playing; when she saw me
  coming in,
  Straightaway she fell down fainting.

DEMEAS.   Well, maybe, perhaps, she thought—

NIKERATOS. Oh! 'Perhaps, perhaps'—you'll kill me.

DEMEAS [*aside*].   I'm responsible for this.

NIKERATOS. What d'you say?

DEMEAS.   I think your story is beyond the bounds of belief.

NIKERATOS. But I saw it.

DEMEAS.   Don't talk drivel.

NIKERATOS.   This is not an empty tale.
I'll go back and—

DEMEAS.   Just a minute. Here's the answer, friend—[NIKERATOS
  rushes into his house] He's gone.
Everything is upside down now. It's the end. When he finds out
All the facts, he'll be so angry, heavens, he will shriek aloud.
He is rough, no finer feelings, always calls a spade a spade.   550
Really, I should have suspected something like this; damn it all.
I deserve to die, by heaven. [NIKERATOS *shouts aloud from in the
  house*] O good lord, that was a shout!
I was right. Fire, fire, he's yelling; threatening to burn the
  child.
I shall see my grandson roasted. Now he's at the door again.

NIKERATOS *rushes out of his house.*

There, the man's a thunderbolt or like a whirlwind

NIKERATOS.   Demeas,
Chrysis is conspiring with them, doing the most dreadful
  things.

DEMEAS. What d'you mean?

NIKERATOS.   She has persuaded wife and daughter to admit
Nothing and she's grabbed the baby, won't let go, and says she
  won't
Hand it over. So don't wonder, if you find I murder her.   560

DEMEAS. Murder Chrysis?

NIKERATOS.   Yes, she's plotting with them.

DEMEAS.   Don't, Nikeratos!

NIKERATOS. Had to warn you this might happen.
                               [*He rushes back into the house*

DEMEAS.   Help, he's melancholy mad.
In he's rushed. How should one cope with such a crisis? I am
  sure
I have never been so flummoxed. Far the best thing is to say
Clearly what has really happened. Heavens, there's the door
  again.

Enter CHRYSIS *from* NIKERATOS' *house, running and holding the baby.*

CHRYSIS. Misery! What shall I do now? Where am I to flee? He will

Take my baby from me.

DEMEAS.   Chrysis, come this way!

CHRYSIS.   Who's calling me?

DEMEAS. Run inside.

Enter NIKERATOS *from his house, armed with a stick.*

NIKERATOS.   You, where're you fleeing?

DEMEAS [*aside*].   Heavens, I shall have to fight   570
A duel today apparently. [*To* NIKERATOS] Who're you chasing?
What d'you want?

NIKERATOS. Demeas, get out! Just let me get the baby in my power,

Then I'll make the women tell me.

DEMEAS.   No.

NIKERATOS.   You're going to hit me then?

DEMEAS. Yes, I shall. [*To* CHRYSIS] Get in, you, quickly.

NIKERATOS.   I shall hit you in return.

DEMEAS. Hurry, Chrysis; he's the stronger.

                    [*Exit* CHRYSIS *with the baby into* DEMEAS' *house*

NIKERATOS.   You began this —Witness, all!

DEMEAS. Take a stick against a freeborn woman! and you're chasing her.

NIKERATOS. You're accusing me quite falsely.

DEMEAS.   So are you.

NIKERATOS.   Bring out the child.

DEMEAS. That's absurd. It's mine.

NIKERATOS.   It isn't.

DEMEAS.   Yes, it is.

NIKERATOS [*to audience*].   O, gentlemen—

DEMEAS. Shout away!

NIKERATOS.   I'll go inside and kill the girl. What else is left?   580

DEMEAS. There, again that wicked notion. I won't let you.
Where're you off to?
Stop!

NIKERATOS.   Don't lay a finger on me!

DEMEAS.   Come, control yourself.

NIKERATOS.   It's clear,
Demeas, you're wronging me and you are in the plot yourself.

DEMEAS. Well then, ask me all about it; don't go bothering the girl.

NIKERATOS. Has your son bamboozled me then?

DEMEAS.   Nonsense! He will take the girl.
No, it's not like that. Come on now, walk around with me a
   bit.

NIKERATOS. I'm to walk around with you?

DEMEAS.   And pull yourself together, friend.
Tell me now, Nikeratos, have you never heard the tragic
Poets tell how Zeus took shape once as a shower of gold* and
   pouring   590
Through the roof seduced a maiden who was shut inside the
   room?

NIKERATOS. Yes, so what?

DEMEAS.   We must be ready, I suppose, for anything.
Has your roof a leak? Consider.

NIKERATOS.   Yes, it mostly leaks. How's that
Relevant to what you're saying?

DEMEAS.   Sometimes Zeus takes shape as gold,
Other times he's simply water. Now you see? He did the deed.
There's the problem solved quite quickly.

NIKERATOS.   You are fooling me.

DEMEAS.   Good lord, no.
I would not do that. But surely you are just as good as him,
Danae's old father, aren't you? If he honoured her, your
   daughter—

NIKERATOS. Moschion has really fooled me, blast it—

DEMEAS.   No, the boy will have her;
Never fear. But what has happened is, be sure, divinely
   sanctioned.   600
Thousands I can name are walking in the midst of us who are
Children of the gods. You think that what has happened is
   unique.
First of all, there's Chairephon,* who dines abroad and never
   pays.

Don't you think that he's a god then?

NIKERATOS.   So it seems; what can I say?
I'll not fight with you for nothing.

DEMEAS.   That's good sense, Nikeratos.
Androcles* lives on for ever, runs and skips and interferes;
Walks around with hair still raven, wouldn't die if it were
     white,
Not if someone slit his gizzard. He's a god, you must admit.
Pray that this may turn out lucky. Burn some incense, sacrifice.
Very soon my son'll be coming for his bride.

NIKERATOS.   There's nothing for it;
I must do what you're proposing.

DEMEAS.   Now you're really showing sense

NIKERATOS. If I'd caught him at the time, tho'—

DEMEAS.   Stop such thoughts and don't get cross.
Go inside and make things ready.

NIKERATOS.   Right.

DEMEAS.   And so shall I.

NIKERATOS.   Then go.

DEMEAS. You're no fool—and I am grateful. Thanks to all the
     gods above,   [*Exit* NIKERATOS *into his house*
None of what I thought had happened proved to have a grain of
     truth.

                                                [*Exit into his house*

CHORAL INTERLUDE

ACT 5

                          Enter MOSCHION, *talking to himself.*

MOSCHION. I was delighted then, when I was freed
     Of that false charge, and thought I'd had
     Some luck. But now I'm more in my right mind
     And I reflect, I'm quite beside myself   620
     And furious at the wrongs my father thought

I'd done. So if there were no difficulty
About the girl and there were not a mass
Of obstacles—my oath, my love, our long
Friendship, by all of which I am held fast,
He'd not accuse me to my face again
Like this, but I'd be off, out of his way,
Leave here for Baktra or for Karia*
And live there as a soldier, spear in hand.
But as it is, I'll not indulge in such
Heroics, for your sake, my dearest girl;   630
It can't be done, and Love, who rules my heart,
Forbids me to. But all the same I must
Not altogether overlook the slight
And take it with a coward's humility.
I want to frighten him, with words at least,
By saying that I'm off to serve abroad.
In future he will always take good care
To treat me with more fairness, when he sees
That I don't take this as a little thing.
But Parmenon's here, just at the right time,
The man I wanted most of all to see.   640

Enter PARMENON *from the country; he does not see* MOSCHION.

PARMENON. Almighty god, in what a foolish way
   I have behaved, and how contemptibly!
   I had done nothing wrong but got into
   A fright and ran away from master's wrath.
   What had I done to justify such fear?
   Let us consider, clearly, point by point,
   Thus: master led a freeborn girl astray;
   Does Parmenon do wrong here? surely not.
   The girl got pregnant; that is not his fault.
   The baby was then brought into our house;
   It's Moschion who brought it in, not me.   650
   One of the household said she'd borne the child;
   What fault has Parmenon committed here?
   Why, none. Why did you scamper then, you fool
   And utter coward? That is ridiculous.

He threatened he would brand me; ah, you've got
There now; it does not make the slightest bit
Of difference, whether it be fair or not
For me to suffer this—not a nice thing
In either case.
MOSCHION. Hey, you!
PARMENON.   Good day to you.
MOSCHION. Stop all this nonsense and go in at once.
PARMENON. What for?
MOSCHION.   To bring me here my army cloak
And sword.
PARMENON.   Bring you your sword?
MOSCHION.   That's right, and get
A move on too.   660
PARMENON.   Whatever for?
MOSCHION.   Go on,
And do what I have told you and don't breathe
A word.
PARMENON. What's up?
MOSCHION.   If I can find a whip—
PARMENON. Oh no. I'm going.
MOSCHION.   Get a move on then.
                    [*Exit* PARMENON *into* DEMEAS' *house*
My father will be here quite soon; he'll beg
Me not to go; that's clear. But for a time
He'll beg in vain; he'll have to; then, when
I decide, I shall give way to him. There's just
One thing—I must be plausible, and that
By god, I simply cannot do. But this
Is it; yes, that's the door; he's coming out.

                Enter PARMENON *from* DEMEAS' *house.*

PARMENON. You're completely out of date with what is
        happening, I believe;*   670
As you have not heard precisely and don't know the way things
        go,
You upset yourself for nothing, drive yourself into despair.
MOSCHION. Where's the gear?

PARMENON.   They are now starting wedding celebrations for you.
   Wine's amixing, incense smoking, sacrifices have begun;
   Offerings already burning in Hephaistos' flame.*
MOSCHION.   The gear, boy?
   PARMENON. It's for you they've long been waiting. Are you off
      to fetch the bride?
   Lucky you! You've no more trouble. So take heart. What do
      you want?
MOSCHION. Villain, you insist on giving me advice?
                              [*He strikes* PARMENON *on the face*
PARMENON.   Help! Moschion,
   What's that for?
MOSCHION.   Run in and quickly bring the stuff I told you to.
PARMENON. Now you've cut my lip.
MOSCHION.   Still talking rubbish, you?
PARMENON.   I'm on my way.
   God, a fine reward I'm given for the news I brought.   680
                  [PARMENON *goes towards* DEMEAS' *house but seeing through the*
                              door the wedding preparations in train, he stops
MOSCHION.   Still here?
PARMENON. They are starting on the wedding, really.
MOSCHION.   That again! Do bring me
   News of something else!   [*Exit* PARMENON *into* DEMEAS' *house*
                            My father will be here in half a minute.
   Just suppose he does not beg me, gentlemen, to stay at home,
   But in rage he lets me go—I never thought of that. Then what?
   Probably he would not do this. But supposing that he did?
   Anything can happen. Heavens, I should look a proper fool,
   If I had to go about and eat my words.

                  Enter PARMENON *from* DEMEAS' *house.*

PARMENON.   There! Here they are—
   Cloak and sword. You take them from me.
MOSCHION.   Give them here. Did anyone
   In the house catch sight of you there?
PARMENON.   No one.
MOSCHION.   No one, are you sure?
PARMENON. Yes, I'm sure.

MOSCHION.   What are you saying? Oh, god blast you!
PARMENON.   On your way!
You just keep on talking rubbish.

Enter DEMEAS *from his house in a state.*

DEMEAS.   Well, where is he? Tell me where.   690
                         [*He sees* MOSCHION *with cloak and sword*
Heavens, what is this?
PARMENON [*to* MOSCHION]. Go quickly!
DEMEAS.   What's the meaning of this gear?
What's the matter? Tell me truly, do you mean to go away?
PARMENON. As you see, he is already marching and is on his road.
Now I too must say goodbye to friends inside; I'm going in.
                                      [*Exit into* DEMEAS' *house*
DEMEAS. Moschion, your anger makes you dearer, and I don't
    blame you
If you are distressed that you have been accused wrongly by
    me.
All the same you must consider who you feel so bitter to.
I'm your father; it was I who took you as a little child,
I who raised you. If your journey through this life has been a
    joy,
I it was who gave you this, so you should tolerate my ways,   700
Even when they've hurt you badly, bearing with me like a son.
I accused you then unjustly; I was misled, wrong and mad.
But remember this, Moschion: though it meant I wronged the
    rest,
It was you alone I thought of, tried to keep all my suspicions
To myself; I did not publish them for enemies to crow.
You're now telling all the world of my mistake, call men to
    witness
What a fool I've been. Moschion, that is not what I expect.
Don't remember this day only in my life when I fell down   710
And forget the days before that. There's a lot I still might say,
But no more. You may be certain, if a son obeys a father
Grudgingly, that's wrong, if readily, all men approve.

Enter NIKERATOS, *talking back to his wife in the house.*

NIKERATOS. Don't annoy me. All's been seen to—baths and
    sacrifice and wedding;
  If the bridegroom ever shows up, he will take the bride and go.
  Help, what's this?
DEMEAS.   I've no idea, friend.
NIKERATOS.   How can you have no idea?
  What's this cloak? Can he intend to do a bunk?
DEMEAS.   That's what he says.
NIKERATOS. He says that! But who will let him, this seducer,
    self-confessed.
  I'll arrest you now, this instant.
MOSCHION.   Go ahead, arrest me, please.
NIKERATOS. Keep on talking nonsense, will you? Drop the sword!
    Be quick about it.
DEMEAS. Moschion, for god's sake, drop it. Do not make him
    angrier.   720
MOSCHION. Let it go then. [*He throws down the sword*] Your
    entreaties have succeeded and your prayers.
NIKERATOS. What! our prayers! Come over here, boy.
MOSCHION.   Are you going to arrest me?
DEMEAS. No, not that! Bring out the bride here.
NIKERATOS.   Do you really think so?
DEMEAS.   Yes!
       [*Exit* NIKERATOS *into his house to fetch* PLANGON
MOSCHION. If you'd done this straightaway, dad, you would not
    have had just now
  All the trouble of that preaching at me.

Enter NIKERATOS *pushing* PLANGON *before him.*

NIKERATOS.   On you go, my girl!
  Now before these witnesses I give this girl to you to hold,
  May she bear you lawful children,* and for dowry I will leave,
  When I'm dead, all my possessions—that, I pray, may never
    be,
  Since I hope to live for ever.
MOSCHION.   Here I take her, hold her, love her.

DEMEAS. All that's left now is to send for lustral water.* Chrysis, come,
　Bring us out the women, bath boy, and the piper.　　　　730

Enter CHRYSIS *from* DEMEAS' *house.*

　　　　　　　　　　　　　　　　　　　Someone give us
Torches, garlands, so that we may bring the bride home in
　procession.

Enter SLAVE *with torches and garlands.*

MOSCHION. Someone's here with all the clobber.
DEMEAS.　　　　　　　　　　　Put a garland on your head,
　Deck yourself as for a wedding.
MOSCHION.　　　　　　　There I am!
　　　　　[Exeunt all in a wedding procession, except for DEMEAS *who*
　　　　　　　　　　　　　　stays to address the audience
DEMEAS.　　　　　　　　　　　You lovely boys,
　Youths and old men, altogether loudly give us the applause
　Loved by Bacchus,* as the token, gentlemen, of your goodwill.
　And I pray the immortal goddess, patron of our finest shows,
　Victory, may always favour all the plays that I put on.

A line which can't be placed is quoted by Phrynichus, (*Eclogae*,
p. 187 Lobeck) as from *Samia*:

　You, bring the frankincense, and you put on
　The fire, Tryphe.

The Arbitration (Epitrepontes)

More than half the play survives, including nearly all the second act, which contains the arbitration scene from which the play takes its name. The text is badly mutilated in many places and restoration is highly speculative. A papyrus recently published (the Michigan papyrus) contains large portions of Acts 3–5, but unfortunately it is much damaged.

Characters

KARION, a cook
ONESIMOS, servant of Charisios
SMIKRINES, father of Pamphile
CHAIRESTRATOS, a friend of Charisios
HABROTONON, a harp-girl, enslaved to a brothel-keeper
DAOS, a shepherd
SYROS,* a charcoal-burner
PAMPHILE, daughter of Smikrines and wife of Charisios
CHARISIOS, husband of Pamphile

Silent characters:

SIMIAS, Karion's assistant
SYROS' WIFE with a BABY
SOPHRONE, Pamphile's old nurse

The scene is set in a village in Attica; two houses are visible: one is that of Charisios, the other of his friend Chairestratos.

ACT I

Of Act I only the end is partially preserved. But the opening scene may be tentatively restored with the help of six short quotations from ancient commentators (OCT, frs. 1–6). In the following reconstruction the supplements, based on the assumption that the scene is expository, attempt to link up these quotations.

Onesimos has been sent to town to hire a cook (Karion) for a party to be given in Chairestratos' house. They enter gossiping with each other.

KARION. For heaven's sake, Onesimos, was not
    Your master, who now keeps the dancing girl*
    Habrotonon, just married?
ONESIMOS.   Yes, he was.
KARION. *Then tell me, do, what's happened? Why's he left*
    His wife? Why is he living with his friend
    Chairestratos? Why has Habrotonon
    Been hired when he's now got a wife at home?
ONESIMOS. *So many questions, Karion! You're much*
    Too nosy. Don't go prying into things
    Which don't concern you.
KARION.   I am fond of you,
    Onesimos; you're nosy too. *Come on,*
    Do tell me why I'm called to cook him lunch
    At someone else's. I like nothing more
    Than knowing everything.
ONESIMOS.   I'll tell you then,
    But you must swear to keep it to yourself.
KARION. *I swear by all the gods I'll never breathe*
    A word to anyone.
ONESIMOS.   *When master was away,*
    His wife proved pregnant and she had the child
    Just five months after they were married. She
    Was desperate and she gave the baby to
    Old Sophrone, who said that she would find
    A home for it. We all knew this, and when

My master had returned, I went to him
And told him everything. For if he learnt
It from some other source, I'd pay for it.
He loves Pamphile but could not forgive
What she had done. And so he left his house
And moved into his friend's and there he stays
With this Habrotonon and simply mopes,
While Pamphile remains in his old home alone.

KARION. *Ah, now I understand. But tell me more;*
How is your master? He'll divorce his wife?

ONESIMOS. I've sprinkled salt on salted fish,* if that
Should happen. *But* why aren't you cooking lunch?
He's long been fretting, lying on a couch.

KARION. *Then I'll get cracking now. I wish you luck.*

> [*Exit into* CHAIRESTRATOS' *house*

ONESIMOS. *And I must go and see how master is.*
I wish he could throw off this lethargy
And take some comfort from this party here.

> [*Exit into* CHAIRESTRATOS' *house*

It seems probable that this scene was followed by a delayed prologue, spoken by some divinity (as in *The Shield*). The conversation
between Onesimos and Karion has given the audience some of
the background, but they still need to know that Charisios is in
fact the father of Pamphile's child, that Sophrone exposed the
child, leaving it to die in a nearby forest, that it was rescued by a
shepherd who gave it to a charcoal-burner whose master is
Chairestratos. Only if the audience knows all this, will they
appreciate the irony of the arbitration scene, in which Smikrines
decides the fate of his own grandson, unawares.

Our text begins again towards the end of a third scene in which
Smikrines is soliloquizing about the ill treatment of his daughter
by Charisios, while Chairestratos is eavesdropping in the background. The first two and a half lines are a quotation from
Stobaeus (*Eclogae* 3. 30. 7) which may belong here, after which we
have thirty-five lines from a papyrus which conclude the first act.

SMIKRINES. An idler who is healthy's far worse off
  Than one with fever; he eats twice as much
  And all for nothing. . . . And the fellow *drinks*
  The most expensive wine. I'm quite amazed   127
  At that. I don't say anything about
  His drunkenness; what I can scarcely believe
  Is that a man can bring himself to drink
  Wine that he buys for two obols a pint.*   130
CHAIRESTRATOS [*aside*]. That's just what I expected. He'll rush in
  And break the party up.
SMIKRINES.   What do I care?
  To hell with him again! He took the dowry,
  Four talents* in hard cash, and doesn't think
  He even needs to live here with his wife;
  He sleeps away from home; he gives the pimp
  Twelve drachmas every day—
CHAIRESTRATOS [*aside*].   Twelve drachmas! yes!
  His knowledge of the facts is quite precise.
SMIKRINES. Enough to keep a man a month and six
  More days besides.
CHAIRESTRATOS [*aside*]. He's got his sums quite right—
  Two obols every day, enough to buy   140
  A starving man some gruel!

Enter Habrotonon from CHAIRESTRATOS' *house;* SMIKRINES, *aborbed*
in his tirade, does not see her.

HABROTONON.   Chairestratos,
  Charisios is waiting for you now.
  Darling, who's this?
CHAIRESTRATOS.   The father of his wife.
HABROTONON. But what's the matter with him, *scowling there*
  Just like some sad *philosopher*, poor man?
        [CHAIRESTRATOS *and* HABROTONON *continue to comment aside on*
                SMIKRINES' *complaints about* CHAIREAS' *behaviour*
SMIKRINES. *He keeps* a dancing girl to *live with him*
  Deserting my own daughter who's his wife . . .
[Lacuna of six lines followed by eight lines of which only single
words survive; supplements highly speculative.]

SMIKRINES. *My daughter must abandon him; he must*
  Give back *the dowry*.
HABROTONON.   *What?* The old man *wants*
  To get the dowry *back?*
SMIKRINES . . . I ask . . .
HABROTONON. But that's not right.
SMIKRINES.   *And when she's left, let him*
  Enjoy his orgies in the night.
CHAIRESTRATOS. . . . Habrotonon?
HABROTONON. But I did not call *you*.
SMIKRINES   .   .   .   .   .   .
HABROTONON. God bless you, don't say 'always'.   160
CHAIRESTRATOS. Oh, go to hell! You'll pay for this, you will.
SMIKRINES. Now *I'll go in* and when I've learnt the facts
  About my daughter's situation here,
  I shall decide how I should tackle him.
                                   [*Exit into* CHARISIOS' *house*
HABROTONON. Are we to tell Charisios he's come?
CHAIRESTRATOS. Let's tell him. What a cunning fox this is!
  He's turning our whole household upside down.
HABROTONON. I wish he'd do the same to lots of homes.
CHAIRESTRATOS. *To lots of homes?*
HABROTONON.   The one next door, at least.
CHAIRESTRATOS. Do you mean mine?
HABROTONON.   Yes, yours.* Come on; let's go
  And tell Chairisios.
CHAIRESTRATOS.   All right, let's go.
  A mob of youths is coming here, quite drunk.   170
  I don't think it's the time to bother them.
                          [*Exeunt* CHAIRESTRATOS *and* HABROTONON *to*
                                           CHAIRESTRATOS' *house*

CHORAL INTERLUDE

ACT 2

The first part of the act is lost, apart from some mutilated fragments from the opening, which appear to be a soliloquy spoken by
Onesimos; the first line and a half of this survives.

ONESIMOS. Thinking that man's predicament is all
    Precarious, I . . .

There follow five lines of which only the first words survive and
then a lacuna of perhaps forty lines, in the course of which
Smikrines must have entered (he is on stage in the background
when our text resumes) and presumably tells in a monologue how
his interview with Pamphile went. Perhaps he had a row with
Onesimos. Onesimos then leaves the stage.

> DAOS, *a shepherd, enters, from the country; he holds a bag of trinkets and is*
> *followed by* SYROS, *a charcoal-burner, and his* WIFE, *who is holding a*
> BABY. *They are in the middle of an argument.*

SYROS. You're trying to avoid what's fair.
DAOS.   And you're
    A rotten blackmailer. You should not have
    What's mine by right.
SYROS.   We need to find a man
    To arbitrate.*
DAOS.   I'll willingly do so.
    Let's have a judge.   220
SYROS.   Who then?
DAOS.   Why, anyone
    Will do for me. My case is just enough.
    What made me offer you a share?
SYROS [*indicating* SMIKRINES].   You'll take
    This man as judge?
DAOS.   Yes, gladly.
SYROS [*to* SMIKRINES].   Would you, please,
    Good sir, spare us a little of your time?
SMIKRINES. Spare time? What for?
SYROS.   We have an argument.

SMIKRINES. What's that to do with me?

SYROS.   We're looking for
A fair man who would arbitrate. So if
You've no objection, settle our dispute.

SMIKRINES. Blast your impertinence! You skive around
In working clothes, while arguing your case.

SYROS. But all the same—It won't take long; it is   230
A simple case. Grant us this kindness, sir;
Please don't despise us. When disputes arise
Justice should always triumph everywhere
And anyone who's there should feel concerned
In this; it is a duty shared by all.

DAOS [*aside*]. I'm tied up with a fairish orator;
Why ever did I offer him a share?

SMIKRINES. Will you abide by what I shall decide?
Speak.

SYROS.   Yes, we will.

SMIKRINES.   I'll hear your case. For what's
To stop me? You speak first, the silent one.

DAOS. I must go back a bit in time, and not   240
Just talk about my dealings with this man,
So that the facts may all be clear to you.
About a month ago, good sir, while I
Was shepherding my flock among the woods
Near here, alone, I found a new-born child,
Left there to die; it had a necklace and
Some other trinkets—

SYROS.   That's what it's about.

DAOS. He will not let me speak.

SMIKRINES.   If you interrupt
Again, I'll thump you with my stick.

SYROS.   That's fair.

SMIKRINES. Speak on.

DAOS.   I shall. I lifted up the child   250
And went away back home with it; I meant
To bring it up; that's what I planned just then.
Night brought reflection, as it does to all;
I reasoned, why should I become involved

With all the trouble to raise up a child?
How shall I pay for it? Why take on all
Those worries? That is how I felt by now.
At dawn I went back to my shepherding.
This man—a charcoal-burner—came along
To the same place, meaning to saw some logs;
I've known him for some time. We had a talk,
And when he saw that I looked glum, he said,   260
'Why's Daos thoughtful?' 'Why?' I said; 'because
I am a busybody', so I told
Him all, how I had found the child and how
I'd taken it. Before I'd even done,
He started begging me, 'Daos, as you
May hope for happiness, please give the child
To me', he kept on saying; 'So may you
Be lucky, and so win your liberty.
I have a wife,' he said, 'who bore a child
Which died', meaning this girl who holds
The baby now.
SMIKRINES [*to* SYROS]. Well, Syros, did you beg?
DAOS [*bursting in before* SYROS *could answer*].
                    He wore out all the livelong day with prayers,   270
Beseeching and persuading me until
I promised. I gave him the child; he called
A thousand blessings on my head and went;
He even took and tried to kiss my hands.
SMIKRINES. Did you do this?
SYROS.   I did.
DAOS.   So he was gone.
Now suddenly he's turned up with his wife,
Demands to get from me the stuff that was
Left with the child—just little things, pure trash,
Worth nothing—and he says he's being done,
Because I will not give them up and claim
That I should keep them for myself. I say
He should be grateful for the share he got   280
By all his prayers and that I should not
Be cross-examined if I don't give all to him.

If he'd been walking with me when I found
These things, a windfall shared by both of us,
Then he'd have taken part and I the rest.
But I found them alone, and then do you think
That you, who were not there, should take the lot
And I have nothing? Last, I've given you
Part of my find.* If you like it, keep it now,
If not, if you have changed your mind, then give
It back to me. Don't do me wrong and think
That you're the loser. You should not get hold   290
Of all, some given willingly by me,
The rest taken by force. I've made my case.

SYROS. He's done?

SMIKRINES.   Did you not hear him? Yes, he's done.

SYROS. Good. Now my turn. He found the child alone
And all he says is right; that's how it was,
I don't deny it, sir. I got this child
From him by my entreaties and my prayers.
In this he speaks the truth. A shepherd then,
One of his mates, to whom he told the tale,   300
Informed me that together with the child
He'd found some trinkets; father, it is these
The baby's here to claim himself—[*to his* WIFE] give me
The baby, wife—Daos, this baby claims
From you the necklace and the other things
By which he may be recognized; he says
That they were put there to adorn himself,
Not to provide for you. And I support
His claim; for I'm responsible for him;
You made me guardian when you gave him me.
Now this, good sir, is what you must decide,
I think, whether this gold and other stuff,
Such as it is, should be preserved intact,
His mother's gift, whoever she may be,   310
Until the child grows up, or that this thief
Should keep it for himself, since he first found
Another's property. Why, then, did I
Not ask you for them when I took the child?

It was not then my right to speak for him.
But now I'm here to claim nothing from you
For my own self. 'A lucky find is shared',
You say? But it is not a 'find', when wrong
Is done to some third party. You are not
Then 'finding' things but simply stealing them.
Consider this point too: perhaps this child   320
May be of higher birth than us; brought up
Amongst us working men, some day he'll feel
Disdain for us, rise up to his true self,
And dare to do some gentlemanly deed,
Hunt lions, bear arms, or run in the great games.
You've watched the tragedies, I'm sure, and know
All this—an aged goatherd, dressed in clothes
Like mine, once found a Neleus and a Pelias,*
And seeing they were grander than himself,
He told them all, how finding them he'd brought   330
Them home. He gave them tokens in a bag,
From which they learnt the truth about their birth,
And those who then were goatherds soon were kings.
If Daos had pinched and sold those tokens off,
To make twelve drachmas for his greedy self,
They would have stayed unknown all time to come,
These mighty princes, born of royal stock.
It really is not fair that I should feed
The child, while Daos takes its only hope
Of rescue, sir, and makes away with it.   340
Why, tokens stopped one man from marrying
His sister, and through them another met
His mother and protected her; a third
Preserved his brother. Nature makes this life
Precarious for all of us; we need
To think ahead, and be on guard, good sir,
Anticipating how to help ourselves.
'If you don't want the baby, give it back',
He says, and thinks he makes a powerful point.
But that's not fair; because you must give up
Some of the child's things, will you attempt

To get the baby too, so you may play
The thief again with more security, 350
Since Luck has now preserved some of its things?
I've had my say. Now judge as you think just.
SMIKRINES. That's easily done. All things that were exposed
Together with the child are his. That is
My judgement.
DAOS.   Fair enough. Whose is the child?
SMIKRINES. My god, I'll not decide it goes to you
Who are defrauding it, but to the man
Who's helping and resisting all your plans
To swindle it.
SYROS.   God bless you, sir, for this.
DAOS. A dreadful verdict! God, it really is.
I found it all and now I'm stripped of all.
He did not find a thing, yet keeps the lot. 360
So must I give the stuff to him?
SMIKRINES.   You must.
DAOS. A dreadful verdict, damn me if it's not.
SYROS. Bring it, be quick!
DAOS.   O god, what misery!
SYROS. Undo the bag and show us; for that's where
You're keeping it. [*To* SMIKRINES, *who is going*] Please wait a
    moment, sir,
For him to hand it over.
DAOS.   Why did I
Entrust the case to him?
SMIKRINES.   Give it, you thief.
DAOS. What shocking treatment!
                              [SYROS *takes the bag and inspects the contents*
SMIKRINES [*to* SYROS].   Have you got it all?
SYROS. I think I have, unless he swallowed some
While I was speaking when he found he'd lost.
DAOS. I never would have thought it possible.
SYROS. Goodbye, kind sir. I wish all judges were
Like you. 370
                              [*Exit* SMIKRINES *to the city*
DAOS.   What scandalous injustice! God!

There's never been a verdict worse than this.
SYROS. You were a villain.
DAOS.   Villain yourself, you'd best
    Keep safe those tokens for the child
    Till he grows up. I'll watch you all the time,
    Be sure of that.
SYROS.   Oh, damn you. Get away.

                            [*Exit* DAOS *to the country*

[*To his* WIFE] You take these things, my dear, and bring them
To Chairestratos, our master. We'll stay
Here now until tomorrow when we'll pay
Our rent and then we'll go back to our work.   380
But first please count the pieces one by one.
Have you a box here? No? Then put them in
Your pocket.

        Enter ONESIMOS *from* CHAIRESTRATOS' *house; he does not at first*
                        see SYROS.

ONESIMOS.   No one's ever seen a cook
    As slow as this. By this time yesterday
    They'd all been at it drinking long ago.
SYROS [*examining the tokens one by one*]. This seems to be a cock, a
        tough one too;
    Here, take it. And this piece is set with stones.
    And here's an axe.
ONESIMOS [*aside*].   What's this?
SYROS.   Here's a gilt ring,
    On iron; the stone's engraved—a bull or goat—
    I can't distinguish which—the letters say
    It's made by one Kleostratos.   390
ONESIMOS [*coming forward*].   Show me.
SYROS. Hey, who are you?
ONESIMOS.   That's it.
SYROS.   That's what?
ONESIMOS.   The ring.
SYROS. What ring d'you mean? I do not understand.
ONESIMOS. Charisios, my master's ring.
SYROS.   You're mad.

ONESIMOS. The one he lost.   [ONESIMOS *takes the ring from* SYROS

SYROS.   Put down that ring, you wretch.

ONESIMOS. Am I to put it down for you?—it's ours.
   Where did you get it from?

SYROS.   Great gods above,
   What trouble! What a job it is to guard
   An orphan's things! The moment anyone
   Turns up he looks as if he'd grab the lot.
   Put down the ring, I say.

ONESIMOS.   Don't you play games
   With me. It is my master's ring, I swear.   400

SYROS [*turning away from* ONESIMOS]. I'd sooner have my throat slit
       than give in
   To him. My mind is made up and I'll sue
   Them one by one. They're baby's things, not mine.

                                    [*He continues to count the tokens*

   [*To his* WIFE] A necklace here—you take it—and a piece
   Of crimson cloth. Take them inside.

                            [*Exit* WIFE *with* BABY *to* CHAIRESTRATOS' *house*

   [*To* ONESIMOS]   Now you,
   What are you telling me?

ONESIMOS.   Charisios
   Is owner of this ring. He lost it once,
   When he was drunk, he said.

SYROS.   My master is
   Chairestratos. Then either keep it safe
   Or give it back to me to take good care of.

ONESIMOS. I'd like to guard the thing myself.

SYROS.   It makes   410
   No odds to me. We're both, I think, en route
   To the same house.

ONESIMOS.   Now they've got company;
   Perhaps it's not the time to tell him this,
   Tomorrow will be better.

SYROS.   I shall wait.
   Tomorrow I am quite prepared to put
   My case to whom you like.

                            [*Exit* ONESIMOS *to* CHAIRESTRATOS' *house*

                                    I've not come off
Too badly even now. I should give up
All else, it seems, and practise law, since that
Is how one keeps one's property today.

                                    [*Exit to* CHAIRESTRATOS' *house*

CHORAL INTERLUDE

ACT 3*

        Enter ONESIMOS *from* CHAIRESTRATOS' *house.*

ONESIMOS. I've started off to go to master and
      Show him the ring more than five times at least,   420
      But when I'm near to showing him and on
      The very brink, I shrink from doing so.
      I now regret I told him anything
      Before; he often says, 'O damn and blast
      The miserable man who told me this.'
      I am afraid he may now make it up
      With his own wife and do away with me
      Who told him this and know a lot too much.
      [*With heavy irony*] I'm doing well, wanting to stir the pot
      With yet more trouble; the trouble's big enough
      That's there already.

        Enter HABROTONON *from* CHAIRESTRATOS' *house, speaking over her
                shoulder to some of the guests inside.*

HABROTONON.   Please leave me alone,   430
      Don't pester me. [*She shuts the door*] Oh dear, it seems I've made
      Myself a fool, unwittingly. I thought
      He'd fall in love with me, but, no, the man
      Just loathes me, dreadfully, won't even let
      Me sit by him but pushes me away.
      Oh dear!
ONESIMOS [*not noticing* HABROTONON]. Shall I return the ring to him

From whom I took it then? That would be odd.

HABROTONON. Poor man! Why does he waste his money so?
For anything he's done I'd qualify
To bear Athene's basket;* oh dear me!
For two days I've been sitting round as chaste   440
As snow.

ONESIMOS.   How could I give it back? Good lord,
I ask you, how?

SYROS *bursts out of* CHAIRESTRATOS' *house.*

SYROS.   Where is he then, the man
Whom I've been chasing round inside? [*He sees* ONESIMOS]
    Here, you,
Return the ring to me, my friend, or show
It to the man you said you would. We've got
To have this settled. I must be away.

ONESIMOS. The situation is like this, my friend;
I'm sure Charisios my master owns
The ring but hesitate to show it him;
I almost make him father of the child,
If I bring him the ring with which it was
Exposed.

SYROS.   How do you make that out?

ONESIMOS.   You ass,   450
He lost it at the Tauropolia*
Some time ago—a women's festival
At night; one must suppose he raped a girl;
She had the baby and quite obviously
Exposed it. So, if someone found the girl
And brought the ring, he'd have clear evidence,
Where now there's muddle and we only guess.

SYROS. That's your concern. But if you mean to start
Blackmailing me and hope I'll pay a price
To get the ring back, then you're off your head.   460
No going shares, as far as I'm concerned!

ONESIMOS. I'm not asking that.

SYROS.   All right. I've got
To go to town now; I'll be back quite soon

To learn what I should do about this next.

[*Exit to city*; HABROTONON *comes forward*

HABROTONON. That baby, which the woman's nursing now,
Onesimos, this charcoal-burner found it?

ONESIMOS. He says so, yes.

HABROTONON.   Dear me, a lovely child!

ONESIMOS. He found my master's ring with it as well, .

HABROTONON. Ah, the poor thing. Then if it really is
Your master's baby, will you watch the child
Brought up to be a slave? You would deserve
To die for that

ONESIMOS.   I tell you, no one knows   470
Its mother.

HABROTONON. And you say he lost the ring
When he was at the Tauropolia?

ONESIMOS. That's so, and drunk according to the boy
Who was attending him.

HABROTONON.   It's obvious
He fell among the women on their own
When they were revelling throughout the night.
When I was there something like that occurred.

ONESIMOS. When you were there?

HABROTONON.   Last year, when I was at
The Tauropolia, and played my harp
For some young girls, and I joined in their games.
I did not know then what a man is like.

ONESIMOS [*ironically*]. I'm sure.

HABROTONON.   By Aphrodite,* I did not.

ONESIMOS. Who is the girl? Do you know?   480

HABROTONON.   I could find out.
The women I was with were friends of hers.

ONESIMOS. Who was her father? Did you find out that?

HABROTONON. I don't know anything, but if I saw
The girl, I'd know her. She was beautiful,
And rich as well, they said.

ONESIMOS.   Perhaps it's her.

HABROTONON. I've no idea. For she was there with us
And wandered off, then she came running back

Alone, in tears, tearing her hair, and, god,
The dress she wore, so fine and pretty, spoiled,
All torn to shreds. 490
ONESIMOS. And did she have this ring?
HABROTONON. Perhaps she did; she did not show it me,
I'll not tell lies.
ONESIMOS. Then what should I do now?
HABROTONON. You see to that. But, if you've any sense
And ask for my advice, you'll make the facts
Plain to your master. If the mother is
A freeborn girl, why keep him in the dark?
ONESIMOS. Habrotonon, let's first discover who
She is. You'll help me, please, to find this out?
HABROTONON. I couldn't, till I know for certain who
The culprit was. For I'm afraid to spin 500
A story to the girls I told you of
And get it wrong. Who knows, another man
Amongst his lot may have had it as a pledge
From him and lost it, or perhaps he put
It in the jackpot as a guarantee
When he was gambling, or perhaps he made
Some bargain, and, hard-pressed, gave up the ring.
Thousands of other things like that occur
When men are drinking. Till I'm sure who was
The culprit, I don't want to look for her
Or say a word about the business.
ONESIMOS. That's very sound. So what is one to do? 510
HABROTONON [*reflects*]. Onesimos, see whether you approve
Of an idea I've had. Suppose I treat
The rape as if the victim were myself
And take the ring and go inside to him—
ONESIMOS. Go on! Now I begin to understand.
HABROTONON. And when he sees me with the ring, he'll ask
'Where did you get it?' I shall say, 'When I
Was at the Tauropolia, and still
A virgin then.' And I'll pretend that all
Her sufferings were mine. Most of the facts
I know myself.

ONESIMOS.   That's really excellent.

HABROTONON. If he's the culprit, he will rush straight in   520
    And so convict himself, and being drunk
    He'll pour it all out first and I shall just
    Agree with what he says and so avoid
    Mistakes by speaking first.

ONESIMOS.   By god, that's brilliant.

HABROTONON. I will avoid mistakes by platitudes
    Girls always use—'You had no shame,
    You went for it all right.'

ONESIMOS.   That's excellent.

HABROTONON. 'How violently you threw me down! My clothes
    Were absolutely ruined,' I shall say.
    Before I do this, I shall go inside   530
    And hold the baby, weep and fondle it,
    And ask the girl who's minding it from where
    It came.

ONESIMOS.   Good heavens!

HABROTONON.   Last of all,
    I'll say, 'So you have got a baby now,'
    And I shall show the ring that we've now found.

ONESIMOS. Habrotonon, you're up to anything,
    A real piece.

HABROTONON.   If it's all proved and he
    Is shown to be the father of the child,
    Then we can search at leisure for the girl.

ONESIMOS. There's one thing you've not said, that you'll be freed.
    For if he thinks you're mother to the child,
    Then obviously he'll buy your liberty.   540

HABROTONON. I don't know that. I'd like it.

ONESIMOS.   Don't you know?
    But will I get some thanks for this myself,
    Habrotonon?

HABROTONON.   By both the goddesses,*
    I shall consider you the cause of all
    My happiness.

ONESIMOS.   Suppose you stop the search
    For her on purpose and you give it up

And leave me in the lurch, what happens then?

HABROTONON. My goodness, why should I? Do you think I long
  For children? Gods above, I only ask
  For freedom. That's the prize I want for this.

ONESIMOS. I hope you get it.

HABROTONON.   Well, do you like my plan?

ONESIMOS. I do, extremely. If you try to cheat,   550
  I'll fight you then. I'll find a way.
  But for the moment let us see if this
  Is really true.

HABROTONON.   So you agree with me?

ONESIMOS. I do.

HABROTONON. Then quickly hand the ring to me.

ONESIMOS. Here, take it.

HABROTONON [*she prays*]. Dear Persuasion, be my friend,
  Be at my side and make the words I speak succeed.

                      [*Exit into* CHAIRESTRATOS' *house*

ONESIMOS. The girl's a clever creature. When she found
  She couldn't get her liberty through love
  And was just wasting all her pains this way,
  She takes another road. But I shall stay
  A slave for ever, snotty, paralysed,   560
  Incapable of making schemes like hers.
  Perhaps I shall get something from the girl,
  If she succeeds; that would be fair—poor fool,
  What empty hopes you have, if you expect
  To earn, from any woman, gratitude!
  I only hope my troubles don't increase.
  My mistress's position's now unsafe.
  For if the girl is found to be freeborn
  And mother of this child, he'll marry her,   570
  Divorcing Pamphile and hoping to escape
  The mess at home this way. But now, I think
  I've dodged the trouble nicely—for this stew
  Was not stirred up by me. Goodbye, I say,
  To meddling! If anybody finds that I
  Have interfered or gossiped, I will let
  Him cut my—balls off. But who's coming here?

It's Smikrines, returning from the town
Again to stir things up. Perhaps he's learnt
The truth from someone. I had best get out.   580
I *do not want* to talk *to him just now.*
Before he sees me I must *be away.*

> [*Exit* ONESIMOS *to* CHAIRESTRATOS' *house*

> *Enter* SMIKRINES *from the city.*

The remainder of this act is badly mutilated; out of 117 lines only
nine are complete; only the first and last words of many lines
survive, of others only a few letters, and there is one lacuna of
fourteen lines. It is impossible to reconstruct the dialogue or even
to be certain of the course of events with any confidence. The
supplements are highly speculative.

The scene begins with a monologue from Smikrines in which
he attacks the behaviour of Charisios. The opening seven lines
have been ingeniously reconstructed (by Jensen) from the
surviving words as follows.

SMIKRINES. *This bloody man has made a fool of us.*
   He is an utter wastrel *and spend-thrift*
   The scandal is the talk of the whole *town.*
   I've come straight *back in fury to find out*
   Precisely *what is happening; they say*
   He sleeps from home and drinks*; shaming* the name
   Of all our family he lives there with the girl.   590

The following fourteen lines give no consecutive sense but
surviving words suggest that Smikrines' denunciation of Charisios
continues until the entrance of the cook, Karion.

At the end of this monologue we have: 'dancing girl . . .
continuous drinking bouts, gambling perhaps . . . I've had enough
of him.'

KARION, *the cook, bursts out of* CHAIRESTRATOS' *house, followed by his*
   assistant, SIMIAS; *he does not see* SMIKRINES, *who overhears him.*

[Of Karion's first seven lines only odd words survive; the following reconstruction is guesswork.]

KARION. *I've cooked for* lots *of parties at the best*
　　Establishments; I've won *high praise.*
　　But never in my life have I received
　　Such treatment. Just as lunch began, a girl
　　Came rushing in alone *and broke it up.*

　　　　　　　　　　　　　　　　　　[*Shouts from inside*
　　What's that? I think they've started quarrelling.
　　[*Shouts into the house*] You'll never get another *cook like me.*
SMIKRINES [*aside*]. Their lunch has plenty of variety!
KARION. I really am unlucky. Now, I don't know why,　　　610
They've come outside and off they scatter home.

　　　　　　The guests come streaming out of the house.

[KARION s*houts after them*] If *you should want* a cook again, you can
　　As far as I'm concerned, all go to hell.
[The following forty-five lines are badly mutilated; supplements
are guesses.]
SMIKRINES [*aside*]. *What's this? Some drunken quarrel, I suppose.*
KARION. *I wonder why they got in such a state.*
　　The girl was carrying a baby; can she be
　　Habrotonon? It's pretty clear that he's
　　The father of the child.
SMIKRINES.　　　　　　　The dancing girl
　　Has borne Charisios *a son! My god!*
　　　　　　　[KARION *sees* SMIKRINES *and explains to him what has happened*
KARION. *When they were having lunch and getting drunk*
　　This girl, who held a baby in her arms,
　　Rushed up to them.

Smikrines replies with a question, e.g. *Did he admit the child was his?*
To which Karion replies (obscurely): '. . . Indeed they have.'
Smikrines seems to have been distressed by this answer: 'Oh dear
. . .'.
　　Then seven lines from Karion, ending with his departure;
judging from the surviving words he may have been speculating
on what would happen next—would Pamphile be turned out and
Habrotonon become mistress of the house?, e.g.

KARION. *Did he decide to* send *a messenger*

To tell his wife that she should take her things
And leave the house? What a to-do! Then what
Will happen next? I long *to find out that.*
It looks as if Habrotonon may now
Become the mistress of the house. Good god!
Whoever would have thought it? Simias,
We must be going.   630

                      [*Exeunt* KARION *and* SIMIAS *to the city*

    CHAIRESTRATOS *bursts out of his house; he does not see* SMIKRINES.

[The following twenty lines are fragmentary; reconstruction is
highly speculative.]

CHAIRESTRATOS.   God, I nearly *burst;*
  I was amazed to see her *give herself*
  Such airs. This morning *she was quiet enough*
  But now she's getting supercilious.
  May I be damned *if she's not got some scheme.*
  I'm nervous *about how this will turn out.*
SMIKRINES [*aside*]. Then *I shall take my* daughter *home. She's not*   640
  Yet had a child* . . .
CHAIRESTRATOS.   *He says he'll* take *her home*
  And start divorce proceedings? Then he'll call
  On us as witnesses? . . .

                [SMIKRINES *sees* CHAIRESTRATOS *and addresses him*
  Charisios [*The remainder of this line and the next are lost.*]
  He is a friend of you lot and he felt
  No shame *at fathering* a baby by
  A whore?

Seven lines follow of which only odd words survive; they may
have contained an angry exchange between Chairestratos and
Smikrines. There follow six lines comparatively well preserved.

CHAIRESTRATOS (?). the life of the unhappy man   654
SMIKRINES. *Good god, you can't say he's* unhappy; [*with heavy irony*] but
  Perhaps I interfere and overstep my rights,
  When I have every reason to remove
  My daughter and to take her home with me.

That's what I'll do. My mind's almost made up.
I testify on oath, Chairestratos,   660
That you with whom . . . I sent . . .
I'll take *away* my daughter . . .
CHAIRESTRATOS. Don't do things which we don't deserve and
    don't
Say . . . saying
SMIKRINES. *His conduct's* scandalous . . .
And he drinks neat wine

Lacuna of about nine lines followed by four lines containing only
odd letters, in which Smikrines may have continued his angry
accusations against Charisios; then Chairestratos seems to have
tried to defend him, saying that he does not enjoy a riotous life.

CHAIRESTRATOS. He hates this dolce vita as it's called.   680
SMIKRINES. He drank with one girl,* with another spent
    The night, and for tomorrow morning he's
    Lined up a third. This way of life has turned
    Many *a household upside down* and brought
    Destruction on many marriages.
    It causes enmity and sicknesses . . .
    While he made merry every single day,
    But I could not persuade *her to leave him.*
    And so let him return the dowry, as
    Is *only right.*
CHAIRESTRATOS. No, Smikrines, not yet.
SMIKRINES. Good god, my daughter won't stay here the tenth   690
    Part of a day. He treats us, his in-laws,
    I swear, as if we're immigrants and on
    The alien register.*
CHAIRESTRATOS [*aside*]. Not even he thinks that.
SMIKRINES. So high and mighty! He will pay for this.
    When he's been ruined in a knocking shop,
    He'll live his life with this fine lady whom
    He's introducing here; he thinks that we
    Don't even know *what's going on.*

                                        [*Exit* SMIKRINES *in a fury*

CHAIRESTRATOS.   Will he
    Keep her* and take the other girl and bring
    Her to his house at once? It's clear he will.
    Now all my hopes* are upside down, it seems.
    But all the same my duty calls and I   700
    Must go to do the task I've been assigned.

                                    [*Exit to the city*

CHORAL INTERLUDE

ACT 4

    Enter SMIKRINES *and* PAMPHILE *in mid-conversation.*

SMIKRINES. I can see no *deliverance from these ills*;
    Pamphile, you must come away *at once*;
    Virtue demands you always flee a rogue.*
PAMPHILE. Oh dear, what is this *that you're telling me?*
    Are you to be my guardian all my life?
SMIKRINES. *You're talking rubbish.* I've no time to lose.
PAMPHILE. In doubtful questions one needs *time and thought.*
SMIKRINES. I've long been telling you *to leave the man.*   710
PAMPHILE. *You tell me to do this just* for my sake?
[Lacuna of two lines.]
    You're saving me? but if I'm not convinced,
    I'll think I'm not your daughter but your slave.
SMIKRINES. What need for words and for persuasion?
    The facts are absolutely plain. They shout
    Aloud, Pamphile. If I have to speak,
    I'm ready and I'll put three points to you;
    There's no way either of you could survive.   720
    He'll live a life of careless pleasure; you
    Will not be happy nor still be allowed
[Three lines mutilated beyond repair, then a lacuna of twenty-three lines, after which Smikrines is still speaking.]
    Then just consider the extravagance:
    He'd pay expenses for the Skira twice,

And for the Thesmophoria* pay twice.
See how it means complete financial ruin. 750
He's had it, hasn't he? All now agree on that
And then consider your position too;
He says he's got to go down to the docks;*
And when he gets there, he will sit around;
You'll be upset and wait about *all night,*
Postponing dinner, hungry, while he stays
Still drinking with that tart; it's obvious
He went *to go and see the dancing girl* . . .

There follow three lines in which only odd words and letters survive, then a lacuna of about 26 lines where a fragment of the Michigan papyrus may belong, which gives us only some isolated words: 'dancing girl', 'money', 'he(?) will learn', 'he(?) is mad'. When the text becomes intelligible again, Smikrines is still speaking; he appears to be expatiating on the situation which will arise if Charisios introduces Habrotonon into their home.

A woman scheming against you . . .
Who will revile you and *do you injury.*
Could *you* bear that? . . .
He will live well . . . and you in misery.
And then she'll have this consolation, 790
She will be scowling at you *all the time*
And giving you advice, assuming every way
The status of a wedded wife. And next
She'll start to push you out. It's difficult,
Pamphile, for a freeborn girl to fight
A battle with a whore; she has no scruples,
Knows more; she feels no shame, can flatter more,
And sticks at nothing. You must believe my words
As though the Pythia* herself *had told*
The future step by step. So if you think
Of all I say like this, you'll never do
A thing which is against your father's will. 800
PAMPHILE.* *Father, should I* express my views on all
The things that you consider for my good
With subterfuge or candidly? Indeed

Your fate *has given you* a wiser mind
Than mine, and *then your motive is* your love,
Protecting me, which *leads* me rather to
Obey you and *give way. But,* father, *no,*
That *seems to me im*possible. Let's drop
All talk of Luck—it's done no wrong to us—
All talk of fallen women. Secondly,
From this (?) . . . *you say that* he's to blame.
But there's no shame *if he enjoys himself*   810
With a few friends (?). Most people know. . .
And say *an honest friend* who's had bad luck
S*hould be esteemed* above *a bad man who*
Is prosperous. Am I to flee from him?
You said just now that you've now broken off
My *marriage, and he'll* come to a bad end
Because of that. Did I *come here* to share
His happiness but if he has *bad luck,*
Am I to have *no* care for him? No, no,
I came to share *his life* . . .   820
He's stumbled? That I shall endure *though I*
May see him living in two houses and
Still clinging to that girl *he's fallen for.*
But if *you give* me to another man
In marriage on condition that I
Shall never *suffer* any pain *or grief,*
My answer is 'No thanks'.* But if it is
Unclear how that *would end,* when I have come
To such a plight,* *I shall endure my lot.*
But she will throw me out? She'll see that I
Am loyal to Charisios, . . . though he   830
Still honours her and keeps *her in the house.*
When *he compares this girl with me, he'll* see
Quite easily which is worse . . .
Will she then slander us? . . .
And if she makes one false accusation . . .

Lacuna of about seventeen lines, in the course of which Pamphile
must have stuck to her determination not to leave Charisios and
Smikrines must have given up and left to fetch Sophrone.

After Smikrines has gone, Pamphile, left alone, may have
reflected on her misery; a quotation from an ancient grammarian
(Scholiast on Euripides, *Phoenissae* 1154) may belong here:

I was all burnt up with tears.

Perhaps she is describing her feelings when she had to abandon
her baby.

When our text resumes Pamphile is still on stage.

> HABROTONON *enters from* CHAIRESTRATOS' *house with the* BABY
> *in her arms;* PAMPHILE *at first does not see her.*

HABROTONON. I'll bring the baby out; poor thing, it has   853
　　Been crying ages. I don't know what is
　　The matter with it.
PAMPHILE. 　　　　　　　Won't any of the gods
　　Take pity on me in my misery?
HABROTONON. When will you see your mother, darling child?
　　　　　　　　　　　　　　　　[*She sees* PAMPHILE

　　But look! Who's here?
PAMPHILE. 　　　　　　　*Enough of this.* I'll go.
　　　　　　　　　　　　　[*She starts towards the house*

HABROTONON. Wait, lady, for a bit.
PAMPHILE. 　　　　　　　　　　You're calling me?
HABROTONON. I am. Please look at me.
PAMPHILE. 　　　　　　　　　　You know me, lady?
HABROTONON [*aside*]. This is the very girl I saw. [*To* PAMPHILE]
　　Darling, hello.
PAMPHILE. But who are you?
HABROTONON. 　　　　　　Come here; give me your hand.
　　Now tell me, sweetheart, did you go last year
　　To watch the Tauropolia *with friends*?
　　　　　　　　　　　[PAMPHILE *suddenly recognizes one of the tokens*
PAMPHILE. Where, lady, did you get the baby you
　　Are holding? Tell me.
HABROTONON. 　　　　　　Darling, do you see
　　Something he's wearing that you recognize?
　　No need to be afraid of me, my dear.

PAMPHILE. Aren't you yourself the mother of this child?

HABROTONON. No, I pretended that, not meaning to
  Injure its mother but to gain some time
  To find her; now I have. I'm looking at
  The girl whom I saw then.

PAMPHILE.   The father? Who is he?   870

HABROTONON. Charisios.

PAMPHILE.   My dearest girl, you're sure?

HABROTONON. I am. But aren't I looking at his wife
  Who lives in there?

PAMPHILE.   That's right.

HABROTONON.   O happy girl,
  Some god has taken pity on you both.   [*A door rattles*
  Someone has banged the neighbours' door on his
  Way out. Take me inside with you to get
  A clear account of everything from me.

                                        [*Exeunt into* CHARISIOS' *house*

Enter ONESIMOS *from* CHAIRESTRATOS' *house and addresses the audience.*

ONESIMOS. He's going a bit mad, my god, he is;
  In fact he is completely off his head;
  I swear he's round the bend. Charisios,
  I mean, my master. Black depression   880
  Has fallen on him or something like that.
  What other explanation could one find
  For what has happened? He was crouched inside
  For ages by the door just now, poor man.
  His wife's papa was nattering to her
  About the business, it seems; I can't
  Describe how he kept changing colour, friends,
  He shrieked aloud, 'My darling, what sweet words
  You say!' and punched his own head hard. He stopped
  A bit and next, 'O what a wife I had,   890
  And what a miserable fix I'm in.'
  And finally, when he had heard it all,
  He went away inside at last and gnashed
  His teeth and tore his hair, beside himself.
  He cried 'I am a sinner', several times;

'I did a deed like this, became myself
The father of a bastard child, and then
I neither felt nor gave the smallest scrap
Of mercy to my wife who'd had the same
Misfortune; I'm a heartless, savage beast.'
He's violent in reproaches of himself,
He stares with bloodshot eyes; he's up the pole.   900
I'm terrified, I'm all dried up with fear.
If he sees **me**, who gave the game away,
When he's like this, he'll kill me, I suppose.
And so I've slipped outside here secretly.
Where can I turn? What can I plan? I'm done.
I've had it. There's the door; he's coming out
O Saviour Zeus, please save me, if you can.

[*Exit* ONESIMOS *into* CHAIRESTRATOS' *house*

Enter CHARISIOS.

CHARISIOS. I led a blameless life, I always watched
  My reputation, pondered what was right
  And wrong, untouched by any vice,
  Beyond any reproach throughout my life—   910
  But now some power has rightly treated me
  As I deserved—I've shown at last that I
  Am human. 'You unhappy man,' it says,
  'You give yourself such airs and talk so big,
  But do not tolerate your wife's bad luck
  For which she's not to blame. I'll show you that
  You've stumbled just the way she did, then she
  Will treat you tenderly, while you insult her.
  So you'll be shown up as a man who was
  At once unlucky and a stupid brute.'
  Did she say to her father then the sort
  Of things you would have said? 'I came to share   920
  His life,' she said, 'and must not run away
  From the misfortune which has struck him now.'
  But you're so high and mighty . . .

[Five lines here mutilated; of the first only one letter survives; supplements speculative]

No better than a savage . . .
If I don't treat her wisely, . . .
                                        in the end
Some power above will punish me for this.
Her father will treat her *abominably*.
But what do I care for him? I'll tell him straight,
'You're not to give us trouble, Smikrines.   930
My wife is not to leave me. Why do you stir
Things up and try to bully Pamphile?
Why do I see you here again?'

   Enter ONESIMOS *followed by* HABROTONON *from* CHARISIOS' *house.*

ONESIMOS.   I'm in
  A thoroughly bad way. Oh dear, oh dear!
  Please, please, don't leave me, lady, in the lurch.
CHARISIOS [*seeing* ONESIMOS]. Villain, you stand there
     eavesdropping on me?
ONESIMOS. I'm not, I swear. I've only just come out.
  But how can I still keep you in the dark?
  My god, *I've done such things for you.* You shall
  Hear all.
[Of the next thirteen lines only the first words survive; the follow-
ing supplements highly speculative.]
CHARISIOS.   *I've always known* that you're
  A loud-mouthed villain—
ONESIMOS.   940
HABROTONON [*comes forward*]. You'll prove *to have* no *knowledge of the*
    facts.
CHARISIOS. *And* who are you *to interfere like this?*
HABROTONON. Not . . .
CHARISIOS. *You and your baby can both go to hell.*
HABROTONON. I'm not the child's mother, *that I swear.*
CHARISIOS. You're not *its mother? Then, good god, who is?*
HABROTONON. You want me *to explain the whole affair?*
CHARISIOS. *Explain it all* at once
HABROTONON.   *I had to find*
  Who was the baby's father, so we tested you—
CHARISIOS. I should have *thrown you out at once.*

ONESIMOS. You should have . . .

CHARISIOS. What do you say, Onesimos? You were 950
Both testing me?

ONESIMOS.   She urged me to, I swear.

CHARISIOS. So you led me astray as well, you crook?

HABROTONON. Don't start a quarrel, darling. Your own wife
Is mother of the baby, no one else.

CHARISIOS. I wish she were,

HABROTONON.   She is, I swear.

CHARISIOS.   What's this
You're telling me?

HABROTONON.   What's this? The simple truth.

CHARISIOS. But is the baby Pamphile's? You said it's mine.

HABROTONON. Yes, yours as well.

CHARISIOS.   It's Pamphile's? Don't please,
Habrotonon, raise up my hopes in vain.   958

There follows a lacuna of about ten lines, then some ten lines in
which Habrotonon says, 'Oh dear, how could I . . . before I knew
it all?' and Charisios replies, 'You're right.' Perhaps Charisios had
asked, 'Why didn't you tell me sooner?' The scene ends with six
unintelligible lines of which only single words survive. Habrotonon
must have convinced Charisios who goes into the house to find
Pamphile and effect a reconciliation.

CHORAL INTERLUDE

ACT 5

The opening of the act is lost. Our text begins with what may be a
soliloquy from Chairestratos, who appears to have fallen in love
with Habrotonon himself but, unaware of the events of the
previous scene, thinks that she is the mother of the child and that
she and Charisios are now in love.

CHAIRESTRATOS.   the opposite, and you,   981
   Chairestratos, must now consider what
   Should happen next; how you can stay his friend,
   Faithful as you have always been? For she's
   No common tart and it's no chance *affair*,
   She's seriously *in love*; she's *had* his child;
   And *in her mind* she's free. Enough of that!
   You must not look at her. First she *must have*
   A talk alone *now* with her dearest love,
   Her sweet Charisios . . .

The next seventy lines are either missing entirely or mutilated
beyond repair. Chairestratos' monologue may have continued for
another ten lines, then Charisios enters with Onesimos. Presumably Chairestratos now learns the truth and is free to woo
Habrotonon. The lacuna is followed by two obscure lines which
end this scene; these are perhaps spoken by Charisios in a monologue following the exit of Chairestratos and Onesimos; if so, 'he'
will refer to Chairestratos, 'a girl like her' to Habrotonon; if this is
right, Charisios is commenting wryly on Chairestratos' behaviour
and saying that Habrotonon is no temptation to him, now he is
reconciled to Pamphile.

CHARISIOS.   *he has no* self-control.
   He'd not have kept his hands from off a girl   1060
   Like her, I'm sure, but I shall not molest her.

There follows a well preserved scene.

   Enter SMIKRINES *and* SOPHRONE, PAMPHILE'*s nurse, from the city.*

SMIKRINES. If I don't smash your head in, Sophrone,
   May I be damned. Will you give me advice
   As well? I'm too precipitate, am I,
   In taking home my daughter, you old bitch?
   Am I to wait till her good man's devoured
   Her dowry and do nothing, only talk,
   About my cash? Is that what you advise?
   Strike quickly—that's the way. Another word
   From you and you'll regret it bitterly.

Is Sophrone my judge? No! When you see
The girl, it's you must make her change her mind.   1070
If not, so heaven help me, Sophrone,
On my way home—you saw that pond we passed?
I'll plunge you in all night and murder you.
I'll force you to agree with me and stop
This arguing. [*he tries the door*] I must knock. The door is locked.
Boy! Boys! Hey, open up! Boys, can't you hear?

ONESIMOS *comes out.*

ONESIMOS. Who's knocking on the door? Oh, Smikrines,
    Old Grumpy, come to get his dowry back
    And take his daughter home.
SMIKRINES.   Yes, blast you, boy,
    It's me.   1080
ONESIMOS. And quite right too. This haste reveals
    A man of brains and careful reasoning,
    And as for stealing dowries, heavens above,
    How quite extraordinary!
SMIKRINES.   By all the gods
    And spirits, may—
ONESIMOS.   Do you suppose the gods
    Have time to deal out good and ill each day
    To every individual, Smikrines?
SMIKRINES. What do you mean?
ONESIMOS.   I'll make it plain to you:
    There're round about a thousand cities now
    And thirty thousand citizens in each.
    Do you suppose the gods destroy or save
    Each one as individuals?
SMIKRINES.   Impossible.   1090
    Your make them live a life of drudgery.
ONESIMOS. 'The gods don't care for us then,' you will say?
    They've lodged in each of us our character
    To be our captain;* this, assigned its post
    Inside us, crushes us, if ever we
    Misuse it, others it saves; that is our god,
    Which is responsible for each man's acts

For good or ill. Propitiate this god
By doing nothing bad or stupid, then
You will fare well

SMIKRINES.   So now my character
Is doing something stupid, you foul rogue?   1100

ONESIMOS. It's crushing you.

SMIKRINES.   What cheek!

ONESIMOS.   But is it right
To take your daughter from her husband then,
Do you think?

SMIKRINES.   Who says it's right? But as things are
It's unavoidable.

ONESIMOS.   You see? The man
Reckons that wrong is unavoidable.
Is anything destroying him except
His character? When you were on your way
Full speed to wickedness, mere chance has saved
You now, and you arrive to find there's been
A reconciliation and the knots
Of trouble all untied. Don't let me see   1110
You, Smikrines, rush headlong in again.
Now drop your accusations and be done,
Go in and take your grandson in your arms.

SMIKRINES. My grandson, rogue?

ONESIMOS.   I see you're really thick
Although you think you're clever. What a way
To guard a marriageable girl! That's how
We come to rear these babies born four months
Before their time, like freaks.

SMIKRINES.   I don't know what
You mean.

ONESIMOS.   You don't? The old girl knows, I think.
My master, at the Tauropolia,
Seized on this girl and dragged her from the dance,
And—Sophrone, you see it? [SOPHRONE *nods assent*] Yes, you
    do.
And so they've recognized each other now
And all is well.

SMIKRINES [*to* SOPHRONE]: What's this, you wicked bitch?

ONESIMOS. 'So nature willed, and nature knows no laws;
　Woman was born for this.'* Don't be a fool.
　I shall recite the whole speech from the play,
　If you don't understand me, Smikrines.

SMIKRINES [*to* SOPHRONE]: You make me livid with your gesturing.*
　You must know well enough what this man means.

ONESIMOS. Of course she knows. You may be sure of this,
　The old girl grasped it first.

SMIKRINES.　　　　　　　　　　What shocking news!

ONESIMOS. There's never been a greater stroke of luck.

SMIKRINES. If what you say is true, the baby then
　Must be the child of some unmarried girl
　Who's *living with Charisios*.*

Of the rest of the play only scattered words survive. Immediately
after Smikrines' last speech Chairestratos enters and says
something about 'this girl' (Habrotonon?); he may have continued
with ten or more lines in which he convinced Smikrines of the
essential facts. Smikrines may then have been reconciled with
Charisios and the play may have ended with the sort of celebration which concludes most of Menander's plays.

There are fragments quoted by ancient authors as from *The
Arbitration*:

1.　Orion, *Anthologia* 7. 8
　You've suffered nothing bad if you pretend
　It did not *happen*.

This possibly comes from the end of the play; it might be
Onesimos answering Smikrines' complaint that he is disgraced by
the birth of a grandchild out of wedlock.

2.　Stobaeus, *Eclogae* 4. 29d. 58
　It's much more shameful for a free man to
　Be made a mockery; but man is born
　To suffer pain.

Could this be from the same scene—Smikrines coming to terms
with his situation?

The Shield (Aspis)

The first two acts of this play are fairly well preserved; the beginning of Act 3 survives in a mutilated state but much is lost. Of acts 4 and 5 we have enough to make a tentative reconstruction of the plot.

Characters

DAOS, an old slave, formerly Kleostratos' tutor
SMIKRINES, Kleostratos' uncle
THE GODDESS CHANCE (Prologue)
A COOK
A WAITER
CHAIRESTRATOS, Smikrines' younger brother
CHAIREAS, Chairestratos' stepson
FRIEND of Chaireas disguised as a DOCTOR
KLEOSTRATOS

Silent characters:

LYKIAN CAPTIVES
COOK'S ASSISTANT (SPINTHER)
Slaves of Chairestratos
KLEOSTRATOS' SISTER?
CHAIRESTRATOS' DAUGHTER?

A young Athenian, Kleostratos, has been serving as a mercenary in Lykia (south-west Turkey). His old tutor,* Daos, who had accompanied him, returns to his home in Athens with the news that he has been killed in action; he brings with him a mass of booty won by his former master and carries Kleostratos' battered shield. Smikrines, Kleostratos' uncle, a miser, at once begins to scheme to get hold of this booty. He plans to do this by marrying

Kleostratos' sister, who will inherit her brother's property (in Athenian law an heiress who had neither a father nor a brother living could be claimed in marriage by her next of kin); but she is already engaged to Chaireas, the stepson of Chairestratos, who is Smikrines' younger brother.

Daos proposes a scheme to outwit Smikrines; Chairestratos is to pretend to be desperately ill. A friend of Chaireas, disguised as a foreign doctor, is to examine the 'patient' and declare that there is no hope. When Chairestratos is 'dead', Smikrines will give up the idea of marrying Kleostratos' sister and transfer his attentions to Chairestratos' daughter, a far richer heiress.

This scheme is put into action and we see Smikrines convinced by the 'doctor' that his brother is dying. The text then becomes fragmentary, but we may guess that Daos continues to tease Smikrines and that he decides to marry Chairestratos' daughter.

In Act 4 there are fragmentary indications that Smikrines agrees that Kleostratos' sister should marry Chaireas. Then Kleostratos enters; he was not dead at all, but captured by the enemy and has now escaped home.

Act 5 perhaps shows Daos relating that Kleostratos and Chaireas are to marry their respective brides. A cook is probably summoned to prepare a wedding feast and Daos and the cook may have combined to punish Smikrines (compare the ending of *The Bad-tempered Man*).

The scene is set in a street in Athens with two houses, one of which belongs to Smikrines, the other to Chairestratos.

ACT I

Enter from the harbour, a train of LYKIAN CAPTIVES *and pack animals carrying booty—gold coins, silver cups and boxes of rich clothes, followed by* DAOS *carrying a badly buckled shield.*

In his opening words Daos apostrophises Kleostratos, his master, whom he left dead (as he thinks) on the battlefield.

Smikrines, who comes out of his house as Daos arrives, overhears him.]

DAOS. *This* is the *saddest* day I've ever spent,
    Dear master; when I reckon up accounts
    I find the balance quite unlike what I
    Had hoped for when I first set out with you.
    I thought you would return from the campaign*
    Safe and in high repute, and then live out
    A life of dignity, holding the name
    Of General or Counsellor; your sister,
    On whose behalf you set off to the wars,
    You'd marry to a husband you approved,
    When you had come back home, long missed and dear.   10
    And as for me, I thought I'd have a rest
    From my long labours, some return for all
    The love I've shown you, as I grew in years.
    But now you've gone, snatched off by death against
    All expectation, O Kleostratos,
    While I, your tutor, have returned and bring
    This shield which did not save you, though you
    So often kept it safe, a gallant soul,
    If any were.
SMIKRINES [*comes forward*]. What unforeseen mischance!
    O Daos.
DAOS.   Terrible.
SMIKRINES.   How did he die?
    What happened?
DAOS.   Smikrines, it's hard to find
    A reason why a soldier should survive,   20
    Easy enough to find why he should die.
SMIKRINES. But all the same, Daos, tell me the facts.
DAOS. In Lykia there is a river called
    The Xanthos; there we'd often been engaged
    In many a battle, always with success;
    The natives had now left the plain and fled.
    But failure sometimes has its use, it seems;
    For he who's had a fall is on his guard.

But our contempt for them had led us on
To be undisciplined in face of what
Was coming; many men had left the camp   30
To sack the villages, lay waste the fields,
And sell the booty which they had secured;
All came away with cash enough.

SMIKRINES.   That's good.

DAOS. My master collected some six hundred coins
Of gold, a fair supply of silver cups,
This mob of captives which you see near by—
And sent me off to Rhodes, instructing me
To leave the booty with a friend and then
Return to him *at once*.

SMIKRINES.   What happened then?

DAOS. I started out at dawn, but on the day   40
I left, the natives seized a hill in front
Of us and held it, unseen by our guards;
They'd learnt from some deserters that our force
Was scattered, and when evening came on
And all inside the camp were in their tents,
Returning from a country which was full
Of every kind of booty, what you'd expect
Occurred—most of them started to get drunk.

SMIKRINES. That's quite disgraceful!

DAOS.   Yes. The natives fell
On them out of the blue, I believe.

[One line deficient, one missing; two mutilated; supplements
speculative.]

SMIKRINES.   *Then how*   50
Did you escape?

DAOS.   *I had already done*
A full day's march and had set up my camp.
About midnight; while I was keeping guard
Over the booty and the prisoners,
Walking around before my tent, I heard
A din, cries of despair, men on the run,
Lamenting, calling each to each by name.
From them I quickly learnt what had occurred.

But luckily there was a little hill,   60
A strong point, there; we all flocked up to it
Together; and more men kept streaming in,
All wounded, cavalry, light armed, and last
The heavy infantry.

SMIKRINES.   How lucky you
Had been sent on!

DAOS.   At dawn we made some sort
Of palisade and waited; those who'd been
Dispersed, making the raids I told you of,
Kept joining us; but after three days' wait
We started off again; for we had learnt
The Lykians were moving all the men
They'd taken to the villages above.

SMIKRINES. You saw him fallen there amongst the dead?

DAOS. Himself I could not recognize for sure;   70
It was the fourth day they'd been lying there—
Their faces were all swollen by the sun.

SMIKRINES. Then how do you know?

DAOS.   He lay beside his shield—
None of the native soldiers, I suppose,
Had taken it, all buckled as it was.
And our good leader then prevented us
From burning all the corpses one by one,
Seeing that it would cause delay to collect
The ashes from each body on its own,
And so he heaped and burnt them in a mass;
Interring them with haste, he soon broke camp.
We slipped away from them, went first to Rhodes,
Then after some days' stay we sailed back here.   80
You've heard it all.

SMIKRINES.   You say you've brought with you
Six hundred golden pieces?

DAOS.   Yes.

SMIKRINES.   And cups?

DAOS. Yes, weighing forty minae*—

SMIKRINES.   No more than that?

DAOS. And you're the heir.

SMIKRINES. What? really, do you think
 That's why I asked you this? Good heavens, no!
 The rest, you say, was stolen?
DAOS. Most of it,
 Except what I took charge of at the start.
 There're clothes and cloaks, and here the mob you see—
 And they're all yours.
SMIKRINES. I'm not concerned with them;
 I only wish he'd lived.
DAOS. I wish he had!   90
 But we must take my sad tidings inside
 And tell it those who least should hear such news.
   [*Exit* DAOS *into* CHAIRESTRATOS' *house, followed by the captives*
SMIKRINES [*shouts after* DAOS]: Then I shall want to talk to you alone
 At leisure, Daos. [*To himself*] Now I think I should
 Go in myself and give some thought to what's
 The gentlest way of treating the bereaved.
      [*Exit* SMIKRINES *into his house*

Prologue*

THE GODDESS CHANCE. If some disaster really had occurred
 For these poor souls, then it would not be right*
 For me to come on next, since I'm divine.
 But as it is, they do not know the truth,
 They're all at sea. But if you put your mind
[Four lines mutilated; supplements speculative.]
 To what I say, you'll learn *the actual facts.*   100
 That fatal day the man they think is dead
 Was with another man, *a friend, who shared*
 His tent. The natives *suddenly* attacked,
 The trumpeter kept sounding the alarm.
 Our men rushed out to help, seizing the arms
 Which were to hand. And so the man who shared
 With Daos' master answered the alarm
 Armed with this shield. He fell immediately.

And since the shield lay there amongst the dead
And since the corpse of the young man swelled up,
So Daos was deceived. Kleostratos   110
Rushed out from there bearing the other's arms
And he was made a captive; he's alive
And very soon he'll come back safe. Well then,
You've learnt enough about that business.
The old man who kept asking things just now,
He's his paternal uncle who's surpassed
The whole of human kind in wickedness;
He doesn't recognize the claims of friends
Or relatives; he's never worried once
About the shameful actions of his life,
But wants to have his hands on everything.
That's all he thinks about. He lives alone   120
With one old woman to look after him.
And where the servant's just gone in next door,
A younger brother of this money-mad
Man lives, who's uncle to Kleostratos
Like him, but truly good in character
And rich; he's married and he has one child,
A daughter. When the young man sailed away,
He left his sister in this uncle's care;
The girls have lived and been brought up as one.
This uncle's a good fellow, as I said,
And when he saw how long Kleostratos
Would be away and that they're not well off,   130
He planned the girl should marry his stepson,
The child his wife had born her first husband;
Two talents' dowry he was going to give,
And meant the marriage to take place this day.
But this disaster that's befallen them
Will throw into confusion all these plans.
For since this wicked uncle heard just now
About six hundred golden coins, and saw
The foreign slaves and baggage mules and girls,   140
He'll want to get his niece, who's heiress now,
Into his power, for that's his right* by age.

But still, he won't succeed but cause himself
A lot of toil and trouble and reveal
To all the world what sort of man he is
And then return to where he was before.
It's only left to tell you all my name.
Who am I then with power to arbitrate
And to direct all this? The goddess Chance.

                                            [*Exit* CHANCE

Enter SMIKRINES *from his house.*

SMIKRINES. Lest anyone should say I'm money-mad,
    I did not even check how much he brings   150
    In gold or ask how many silver cups;
    I did not number any of the stuff,
    But gladly let them take the lot inside.
    For they habitually take every chance
    To say the worst of me. But I shall have
    An accurate account, as long as those
    Who carry it are slaves. In any case
    I think they'll all be willing to abide
    By law and justice, and, if not, no one
    Will let them have their way. I want to warn
    Them not to hold this wedding which they plan.
    Perhaps it's odd even to mention this;   160
    Now that bad news has come, they're not concerned
    With weddings. Still, I'll knock and call out Daos;
    For he alone will heed what I've to say.

As he moves towards CHAIRESTRATOS' *house, enter* DAOS *from the house,
    talking over his shoulder to the women lamenting inside.*

DAOS. You certainly deserve to be excused
    For your behaviour but, as things are now,
    Just try your best to bear the blow we've had
    Like rational beings.
SMIKRINES [*comes forward*]: Daos, here I am
    To see you.
DAOS.   Me?
SMIKRINES.   Yes, certainly, that's right.

[*Sententiously*] I only wish he'd lived and managed this,
    As was his right, and, when I died, become
    The heir to my possessions, as the law   170
    Prescribes.
DAOS.   I wish he had. So what?
SMIKRINES. You ask? I'm oldest of the family.
    And yet I must put up with being wronged
    And see my brother always do me down.
DAOS. You really mean this?
SMIKRINES.   Yes, my friend, he goes
    Beyond all bounds, and treats me just as though
    I were a slave or illegitimate;
    He's started to arrange this marriage now,
    Giving the girl to god knows who, without
    Consulting me or asking me, when I'm
    The same relation to her as himself.
DAOS. What then?
SMIKRINES.   I'm angry when I see all this.   180
    Since he behaves to me as if I were
    Quite unrelated, this is what I'll do:
    I shall not leave my property for them
    To plunder but shall follow what some friends
    Advise and take this girl as wife myself.
    For this, I think, is what the law prescribes,
    Daos. You should've thought yourself how this
    Could be effected properly; you are
    Not uninvolved.
DAOS.   The saying 'Know yourself',*
    Is, Smikrines, I think, profoundly true.   190
    Let me abide by it. Refer to me
    And ask my views on all that fits a slave
    Who's honest
[Lacuna of two lines, then four lines fragmentary; supplements speculative.]
           but don't question me on things
   That don't concern me.
SMIKRINES.   There's restraint for you!
DAOS. But if you *want from me a sure account*

Of your affairs, you can *examine* all
The servant girls and slaves *with whom I then*
Received the gold. As for the goods he won,
They are all sealed; the contracts which he made
Abroad I can explain; and I will show,
If I am told to, one by one, where each
Was made, and how, and who were witnesses.
But, Smikrines, when it's inheritance   200
And marriage to an heiress, family,
And differences in kin that you discuss,
Don't drag in Daos. You yourselves must deal
With free men's business, whose concern it is.

SMIKRINES. Good heavens, do you think I have no heart?

DAOS. I am a Phrygian. A lot that's thought
All right amongst your people seems to me
Quite wrong, and vice versa. Why should you
Give heed to what I say? No doubt your views
Are far superior.

SMIKRINES.   You seem to me
To tell me, more or less: 'Don't bother me.'   210
Something like that. I understand. I'd best
Go into town and talk to one of them,
If no one is at home.

DAOS.   There's no one in.

                          [*Exit* SMIKRINES *to the city*

O Chance, what a fine master I once had,
And what a sod you mean to give me now!
How have I wronged you to deserve all this?

Enter COOK *and his assistant,* SPINTHER, *from* CHAIRESTRATOS' *house.*

COOK. If ever I do get a job of work,
    Somebody dies and I must scuttle off
    Without my pay, or else one of the household,
    Who has got pregnant secretly, gives birth,
    And then they scratch the party suddenly,
    And I am on my way. Oh, what bad luck!

DAOS. Lord, Cook, for heaven's sake, be off with you.   220

COOK. And what d'you think I'm doing now? Boy, take

The knives and hurry up.

> [*The* COOK *then addresses the audience*
>
> After ten days at last

I got a job worth three drachmas and came;
I thought I'd got the cash in hand; some corpse
Arrives from Lykia and steals the lot
From me by force. [*He turns to the boy*] You good-for-nothing
  boy,
You see the household's had a tragedy,
The women weeping and beating their breasts,
And then you come out with an empty flask?*
Remember what a chance you had. I've got
An honest Aristeides* not a Spark   230
To serve me. Well, I'll see you go without
Your dinner.

> [*He looks round for the* WAITER *and adds ironically*
>
> But the waiter means to stay

Around maybe to get a bite of lunch.

> [*Exeunt* COOK *and* ASSISTANT *to the city*

Enter WAITER *from* CHAIRESTRATOS' *house, talking to the women inside.*

WAITER. If I don't get my pay, I'll beat my breast
  As hard as you.
DAOS.   Go on! *Now* no one *needs* this man.
[Lacuna of 1–2 lines.]
WAITER [*aside*]. Daos is here. What's he announcing then?
  [*To* DAOS] *That I must go away, you idiot?*
DAOS. That's right.
WAITER.   God blast you then! You've done a thing
  Like this, you loony! All this gold you had
  And slaves, and yet you've come and brought them back   240
  For master? And you didn't run away? From where
  Do you come then?
DAOS.   From Phrygia.*
WAITER.   Oh well,
  You're useless then, and queer. We Thracians are
  The only men, and Getans are brave types,
  By god.

DAOS. That's why the mills* are full of you.
  Be off with you and leave our door. For I can see
  Another crowd of men approaching here;
  They're drunk.

> [*Exit* WAITER *to the city*

Enter CHORUS. DAOS *addresses the* CHORUS.

> Go on, you're right! Since no one knows
  What Chance may bring, enjoy life while you can.

> [*Exit* DAOS *to* CHAIRESTRATOS' *house*

CHORAL INTERLUDE

ACT 2

Enter SMIKRINES, CHAIRESTRATOS, *and* CHAIREAS *from the city.*

SMIKRINES. Well then, Chairestratos, what do you say?   250
CHAIRESTRATOS. First, my good brother, we must organize
  The funeral.
SMIKRINES.   That shall be organized.
  But after that, don't you betroth the girl
  To anyone. That's not your business
  But mine. I am the elder. You've a wife
  In there, and daughter. I must have the same.
CHAIRESTRATOS. But Smikrines, have you no sense at all
  Of decency?
SMIKRINES.   Heavens, what do you mean?
CHAIRESTRATOS. At your age do you mean to marry this
  Young girl?
SMIKRINES.   At my age?
CHAIRESTRATOS.   Yes, you seem to me
  A lot too old.
SMIKRINES.   Am I the only man
  To marry when he's getting on in years?
CHAIRESTRATOS. But, Smikrines, do treat the business

With some humanity. Here's Chaireas
Was going to marry her, who was brought up
Together with her. What am I to say?
You need not lose a thing; take all this stuff,
And be the lawful owner of the lot;
We give it all to you. But let the girl
Without the property be bride to one
Of her own age. I'll give from my own purse
A dowry of two talents.

SMIKRINES.   Lord, do you think
You're talking to a half-wit? What do you mean?   270
Am I to take the property and let the girl
Go to this boy, so, if they have a son,
I'm sued for restitution of his rights?*

CHAIRESTRATOS. Is that what you suppose? Forget it then.

SMIKRINES. 'Suppose', you say? [*Snorts*] Send Daos here at once
So he may give me a full list of all
The goods he's brought with him.

CHAIRESTRATOS.   What should *I say*
Or what should I have done?

[Three lines badly mutilated; supplements speculative.]

SMIKRINES.   There's *nothing you*
Could say or do to make me change my plan.

                          [*Exit into his house;* CHAIREAS *comes forward*

CHAIRESTRATOS. *God help me! Will this villain have his way?*
[*To* CHAIREAS] *I* always *thought that* you would take this girl,
Kleostratos would marry my own child,   280
And I would leave you heirs to all I have.
I wish I could leave life at once, before
I see things that I never thought to see.

                          [*Staggers into his house in a state of collapse*

CHAIREAS. Well, first, perhaps, it's right, Kleostratos,
To pity you and mourn your fate—then mine.
For none of these has had bad luck like mine.
I fell in love, a love I did not choose,
With your own sister, dearest of mankind;
Nothing I did was wild, despicable,   290
Or wrong; I followed proper form and asked

Your uncle whom you left in charge and my
Own mother, who was looking after her,
To give her hand to me to be my wife.
I thought that I was blessed in life, I thought
I'd really reached my goal. But now no more,
In future I can't even look at her.
The law will put her in another's charge
And judge my claim as nothing from now on.

Enter DAOS *from* CHAIRESTRATOS' *house, talking over his shoulder to*
CHAIRESTRATOS.

DAOS. Chairestratos, you're not behaving well.
Stand up. Don't lie down in despair like that.   300
                              [*He turns and sees* CHAIREAS
Come, Chaireas, and comfort him, and don't
Let him give up. The hopes of all of us depend
On him. Open the door and show yourself!
Will you betray your friends, Chairestratos,
So cravenly?

             CHAIRESTRATOS *staggers out of his house.*

CHAIRESTRATOS. Daos my boy, I'm ill.
Events have brought on me a black despair.
By god, I'm not myself, I'm almost mad.
For now my noble brother's driving me
Distracted by his wickedness. He means
To marry her himself!
DAOS.   To marry her?   310
Will he be able to?
CHAIRESTRATOS.   That's what he says,
The noble gentleman, and that despite
My giving him all that my nephew sent.
DAOS. The filthy swine!
CHAIRESTRATOS.   Yes, swine indeed. By god,
I'll put an end to life, rather than see
This happening.
DAOS.   Then how could one outwit
The utter cad?

CHAIRESTRATOS.   It's very difficult.

DAOS. Yes, difficult,and yet it can be done.

CHAIRESTRATOS. It can?

DAOS.   What's more, by god, it is a thing
   Worth fighting for.

CHAIRESTRATOS.   If anyone's begun

[One line mutilated, lacuna of one or two lines, three more mutilated; supplements speculative.]

   A scheme to stop these plans, for heaven's sake,   320
   Let him speak out. Daos, what can we do?

DAOS. *He'll get* two talents *by his present plans,*
   But if we give him hope *of getting more,*
   You'll see him rushing for the prize at once
   In headlong haste, quite up the pole and wild
   With glee, and then you'll easily handle him.
   He'll only see and look for what he wants,
   And so he'll be no rational judge of truth.

CHAIRESTRATOS. What are you getting at? Explain yourself.
   I'm ready to do everything you want.

DAOS. You must play out a sad and tragic scene.
   For what you said just now—that you had sunk   330
   Into a deep despair, resulting from
   The suffering of poor young Chaireas
   And of the girl you were to give to him,
   And from the sight of this young man in black
   Despair, the boy you thought of as your son—
   Must all seem true, that you've been struck
   By one of those quite sudden illnesses;
   Sickness results in nearly every case
   From grief. And I know well your character
   Is prone to bitterness and melancholy.
   And then we'll call some learned doctor in,   340
   Who'll say your illness comes from pleurisy
   Or inflammation of the diaphragm
   Or else some other ill which carries men
   Off quickly.

CHAIRESTRATOS. Then?

DAOS.   Then suddenly you're dead!

We shout, 'Chairestratos is gone' and beat
Our breasts before the doors. You'll stay inside,
Shut up; outside a shape to represent
Your corpse, all covered up, will lie
In state.

CHAIRESTRATOS [*to* CHAIREAS]. You grasp what he is getting at?

CHAIREAS. By god, no, not a word.

CHAIRESTRATOS.   No more do I.

DAOS. Your daughter then becomes an heiress too,
Just like the girl whose case is in dispute.
But you're worth sixty talents more or less,   350
And she's worth only four. Old greedy guts
Enjoys the same relationship to both—

CHAIRESTRATOS. Ah, now I understand.

DAOS.   You must, unless
You're thick. He'll gladly give her to the first
Who asks before three thousand witnesses,
And take your daughter—

CHAIRESTRATOS.   He'll regret it then

DAOS.—As he imagines, and he'll organize
The whole household, go round with keys, put seals
On all the doors, dreaming the while of wealth.

CHAIRESTRATOS. And what about my dummy?

DAOS.   That'll lie here.
And we shall all sit round it in a ring,   360
And take good care that he comes nowhere near.

[Lacuna of two or three lines, then eight lines mutilated; supplements highly speculative.]

There're lots *of other things that could occur;*
If someone carries off some of your goods
While you are 'dead', when you revive and find
Them gone, then you can *call* your friends *and get*
A proof *of who* has visited the house.
Suppose it was some man in debt. If *you can prove*
It, you exact the double fine *for theft.*

CHAIRESTRATOS. Daos, your scheme *is excellent;* it suits
Me well. What heavier punishment could you
Devise for such a sinner?

DAOS. I'll exact 370
A punishment some time worth all the pain
He's brought on you, I swear by god, I will.
For as the proverb truly says, 'The wolf
Gapes wide his jaws but goes empty away.'
But now's the time for action. Chaireas,
You know some foreign quack who'll see the joke,
A bit of an impostor?
CHAIREAS. No, I don't.
DAOS. You really should.
CHAIREAS [*reflects*]. What do you say to this?
I'll go and fetch one of my friends and beg
A wig and cloak and stick for him, and he
Will play the foreigner as best he can.
DAOS. Be quick about it. [*Exit* CHAIREAS *to the city*
CHAIRESTRATOS. What am I to do?
DAOS. That's all decided. Die, and good luck to you. 380
CHAIRESTRATOS. I will. Let no one leave the house, but stay
On guard like men.
DAOS. Who shall be in the know?
CHAIRESTRATOS. Only my wife must know and the two girls,
So they don't weep true tears, but let the rest
Inside insult me when they think I'm dead.
DAOS. You're right. Let someone take our patient in.
[CHAIRESTRATOS *is helped off stage by slaves into his house*
The 'tragedy' will certainly provide
Some pretty fun, excitement too, when once
It starts; let's hope our doctor's plausible. 390
[*Exit into* CHAIRESTRATOS' *house*

CHORAL INTERLUDE

ACT 3

Enter SMIKRINES *from his house.*

SMIKRINES [*ironically*]. He has been quick in bringing me the list!
  He has been most considerate to me!
  Daos is on their side. That's good, by god;
  He has done well. I'm glad that now I have
  A fine excuse to stop checking this stuff
  So altruistically and have a look
  For my own interests; for what he's kept
  Concealed is surely double what he's shown.
  I know the dodges of this pesky slave.

  Enter DAOS *from* CHAIRESTRATOS' *house, putting on a show of
  frenzied lamentation; he pretends not to see* SMIKRINES *and tears up
  and down the stage, quoting from tragedies.*

DAOS. O gods, what dire disaster's struck us now!   400
  I never would have thought a man could go
  Down hill so fast. A raging thunderbolt
  Has struck our house.
SMIKRINES.   Whatever does he mean?
[Lacuna of two lines; three more mutilated; supplements guess-
work.]
  He's acting like a perfect lunatic.
DAOS. *No man can well express our suffering,*
  Only *a poet whom the Muse inspires.*
  'How can a mortal fight with chance divine?'
SMIKRINES. The man *is round the bend. That's plain enough.*
DAOS. *'There is no man who's happy in all things.'**
  Again, that's very good. O honoured gods,
  What unforeseen and *tragic* happenings!
SMIKRINES. Daos, you wretch, where are you running?
DAOS.   Here's one:
  'It's chance not prudence rules the fate of men.'   410
  That's excellent. 'God plants the guilt in men,
  When it's his will to blast a house entire.'
  And Aeschylus, great—

SMIKRINES.   Miserable wretch,
  Still quoting saws?
DAOS.   'No faith, no reason, dire—'
SMIKRINES. He'll never stop?
DAOS.   'What is incredible
  In mankind's ills?' says Karkinos. 'For God
  Can in one day cast down the happy man
  To misery.'   [*He suddenly pretends to notice* SMIKRINES
              Yes, Smikrines, all these
  Are certainly well said.
SMIKRINES.   What **do** you mean?
DAOS. Your brother—God, how shall I tell you this—   420
  Is all but dead.
SMIKRINES.   The man who only now
  Was talking to me here? What happened to him?
DAOS. Bile, grief, derangement, and a choking fit.
SMIKRINES. Good god, how terrible!
DAOS.   'There is no word to tell,
  No chance so dread—'
SMIKRINES.   You're wearing me to death.
DAOS. 'Disasters strike us unforeseen, for so
  The gods ordain.' The one's Euripides',
  The other's Chairemon's, not poets whom
  You'd count as second rate.
SMIKRINES.   A doctor's come?
DAOS. No, Chaireas has gone to fetch one.
SMIKRINES.   Which?

        Enter CHAIREAS' FRIEND, *disguised as a the 'doctor'** with
                 an* ATTENDANT *from the city.*

DAOS. This one, it seems. [*Goes to meet the* DOCTOR] Do hurry,
    friend.   430
DOCTOR.   *I am.*
DAOS. 'Sick men are helpless, and so hard to please.'
        [*Exeunt* DOCTOR *and* ATTENDANT *into* CHAIRESTRATOS' *house,
                        followed by* DAOS *and* CHAIREAS
SMIKRINES. If they see me, they'll say I've hurried here
  Delighted by the news; I'm sure of that.

And he himself would not be glad to see me.
But still, it would seem odd *if* I did not
So much as ask *about his health; I'd best*
Go on and see what's happening in there.

[Lacuna of seventeen lines, all of which we do not attempt to fill.
The remainder of the act is more or less badly mutilated; supplements speculative.]

        [SMIKRINES *moves towards* CHAIRESTRATOS' *door but meets the*
               DOCTOR *and his* ATTENDANT *coming out of the house*]

SMIKRINES. *Doctor, how is he? Is there any hope?*

DOCTOR. *I dinna like th' appearance of* his bile,
   And he's sae weak now *he can scarcely breathe.*   440

SMIKRINES. *What is this sickness?* I *don't* understand.

DOCTOR. *It's meningitis; sae the symptoms show.*

SMIKRINES. *That's clearer to me; now* I understand.

DOCTOR. His very diaphragm *is noo inflamed,*
   I beleeve. Phrenitis is the name we gee
   To this.

SMIKRINES. I understand. What happens next?
   Is there no hope that he can now survive?

DOCTOR. I maunna offer ye fausse comfort, man;*
   Sic' maladies are fatal.

SMIKRINES.   No, don't give
   Me comfort, doctor, but just speak the truth.

DOCTOR. There is nae way at all the man will live.   450
   He's vomitin' up bile; *the sickness* clouds
   His mind and he sees nothing with his eyes.
   He keeps on foamin' at the mouth. He looks
   Like one who will be carried to the grave
   Quite soon.

SMIKRINES.   *My god, this is too terrible.*

DOCTOR [*to his* ATTENDANT]. Laddie, let's gang; we're off.

              [*The* DOCTOR *and his* ATTENDANT *start to move off*

SMIKRINES.   Doctor, hey, you!
   Stop, wait a bit.

DOCTOR.   Ye callin' me?

SMIKRINES.   I am.
   Come over here a little from the door.

DOCTOR. *I've told ye all*; ye canna force the gods.

SMIKRINES.*You ought to* pray *that he may yet get well.*
  Doctors can make mistakes; they're often *wrong.*

DOCTOR. Mock, *if you like*, but let me tell ye this:
  There's nae man kens the art as well as I.

                                    [*He takes a close look at* SMIKRINES
  Ye seem to me yosel' *to nae be well*;
  Consumption threatens ye; ye look like death.

    [*Exeunt* DOCTOR *and* ATTENDANT *to the city,* SMIKRINES *withdraws*
                                           to the back of the stage

DAOS. No doubt the women are now pilfering
  Like soldiers plundering a captured town.
  Neighbours are given orders through the drains.*

                                    [*Seeing* SMIKRINES
  There he is. I'll stir him up, but as I
  Was doing . . .

There follows a lacuna of over 200 lines, including the end of this
act and the beginning of Act 4. Daos, it seems, proceeds to stir up
Smikrines by further teasing. Smikrines presumably decides to
marry Chairestratos' daughter, as Daos forecast in Act 2.

CHORAL INTERLUDE

ACT 4

The beginning of Act 4 is lost in the lacuna. We then have twenty-
three part-lines which make no consecutive sense, but they enable
us to guess how the plot developed. Smikrines and Chaireas are in
conversation. Smikrines says: 'They are shouting "He is gone!" ',
i.e. Chairestratos is dead . . .', 'The man is dead . . .'. Later
Smikrines speaks of 'betrothing'; presumably he is agreeing to
betroth Kleostratos' sister to Chaireas, while he himself will marry
Chairestratos' daughter. He appears to say, 'I am ready to produce all *the money* you demand'. Smikrines and Chaireas now leave
the stage and Kleostratos, safely returned, as Chance prophesied
in the Prologue, enters from the direction of the harbour.

There follow twenty half-lines which do, with heavy supplementation, make some sort of consecutive sense.

KLEOSTRATOS. Greetings, my dearest land. I pray to you   491
  Now I've survived so many *sufferings*.
  But though I'm *safe* back home, I see *one thing's*
  Still lacking to complete my preservation.
  And yet if Daos luckily escaped
  And he is here, then I should think myself
  The happiest of men. But I must knock
  The door.

                                                [*He knocks*

DAOS [*from inside the house*]. Who's knocking at the door?
KLEOSTRATOS.   It's me.
DAOS. Who do you want? *The master* of the house   500
  Is *lately* dead.
KLEOSTRATOS.   He's dead? unhappy man!
DAOS. *So go away at once and* don't distress
  The mourners.
KLEOSTRATOS.   Uncle! *you've been snatched from us!*
  Open the door for me, you wretched man.

                DAOS *opens the door and comes out.*

DAOS. *Did you not hear me tell you 'Go away'?*
                        [*He suddenly recognizes* KLEOSTRATOS
  My god, it's my young master *back from the dead.*
KLEOSTRATOS. Daos, what did you say? *Is uncle dead?*
DAOS. *No, he's alive and well. Don't mourn for him.*
                        [DAOS *embraces* KLEOSTRATOS
  At last I hold *you in my arms . . .*

The remainder of the act, not more than twelve lines, is lost, apart
from isolated words. From these it may be tentatively deduced
that Daos briefly explains the situation to Kleostratos, who says
'Open up the house'; and someone says 'Awake'; perhaps
Chairestratos awakes from his 'death'; the ruse is over.

Act 5 is even more fragmentary; only half-lines survive,
which make no consecutive sense. The following reconstruction is
highly speculative. The act seems to have begun with someone

(Daos?) describing in a monologue(?) the happy events inside Chairestratos' house: 'The women are delighted' . . . 'A double wedding's taking place; *Chairestratos is giving* his own daughter *to Kleostratos* and his niece *to Chaireas.*' . . . '*he intends to leave* all his property *to them* . . . and in the end he'll have the lot (? . . .'.

Then Chaireas enters and learns of Kleostratos' safe return.

DAOS. Here he is, by god . . . Come to me, Chaireas.
    Kleostratos is safe . . .   530
CHAIREAS. . . . I thought *that he was dead* . . . Then where is he?
DAOS. Here . . . And you can take him in your arms and embrace
    your friend.

> [*Exit* CHAIREAS *into* CHAIRESTRATOS' *house.* DAOS *sees*
> SMIKRINES *approaching*

DAOS. He is approaching, talking *to himself.*
    It's plain he's going to give a wedding feast.
    . . . if one beats him frequently . . .
    I make him better behaved.
    I must somehow *punish the man.*

DAOS *withdraws and* SMIKRINES *enters, still ignorant of* KLEOSTRATOS' *return and* CHAIRESTRATOS' *'resurrection' and still planning to marry* CHAIRESTRATOS' DAUGHTER, *promising to give* 'to CHAIREAS what he wants' (*in compensation*).

SMIKRINES (?). For me the betrothal involves this   540
    . . . and before witnesses
    . . . and to Chaireas what he wants.
    For I . . . this fortune . . .
    If *no one* troubles me . . .

[There follows a lacuna of about eighty lines.]

A papyrus fragment may belong here (Papyrus Berolinensis 1128), in which Daos may be teasing Smikrines by describing the scene at Chairestratos' 'death-bed':

SMIKRINES. (*reflecting on the 'death' of* CHAIRESTRATOS). . . . *Although un*just, the law
    Must be obeyed, just like a tyrant's word.
DAOS. The girl was there as well, lamenting at
    His fate; she whispered, 'Father, father,' and
    'Enfold me, father, in your arms . . .

SMIKRINES. *I must reflect* upon the situation
    Chance has now given me.   [*Exit into his house*
DAOS [*aside*].   And *you'll* not *prove*
    To have good judgement in a situation
    That is good. (??)

The conclusion is lost; no doubt Smikrines got his just deserts, perhaps in a scene like that in the last act of the *Dyskolos*, in which Daos and the Cook punish him by cruelly disillusioning him. And, if Menander's other plays are any guide, the play would have ended in a celebration of the weddings of Kleostratos to Chairestratos' daughter, and Chaireas to Kleostratos' sister.

A fragment (OCT 1) is quoted from this play by Stobaeus (*Eclogae* 4. 8. 7), which we cannot place in context:

        Oh thrice unhappy men,
In what do they do better than the rest
Of us? How pitiable is the life
They must endure who guard the forts or hold
The citadels. If they suspect that all
Can easily get at them with daggers in
Their hands, then what a dreadful price they pay!

The Girl with the Shaven Head
(Perikeiromene)

About half this play survives on five papyri and one parchment codex.

Characters

POLEMON, a soldier

SOSIAS, his servant

GLYKERA, his mistress, later his wife

DORIS, her maid

MOSCHION, a young man in love with Glykera, who turns out to be
    her twin brother

DAOS, his servant

PATAIKOS, an old man, who turns out to be the father of Glykera
    and Moschion

MISAPPREHENSION, a divinity, speaker of the Prologue

Silent characters:

HABROTONON, a piper

A COOK

POLEMON'S 'ARMY' OF SLAVES

Characters who do not appear in surviving fragments:

MYRRHINE, Moschion's foster-mother

PHILINOS, Myrrhine's husband(?)

*The scene is a street in Corinth, with two neighbouring houses, one belonging to
Polemon, a mercenary who has just returned from service abroad, the other to
Myrrhine, Moschion's foster-mother.*

The first 120(?) lines of the play are missing.

Our text begins in the middle of a Prologue, spoken by Misapprehension. This is a 'postponed' prologue, as in *The Shield*. Before it there must have been a scene in which Glykera may have rushed onto the stage from Polemon's house directly after her hair had been cut off, followed by Polemon and Sosias. From the ensuing dialogue, the audience may have learnt that Sosias, sent ahead by Polemon to announce his return from abroad, had seen Moschion embracing Glykera; we learn from the Prologue that Sosias described to Polemon what he had seen. At the end of the scene Glykera must have returned to Polemon's house and Polemon and Sosias go off to the house of a friend.

A wall-painting of second century AD from a house in Ephesus inscribed 'Perikeiromene' illustrates the lost opening scene. There are three figures; on the left stands a women whose cloak is raised to conceal her hair (Glykera, just after Polemon has cut off her hair); in the centre a young man wearing a military cloak sits staring gloomily into the distance (Polemon); on the right stands a figure with his right arm raised in an emotional gesture (Sosias, distressed by Polemon's behaviour—see lines 172 ff.).

Not much of the Prologue appears to be lost but in the missing lines Misapprehension may have explained some important facts which the audience must know: that Pataikos' wife had twins which he exposed when she died in childbirth; the twins were found by an old woman, who kept the girl (Glykera) and gave the boy (Moschion) to a rich woman (Myrrhine).

MISAPPREHENSION.   .   .   .   .   .

One of the twins she found she wished to keep   120
Since she was keen to have the girl herself,
The other one she gave to a rich friend,
A lady who was longing for a son;
She lives in this house here. So that was that.
Years passed, the war began,* Corinth's distress
Increased; the woman was quite soon reduced
To poverty; the girl, whom you've just seen,
Was now grown up; a lover then appeared,
The impetuous young man you saw, by birth

Corinthian; she gave the girl to him   130
As her own daughter; she was failing now
And she foresaw that she was near life's end,
And so she did not hide the work of chance
But told the lass how she had rescued her,
And giving her the baby clothes in which
She'd found her, she explained about her still
Unknown blood brother too; allowing for
The flukiness of human life, she saw
That he was now her only relative,
If she should ever be in need of help;
And she was also on her guard in case
Some unintended trouble fell on them   140
Through me, Misapprehension, since he,
She saw, was always drinking and was rich,
While she was young and pretty, and the man
That she was left with unreliable.
And so she died. And then not long ago
The soldier bought this house. The girl now lives
Next door to her own brother but has not
Revealed the fact; he seems so grand, she does
Not wish to spoil his way of life but wants
Him to enjoy the gifts that fortune's given.   150
But she was accidentally seen by him,
A rash young fellow, as I said before,
And always hanging purposely around
Their house; she happened to be sending off
Her maid somewhere that evening; he saw
Her standing at the door, he ran straight up
And kissed her and embraced her in his arms.
Knowing he was her brother, she did not
Run off. The slave came by and saw them there.
The rest he's told you, how the boy went off
Saying he'd like to see her when she had
The time, while she stood there in tears and sobbed   160
Because she was not free to act like that.
I've lit this fire to help the future on,
So that her man should get into a rage—

He's not like this by nature but I led
Him on, to start the revelations—and
That they should find their family at last.
If any was disgusted at all this
And thought what's happened a complete disgrace,
Then he must change his mind. By will of god
Evil can quickly turn to good. Farewell,   170
My friends; be kind to us and watch the rest.

[*Exit* MISAPPREHENSION

Enter SOSIAS *from the city.*

SOSIAS. Our swaggering soldier, as he was just now,
The man who won't let women keep their hair,
Is lying on a couch and weeps. I have
Just left them getting lunch prepared and all
His friends have gathered there to help him bear
His grief more easily. As he had no way
Of hearing what was happening at home,
He's sent me out on purpose just to fetch
His cloak, not really needing anything;
He simply wants to make me take a walk.   180

Enter DORIS *from* POLEMON'*s house; she speaks back to*
GLYKERA *inside; she does not see* SOSIAS.

DORIS. Madam, I'll go and see what's happening.
SOSIAS [*aside*]. Here's Doris. How she's grown! How well she
       looks!
    These women lead a pleasant sort of life,
    That's clear enough. I'll go.

[*Exit into* POLEMON'*s house;* DORIS *goes up to* MYRRHINE'*s door*
DORIS.   I'll knock; there's none
    Of them outside. Unlucky girl, who takes
    A soldier as her partner! They are all
    Quite lawless, none that you can ever trust.
    O mistress, how unfairly he is treating you!
    Boys!* He'll be glad to learn that she's in tears;
    That's what he wanted.   [*The door is opened*
DORIS. Boy, please go and tell . . .   190

Lacuna of about seventy lines, in the course of which Doris must have asked Myrrhine to give refuge to Glykera. Myrrhine must have consented and Glykera left Polemon's house for Myrrhine's.

When the text resumes Daos, the slave of Myrrhine, is speaking. His first surviving word, 'boys', may be addressed to slaves carrying Glykera's luggage into Myrrhine's house. He then sees the Chorus approaching; as usual they are drunken youths.

DAOS.   .   .   .   .

 Boys! Here's a crowd of youths approaching, drunk.
 High praise to mistress; she's taking the girl
 Into our house. That's like a proper mother.
 I must look for master;* for I think it's time   265
 He got back here as fast as he can come.

           [*Exit to the city*

CHORAL INTERLUDE

ACT 2

Enter MOSCHION *and* DAOS *from the city;* DAOS *must have told*
MOSCHION *that* GLYKERA *has taken refuge with* MYRRHINE *and*
claimed credit for it.

MOSCHION. Daos, you have often brought me news which had no
 grain of truth;*
 You're a goddam liar, Daos; if you're kidding me again—
DAOS. String me up, sir, if I'm kidding, straightaway.
MOSCHION.   That's much too mild.
DAOS. Treat me as an enemy then. If it's true, though, and you
 find   270
 She's inside, it's I who've managed all this business for you;
 Moschion, it's I persuaded her to come here at the cost of
 Endless words and got your mother for your sake to take her in
 And to carry out your wishes. What then shall become of me?
MOSCHION. Daos, think what kind of lifestyle would most please
 you? Think and say.

DAOS. Best perhaps to be a miller?

MOSCHION [*aside*].   Off he'll go straight to the treadmill.*

DAOS. Don't suggest a manual trade, sir.

MOSCHION.   I should really like to

Make you Minister of Greek Affairs and, more,   280
  commander of the troops.

DAOS. I don't care for mercenaries, who would quickly slit my
  throat,

If by chance they caught me stealing.

MOSCHION.   But *you'll steal* by farming contracts;*

Undetected you will profit to the tune of seven talents

Out of every eight you farm out.

DAOS.   Moschion, what I should like is

Just to keep a general store here, or to sit round in the market

Selling cheese; I swear *I would not care* about becoming rich.

That's the life that suits me really, that is what I would prefer.

MOSCHION. What a godless way of living you suggest! I know a
  saying:

'May no good old woman ever be reduced to selling honey!'*

DAOS. What I want is a full belly; that, I say, is well deserved,

After all the things I've told you.

MOSCHION.   Certainly you've proved no fool.

Off you go and sell your cheeses. Work away.   290

DAOS.   Thanks very much.

'Amen to that', so goes the saying. Master, come and open up.

        [*Goes over to* MYRRHINE*'s door*

MOSCHION. So I must. You're right, I need to talk her round and
  have the laugh

Over this goddamned commandant with his dandy helmet
  plume.

DAOS. Absolutely.

MOSCHION.   Go in, Daos; be my spy of everything,

What she's doing, where's my mother, how they're ready to
  receive me.

There's no need to spell it all out. You are clever.

DAOS.   Right, I'll go.

MOSCHION. Daos, I will walk around here, waiting for you, by the
  doors.   [*Exit* DAOS *into* MYRRHINE*'s house*

When I went to her last evening, certainly she showed a hint;
I ran up; she did not scamper, took me in her arms and hugged
    me.   301
So it seems I'm not bad-looking nor, I think, poor company;
All the girls in fact adore me; but I quickly ask forgiveness
For this boasting.*

Enter DAOS.

DAOS.   Moschion, she's bathed; she's sitting—
MOSCHION.   Darling girl!
DAOS. Mother's organising something, bustling round. And lunch
    is ready.
    Judging from their preparations now they're waiting just for
    you.
MOSCHION. They've been waiting long for me then? I'm attractive.
    Did you say
    I was here?
DAOS.   Good heavens, never.
MOSCHION.   Then go in and tell them now.
DAOS. As you see, I'm on my way, sir.   311
                                    [*Exit into* MYRRHINE's *house*
MOSCHION.   She'll be shy, that's obvious,
    When we enter, and she'll cover up her face, for that's the way
    Girls behave. But when I enter, I must straightaway kiss
        mother,
    Win her over absolutely, bring myself to flatter her,
    Make it look as if she only were the object of my life.
    She has treated the whole business just as if it's her concern.
    There's the door. There's someone coming.

Enter DAOS.

                                What's the matter, boy? How nervous
Are the steps you take towards me!
DAOS.   Yes, by god, they're really nervous.
It is quite extraordinary. When I went and told your mother
You were here, at once she shouted, 'None of that! How did he
    know?
I suppose it's you who told him she had taken refuge here   320

In her panic. That's the answer. Damn you, boy, get out, at
  once.'
Gods above, all's stolen from you, snatched from right under
  your nose.
She was not the least delighted when she heard that you were
  here.
MOSCHION. You have done for me, you villain.
DAOS.   That's absurd. Your mother rather—
MOSCHION. What d'you say? She did not take her in by her own
  choice, or what?
Not for my sake? You persuaded her to come to me, you said.
DAOS. *I* told *you* that I'd persuaded her to come? Good god, no,
  never.
Master, *you accuse me falsely.*
MOSCHION.   Did you not maintain just now
  You had helped persuade my mother for my sake to take her
    in?   330
DAOS. Well, you see, I did say that, yes, I remember.
MOSCHION.   And you thought
  That it was for me she did this?
DAOS.   No, I can't say that, but I did
  Try to urge her—
MOSCHION.   Very well then. Come with me.
DAOS.   Where to?
MOSCHION.   Not far.
  You will learn.
DAOS.   I'll tell you something, Moschion; at that time I—
             [MOSCHION *starts to drag* DAOS *off to punish him*
  Wait a bit.
MOSCHION.   You're talking nonsense.
DAOS.   No, I'm not, I swear I'm not;
  Only listen. Perhaps the truth is she, maybe, you understand,
  Does not want things to develop in a rush, all anyhow,
  But before you know her feelings, needs to hear what you've to
    say.
  That's it. She's not come here like a call-girl or a wretched
    whore.   340
MOSCHION. Now, I believe, Daos, you're talking sensibly again.

DAOS.   Then test it.
> You, I think, know what the score is; she has left her home and
>   lover—
> That's no nonsense; if you're wanting three or four days'
>   happiness,
> Somebody will give it to you. She imparted this to me;
> Now it's time for you to hear it.

MOSCHION.   Where am I to leave you, Daos,
> Bound securely? You are making me go round in endless
>   circles.
> You were just convincing me, and now you've babbled crap
>   again.

DAOS. You won't let me think in quiet. Change your plan to some
>   extent;
> Go in now respectably.

MOSCHION.   Leaving you to run away?

DAOS. Yes, of course. You realize, don't you, I am well supplied
>   with cash   350
> For a journey?

MOSCHION.   *Stop this nonsense. Come along with me, my boy.*

DAOS. You go in; you might succeed in putting straight some of
>   this mess.

MOSCHION. Willingly. You've won, I grant you.

> > > > > *[Exit* MOSCHION *into his house*

DAOS.   I was nearly done, by god.
> Now I'm numb with terror—things are less straightforward
>   than I thought.

Enter SOSIAS *from the city, carrying* POLEMON'*s sword and military cloak;
he does not notice* DAOS.

SOSIAS. He's sent me back here with his cloak and sword
> To see what she is doing and report.
> I am within an ace of telling him
> I found her lover in the house, so he
> May jump to it and run here—so I would,
> Did I not pity him with all my heart.
> I'm sure I've never seen my master so

Distressed, a nightmare! What a welcome-home!   360

> [*Exit into* POLEMON'*s house*

DAOS. The soldier has arrived. My god, things are
Extremely difficult, they really are.
And I have not considered yet the point
Which really matters—if my master* comes
Back from the farm more quickly than we thought,
What chaos he will cause when he appears.

> *Re-enter* SOSIAS *from* POLEMON'*s house; he shouts back into the*
> *house to* DORIS.

SOSIAS. You've let her go, you wicked animals,
    You've let her leave the house!
DAOS [*aside*].   The fellow's back;
    He's furious. I'll get out of the way

> [DAOS *withdraws*

SOSIAS. It's plain she's gone straight to the neighbour's house
    To join her lover, telling us both loud   370
    And long to go to hell.
DAOS [*aside*].   The soldier takes
    A prophet* round with him; he's hit the mark.
SOSIAS. I'll go and knock.

> [*He goes to knock on* MYRRHINE'*s door;* DAOS *intercepts him*

DAOS.   You miserable man,
What do you want? Where are you going to?
SOSIAS. Are you from here?
DAOS.   Perhaps I am. But why
    This interference?
SOSIAS.   Gods above, are you
    Quite mad? You dare to keep a freeborn girl
    Locked up against her legal guardian's will?
DAOS. You scoundrel, yes, you liar, who assume—
SOSIAS. Do you imagine that we have no guts
    And that we're not true men?
DAOS.   That's right, you're not
    Worth twopence; when a tinpot* general   380
    Has under his command men such as you,
    We'll easily fight with you.

SOSIAS.   Good god, this is
  Outrageous! Tell me whether you admit
  You've got her?
                    [SOSIAS *calls, unsuccessfully, to a passer-by to be his witness*
                  Hey, you passer-by, come here!
  The man who should have been my witness has
  Gone rushing off. [*To* DAOS] Do you admit you've got her?
DAOS. No, we have not.
SOSIAS.   But she's inside the house.
  I'll see that some of you shed tears for this.
  Who do you think you're playing games with, you
  Tell me? What is this nonsense? We shall sack
  This wretched little house of yours straight off.
  So get her lover armed!
DAOS.   Poor man, you are a case,   390
  Waiting so long as though she were with us.
SOSIAS. Our doughty lads* will tear the place to bits
  Before you have the time to spit, although
  You say we're not worth twopence.
DAOS.   That was just
  A joke. You are a shit!
SOSIAS.   Such civilized
  Behaviour!
DAOS.   But we've not got her.
SOSIAS.   Good grief!
  I'll get my pike.
DAOS.   Oh, go to hell! I'm off
  Inside since you seem like *a lunatic.*

                                        [*Exit into* MYRRHINE*'s house*

            Enter DORIS *from* POLEMON*'s house.*

DORIS. Here, Sosias!
SOSIAS.   Doris, if you come near
  Me, I will do you mischief. You yourself
  Are most to blame for all this business.
DORIS. God bless you, tell him she was terrified   400
  And that she's taken refuge somewhere with
  A lady.

SOSIAS.   With a lady? terrified?

DORIS. That's right. She's gone to Myrrhine next door,
  I swear by all my hopes of happiness.

SOSIAS. You see where she has gone? It's here, it's where
  Her darling lives.

DORIS.   She's not employed as you   405
  Imagine, Sosias.

SOSIAS.   Be off with you,
  Get out. *You're telling me* a pack of lies.

The conclusion of this act, about thirty lines, is missing. Sosias and
Doris must have continued arguing until Sosias goes off to tell
Polemon that Glykera has taken refuge in Myrrhine's house and
Doris goes to fetch Pataikos to help Glykera.

CHORAL INTERLUDE

ACT 3

The opening, about thirty lines, is missing. When our text
resumes, Sosias has returned with Polemon and his 'army', con-
sisting probably of no more than a couple of slaves and the pipe-
girl Habrotonon. Pataikos is with them, trying to persuade
Polemon and a drunken Sosias to calm down.

SOSIAS. He's* come from them; he's had a bribe, believe me.   467
  He is betraying you and your whole force.

PATAIKOS. Oh, go away and have a sleep; do stop
  This brawling; you're not well. [*To* POLEMON] I'll talk to you,
  You are less drunk.

POLEMON.   Less drunk! I've had no more
  Than half a pint maybe, since I foresaw
  All this, worst luck, and kept myself prepared
  For what was coming.

PATAIKOS.   Good. Take my advice

POLEMON. What is it you are telling me to do?

PATAIKOS. That's a fair question; now I'll tell you all
  The rest.

SOSIAS [*drunk*]. Habrotonon, signal the charge!

PATAIKOS. First send away this fellow and the slaves
 He's brought.

SOSIAS [*to* POLEMON]. You're making a fair mess of things.
 He'll have a truce, when you could take the girl
 By force.

POLEMON.   This man here is advising me—

SOSIAS. Pataikos? He's destroying us—he's not   480
 Our leader.

PATAIKOS.   Oh, for god's sake, go away.

SOSIAS [*moving off*]. I'm off. Habrotonon, I thought that you
 At least would act. You know some useful skills
 In sieges; you can climb up an erection*
 And hold your target tight in your embrace.

         [*She turns away, insulted*
 Now where're you going, darling? You're ashamed?
 You're not upset by what I said, I hope?

       [*Exeunt* SOSIAS, HABROTONON *and the* 'ARMY'

PATAIKOS. If, Polemon, the situation is
 What you maintain, and she's your wedded wife—

POLEMON. What a thing to say, Pataikos!

PATAIKOS.   But it makes
 A difference.

POLEMON [*shouts angrily*]. I consider her my wife.

PATAIKOS. Don't talk so loud. Who gave the girl to you?

POLEMON. Who gave her me? She did herself.

PATAIKOS.   All right.   490
 Perhaps she liked you, but does so no more;
 And she's gone off because you did not treat
 Her decently.

POLEMON.   What's that? I didn't treat
 Her decently? By saying that you've hurt
 Me most of all.

PATAIKOS.   You love her, I'm quite sure.
 So what you're doing now is lunacy.

      [POLEMON *turns to rush into* MYRRHINE's *house*
 Where do you think you're going? Who do you mean
 To fetch? She is her own mistress, you know.

Unhappy lovers have but one resource—
Persuasion.

POLEMON.   But he seduced her when
I was away—is he not wronging me?

PATAIKOS. He wrongs you, yes, so you can lodge complaint,*   500
If ever you discuss the case with him;
If you resort to violence, you will lose
Your plea. For his offence entitles you
To lodge complaint but not to take revenge
Yourself.

POLEMON.   Not even now?

PATAIKOS.   Not even now.

POLEMON. My god, I don't know what to say, except
That I shall hang myself. Pataikos, she's
Abandoned me; Glykera! she's abandoned me.
But if that's really what you now advise—
You know her and you've often talked to her—
Go to her then and have a talk with her;
Be my ambassador, I beg you, please.

PATAIKOS. I'll do what you suggest.   510

POLEMON.   You're good
At speaking, I suppose, Pataikos.

PATAIKOS.   Yes,
I'm pretty good.

POLEMON.   Really, you must be good,
Pataikos; that's the only way to save
My bacon. If I've ever done her wrong,
If I don't keep on trying every way
To please her—if you saw the finery
I've bought for her—

PATAIKOS.   No thanks.

POLEMON.   Do have a look.
Pataikos, please. You'll pity me the more.

PATAIKOS. Heavens above!

POLEMON [*going towards his door*]. Do come! Such lovely clothes!
How beautiful she looks dressed up in one
Of these! Perhaps you have not seen her in—   520

PATAIKOS. Oh yes, I have.

POLEMON.   And then how tall she is,
A sight for one's sore eyes. But why do I
Bring in her height? That's quite irrelevant;
I'm mad.
PATAIKOS.   You're not.
POLEMON.   I'm not? You must see them,
Pataikos. Come this way.
PATAIKOS.   Go on. I'll come.

                    [*Exeunt into* POLEMON'*s house*

Enter MOSCHION *from* MYRRHINE'*s house and shouts at the retreating
figures of* POLEMON *and* PATAIKOS.

MOSCHION. To hell with you! be off and quickly too.
They came with lances but they've scuttled off.
They could not even crush a swallow's nest;
What useless bums they are—malicious toads!
He said that they had mercenaries with them,   530
But now these famous mercenaries prove
To be nothing but Sosias alone.

                    [*He turns to address the audience*

Of all the unhappy men our age has seen—
And there has been a good big crop of these
Throughout all Greece for reasons I don't know—
Of all these thousands, I am sure there's none
Alive as miserable as me. As soon
As I went in there, I did none of what
I usually do; I didn't go to see
My mother, didn't send for any of
The servants, but went into a room away   540
From everyone and lay myself down, quite
Absorbed in thought; and I sent Daos in
To tell my mother I had come, just that,
But he paid little heed to me; he found
Their lunch was on the table and so he
Just gorged himself; and all that time I lay
Alone and kept on saying to myself,
'Soon mother will be here to bring me word
From my beloved, saying on what terms

She'll meet with me.' And I was practising   550
A speech . . .

There follows a lacuna of about 160 lines, including the end of this
act and the opening of Act 4. Moschion's monologue must have
continued as he has to explain why he is the most unhappy of all
men alive; perhaps he went on to say that Myrrhine came to him
and told him that it was impossible for him to marry Glykera (she
may have told him he was a foundling but did not reveal that
Glykera was his sister; for when he appears in the next act, he
does not know this; he says then: 'On reflection I think it not
impossible that my real mother exposed a daughter born to her at
the same time as me, and she (Glykera) is then my sister.')

CHORAL INTERLUDE

ACT 4

The opening of the act is missing. Our text resumes with Pataikos
in conversation with Glykera; Pataikos, who still does not know
that he is the father of Glykera and Moschion, is acting as go-
between for Polemon; she is defending herself against the charge
of trying to seduce Moschion.

GLYKERA. *What* could I *gain*, my dear, by running to
    His mother here? Do you consider that?
    Was it to make him take me as his wife?   710
    [*ironically*] His standing in society* and mine
    Are just alike. Not that, but so that he
    Should keep me as his mistress? In that case
    I would try hard to keep his family
    Deceived, and so would he. Would he rush in
    And lodge me here in his own father's house?
    Have I been such a fool that I thus chose
    To rouse *his mother's* hatred and leave you
    Suspecting us *of misbehaviour*,
    Suspicions which can never be erased?

You think, Pataikos, I can feel no shame?
You've come convinced of this and you supposed
I really was like that?

PATAIKOS.   Heaven forbid!   720
I only wish that you could prove that what
You say is true. I *believe your words myself.*

GLYKERA. But all the same you must go back and tell
Him to abuse some other girl from now.

PATAIKOS. *He never meant to do this* dreadful thing.

GLYKERA. It was abominable *and not the way
A decent man would treat* a servant girl.

A lacuna of about sixteen lines. When the text resumes, Glykera
has cooled down and is telling Pataikos she has some tokens which
show who her parents were.

GLYKERA. I had those things *from her, tokens which showed*   742
Me who my father and my mother were;
I've always kept them close and guarded them.

PATAIKOS. What do you want?

GLYKERA.   I want to fetch them here.

PATAIKOS. Have you completely given up the man?
What do you want of me?

GLYKERA.   My dearest friend,
You must do this for me.

PATAIKOS.   It shall be done,
Although it is absurd. You should have thought
The whole thing through.

GLYKERA.   I know what's best for me.

PATAIKOS. You're set on this? Which of the servant girls
Knows where these things are hidden?   750

GLYKERA.   Doris knows.

PATAIKOS [*shouting*]. Hey, someone call out Doris. [*To* GLYKERA]
All the same,
Glykera, for heaven's sake, *be ruled by me
And pardon him* on terms I now suggest.

Enter DORIS *in tears from* POLEMON'S *house.*

DORIS. Oh, mistress!

GLYKERA.   What's the matter?
DORIS.   Misery!
GLYKERA. Please, Doris, bring me out the box in which
  I keep my needlework; you know the one,
  Of course you do; the one I gave you to
  Look after. Why're you crying, you poor thing?
                                    [*Exit* DORIS *to fetch the box*
PATAIKOS. Good god, it's quite extraordinary.
  Nothing *in human life's past belief* . . .   760

A lacuna of about seven lines, in which Doris must have returned
with the box and Pataikos began to examine its contents. He must
have said that he had recognized a figure embroidered on some
clothes 'which I saw then', i.e. when Polemon was showing him
Glykera's wardrobe; perhaps this recognition was the extraordinary experience of which he spoke above.

He is now examining the embroidery which Doris has brought
in the box.

  .   .   .   .

  Which I saw then. Next door to this there stands
  A goat or ox or some such beast?
GLYKERA.   My dear,
  It is a stag and not a goat.   770
PATAIKOS.   It has
  Some horns, I'm sure of that. And third there's here
  A winged horse. This is the needlework
  Of my unhappy wife, poor dear.

Enter MOSCHION *from* MYRRHINE*'s house; he does not see* PATAIKOS *and*
  GLYKERA; *he is musing on what he had learnt from his foster-mother.*

MOSCHION. When I reflect on this, I think it's not
  Impossible that when my mother bore
  Me she exposed with me a daughter born
  At the same time. If that's what happened and
  She is my sister, I am doomed to misery.
PATAIKOS. Good god, what members of my family survive?*
GLYKERA. Ask what you want and learn the truth from me.   780
PATAIKOS. Tell me from where you got the things you have?

GLYKERA. These were the clothes I wore when I was saved.

MOSCHION [*aside*]. Let me draw back a bit; tossed by the storms
   Of life I've reached the crisis of my fate.

PATAIKOS. Did you lie there alone? Please tell me that.

GLYKERA. Oh no. A brother was exposed with me.

MOSCHION [*aside*]. Ah, there's the answer to one thing I ask.

PATAIKOS. How were you parted from each other then?

GLYKERA. I've heard, and I could tell you all. But ask
   About myself; for that I may explain.   790
   The rest I swore to her* I'd not reveal.

MOSCHION [*aside*]. Her words confirm quite clearly what I feared.
   'She swore to mother.' Where does that leave me?

PATAIKOS. Who was it took you up and cared for you?

GLYKERA. A woman did, who saw me lying there.

PATAIKOS. What record did she tell you of the place?

GLYKERA. A spring, she said, a place shadowed by trees.

PATAIKOS. The very place the man who left you said.

GLYKERA. Who was this man? Please tell me if you may.

PATAIKOS. It was a slave who left you in that place,
   But I it was who shrank from rearing you.   800

GLYKERA. You, my own father, cast me out? But why?

PATAIKOS. The ways of chance, my child, are often strange.
   Your mother died quite suddenly when she
   Bore you, and just one day before, my girl—

GLYKERA. Whatever happened? How I shake with fear!

PATAIKOS. Long used to plenty, I lost everything.

GLYKERA. All in one day? How? God, how terrible!

PATAIKOS. I heard the ship which gave us all our needs
   Was sunk beneath the wild Aegean waves.

GLYKERA. How your misfortune grieves me!

PATAIKOS.   I believed   810
   In poverty I'd be an utter fool
   To bring up children who would be a drag.
   Tell me of all *the other tokens*, child.

GLYKERA. Which one?

PATAIKOS.   *I want to hear about them all.*

GLYKERA. *That's what you want? Then all* shall be revealed.
   There were some necklaces, a little brooch

With precious stones left to identify
The babies there exposed—
PATAIKOS. Let's look at them.
GLYKERA. Those I no longer have.
PATAIKOS. What's that you say?
GLYKERA. *I must suppose my brother has them now.*
MOSCHION [*aside*]. This man must be my father, it appears.
PATAIKOS. Could you describe the things?
GLYKERA. A crimson belt— 820
PATAIKOS. That's right.
GLYKERA. With dancing maidens worked on it.
MOSCHION [*aside to himself*]. Now don't you know the truth?
GLYKERA. A gold head-band,
And last a see-through cloak. I've told you all.
PATAIKOS. I will hold back no longer. Darling girl!

[*He embraces her*

MOSCHION [*aside*]. If I'm *his son, why should they not embrace*
Me too? I've been here and *have heard all that*
They said to one another.

[*He goes forward*

PATAIKOS. God, who's this?
MOSCHION. Who am I? *I'm your son . . .* 827

The end of this act and the beginning of the last act are missing, between 100 and 200 lines; in the last part of Act 4 Moschion must have been accepted as Glykera's lost brother and Pataikos' son.

ACT 5

When our text starts again Polemon is convinced that he has lost Glykera for ever; he now knows that she is a freeborn girl, the daughter of Pataikos, and supposes that she will have nothing more to do with him. But, unknown to him, Glykera loves him and he has a champion in Pataikos, who has agreed that she shall marry him. Polemon is on stage talking to Doris.

POLEMON.   .   .   .   .
To hang myself.

DORIS.   Oh, don't do that. Oh dear!   976
POLEMON. What shall I do then, Doris? How can I
    Live on without her, doomed to misery?
DORIS. She will come back to you—
POLEMON.   *You really think so?*
DORIS. If *from now on* you try your best *to do*   980
    The decent thing—
POLEMON.   I shall not fail to try,
    You may be sure of that.
DORIS.   You must.
POLEMON.   Well said!
    Go in to her.   [*Exit* DORIS *to* MYRRHINE'*s house*
                    Tomorrow, Doris, I
    Shall set you free. But hear what you must say—
    She's gone. *Oh darling*, how you've conquered me!
    It was your brother that you kissed and not
    A lover. Mad with jealousy, a man possessed,
    I thought that I was wronged and straightaway
    I acted like a drunken sot. And then
    I meant to hang myself—a good thing, too.

                    Enter DORIS.

    Oh dearest Doris, what's the news?
DORIS.   It's good.
    She's coming to you.
POLEMON.   Did she laugh at me?   990
DORIS. Oh no, she was just putting on a dress.
    Her father was still asking questions. You
    Must now be quick and make a sacrifice
    To celebrate the happy news we've had
    Of her good luck.
POLEMON.   By god, you're right. The cook
    Is here. Tell him to sacrifice the pig.
DORIS. But where's the basket* and the rest we need?
POLEMON. The basket you can deal with later on.
    Let him kill the pig. Or better, I myself
    Shall do the job. I'll take a garland from
    The altar here and put it on my head.

DORIS. You're much more likely to convince her dressed   1000
    Like that.
POLEMON.   Bring out *my darling Glykera!*
DORIS. She was about to come, *her father too.*
POLEMON. Her father! What am I to do?
                  [*The door sounds; exit* POLEMON *in a panic*
DORIS.   Oh dear!
    He's hopped it. Who'd have thought a creaking door
    Was such a danger? I'll go in myself
    To help with anything that needs be done.
                      [*Exit into* POLEMON'*s house*

      Enter PATAIKOS, *talking over his shoulder to* GLYKERA.

PATAIKOS. I like your 'I shall now be reconciled
    With him' a lot. When you've been fortunate,
    To make a peaceful settlement's the sign
    Of a true Greek. Now someone run at once
    And call him out.
POLEMON [*coming out of the house*]. I'm coming. I was just   1010
    Making a sacrifice for her good luck
    Since I had heard that Glykera had found
    Her family.

        Enter GLYKERA *from* MYRRHINE'*s house.*

PATAIKOS.   You're right. And now you must
    Hear what I have to say. I give this girl
    To you in marriage, so that she may bear
    You lawful children.*
POLEMON.   I accept her hand.
PATAIKOS. And give three talents' dowry.
POLEMON.   You are kind.
PATAIKOS. Henceforth forget your soldier's role, so you
    May never more rush into things again.
POLEMON. Good god, shall I, who nearly came to grief
    Just now, rush into things again? I shall
    Not even find a fault in Glykera.
    My darling, only make it up with me.   1020
GLYKERA. Your drunken rage has now turned out to be

The first beginning of our happiness.
POLEMON. You're right.
GLYKERA.   And so all is forgiven now.
POLEMON. *That's really kind*. Pataikos, join with us
   In making sacrifice.   [*Exit into his house with* GLYKERA
PATAIKOS.   I must pursue
   Another wedding now; I want my son to wed
   Philinos'* daughter. Gods above and Earth . . .

The concluding few lines of the play are missing; it may have
ended with arrangements for a party of celebration, as, for
instance, in *The Bad-tempered Man* and *The Girl from Samos*.

Two quotations from ancient authors:

1. Stobaeus, *Eclogae* 2. 33. 6
   So welcome is a friend who feels like me.

Perhaps this is Polemon praising Pataikos for acting as his
'ambassador' to Glykera.

2. Photius a 2475
   But still, you show them to the woman and . . .

Perhaps Pataikos is telling Glykera to show her tokens to
Myrrhine so that she may compare them with Moschion's.

The Man she Hated (Misoumenos)

About 600 lines or part-lines of this play survive from thirteen different papyri (it appears to have been one of Menander's most popular plays), but the fragments are so damaged and scattered that even our knowledge of the plot is incomplete.

Characters

THRASONIDES, a captain of mercenaries
GETAS, his slave
KRATEIA, a girl captured and loved by Thrasonides
DEMEAS, Krateia's father
KLEINIAS, a friend of Demeas
SYRA(?), an old woman, Kleinias' slave
KRATEIA'S NURSE (Simiche?)
A COOK
KRATEIA'S BROTHER

The scene is a street in a city (perhaps Athens) with two houses, one that of Thrasonides, the other that of Kleinias.

[The line numbers are those of Loeb text vol. ii.]

The general outline of the plot is clear: Thrasonides, a captain of mercenaries, has recently returned home to Athens(?) from a campaign in Cyprus; there he had acquired a girl called Krateia; he fell in love with her but she refuses him, because she believes he has killed her brother, and he will not force her. Krateia's father, Demeas, arrives from Cyprus in search of her and stays with Thrasonides' neighbour, Kleinias. He meets and recognizes Krateia; Thrasonides reluctantly agrees to ransom her. Krateia's brother then appears on the scene, and Krateia herself accepts

Thrasonides' hand in marriage. But some fragments suggest a sub-plot, the nature of which we can scarcely glimpse.

ACT I

THRASONIDES *stands outside the door of his house on a cold, wet night.*

THRASONIDES. O Night, of all the gods it's you that play
　　The greatest part in Love; it's in the night
　　Most words of love are spoken, thoughts arise
　　Filled with desire—Night, have you ever seen
　　A man more miserable than me, a more
　　Unhappy lover? Here I stand before my doors
　　In this dark alley; up and down I walk,
　　This way and that, till now, as midnight nears,
　　When I could be in bed and hold my love
　　Close in my arms. She's in my house and I　　　　　10
　　Could take her; and I long to, quite as crazed
　　As any lover—but I don't. I choose
　　To stand beneath the open sky although
　　It's winter, shivering, while I talk to you.

　　　　Enter GETAS *from the house and watches his master.*

GETAS [*aside*]. Good god, not even the proverbial dog*
　　Should go outside *when it's as cold as this.*
　　My master strolls around as if it were
　　High summer spouting philosophy.
　　He'll do for me. He must be made of oak . . . .
[Two lines mutilated—'spending his time' . . . 'the door']　　20
　　Unhappy man, why aren't you now asleep?
　　You wear me out with all this tramping round.
　　Or are you sleepwalking? [*To* THRASONIDES] Stop, if you are
　　Awake and see me.
THRASONIDES. 　　　　　Getas, you've come out
　　As well? Why's that? Did someone tell you to?
　　I never did. Or is this some idea of yours?
GETAS. God, no; I had no orders—they're asleep.

THRASONIDES. It looks as if you've come to care for me.

GETAS. Come in, you lucky man;* it's late. You've had
   Good luck in everything.

THRASONIDES. Who? Me? I'm most
   Unlucky, Getas, treated terribly. 30
   I have not had *a chance* to see you yet;
   It's only yesterday you got back home
   After so long.

GETAS. Why, when I left the camp
   And started off, *you seemed* happy enough.
   But since I had the job of bringing home
   The spoils, I've got back last. What's bugging you?

THRASONIDES. I'm being piteously abused.

GETAS. By whom?

THRASONIDES. My captive girl. I bought her, made her free,
   Appointed her the mistress of my house,
   And gave her gifts of servants, gold, and clothes,
   Thought her my wife— 40

GETAS. Then how does she abuse you?

THRASONIDES. I am ashamed even to tell you that.
   The snake! The monster!

GETAS. Tell me, all the same.

THRASONIDES. She feels a strange loathing for me—

GETAS [*aside*]. Good lord!
   Magnetic poles!* [*To* THRASONIDES] You think she hates you!
   What
   A strange idea!

THRASONIDES. Or do you think that this
   Is what one might expect of human nature?

GETAS. She's not in charge . . .

After four lines of which only a few letters survive, Thrasonides is
speaking and seems to be describing how he has tested Krateia's
feelings for him.

THRASONIDES. .   .   .   .
   I wait for when the sky is pelting rain 50
   At night, lightning and thunder, and I lie
   In bed holding her in my arms.

GETAS.   Then what?

THRASONIDES. I shout, 'Dear girl', and say I've got to go
  At once to see a man, and give some name.
  Then any wife would surely say: 'Poor man,
  It's raining hard. To see a man, you say? . . .

Twenty-eight lines follow which are too damaged to give sense; it
seems that Thrasonides continues to explain his relationship with
Krateia and Getas intervenes, perhaps saying that she is too
petted and extravagant. When our text resumes, badly damaged,
Thrasonides is still reporting his appeals to Krateia.

THRASONIDES. And so she is.* 'My darling, give *your heart*   85
  To me. If you despise me, *you will fill*
  Me straightaway with jealousy and pain
  And madness.'

GETAS.   Why, you poor unhappy man!

THRASONIDES. 'If only you vouchsafed a friendly word,
  I'd sacrifice to all the gods in thanks.'

GETAS. Then what could be the reason? You are not   90
  Completely unattractive, one might say,
  Though certainly your meagre soldier's pay's
  A snag. But then to look at you do have
  Some real charm. Yet you bring home a girl
  Who's in her prime *and she refuses you.*

THRASONIDES. Damn you! We must find out what it's about
  And show the necessary cause of this.

GETAS. Well, master, women are a filthy lot—

THRASONIDES. If you don't stop—

GETAS.   From what you're saying, sir, . . .
  She's purposely indulging in some game
  At your expense; *a woman's character's*   100
  Not always logical . . .

There follows a gap of a hundred or more lines where there may
have been a postponed prologue in which some deity explained
the facts the audience needed to know: Demeas had a daughter,
Krateia, and a son; Krateia was captured in the course of the war
in Cyprus and enslaved; she was bought by Thrasonides, who fell
in love with her. The son was thought to have been killed in the

fighting by Thrasonides (he had this son's sword and perhaps boasted that he had killed the man who had owned it); hence Krateia's loathing of Thrasonides.

A scrap of papyrus containing eight half-lines may belong to a further conversation between Getas and Thrasonides; these may be the end of the act leading to the choral interlude; Getas(?) says, 'I'm going in . . . *I see* some muggers as I walk around *who're threatening* me . . . avoiding them'.

ACT 2

A badly mutilated fragment of ninety-four lines may belong to the earlier part of this act; the first fourteen lines of this fragment seem to start with another conversation between Thrasonides and Getas; then Thrasonides tells Getas to go in and, left alone, has a short monologue on his sufferings
('pity for me'). Then Thrasonides goes off, perhaps to join a party elsewhere (see Act 3, p. 169)

At some time during this act, Thrasonides threatened to commit suicide and Getas removed all the swords in the house to that of his neighbour Kleinias. Two clues on this are given in quotations from ancient authors:

OCT fr. 2. Arrian, *Discourses of Epictetus* 4. 1. 19

Then what does Thrasonides say?

> A cheap young slave-girl has made me her slave,
> Who've never been enslaved by enemies.

And then he asks for a sword and is angry with the man who out of kindness will not give it him.

OCT fr. 6. Pollux 10. 145 f.

> The swords have disappeared.

Presumably spoken by Thrasonides when he finds there are no swords in the house.

When Thrasonides leaves the stage, Demeas appears, just arrived

from Cyprus. In his opening monologue he may have said that he
had received a letter from a friend, Kleinias, about Krateia ('a
letter about her'). He approaches Kleinias' door and knocks; the
door is opened by another character, probably Syra, an old
woman who is a servant of Kleinias (she does not know him and
addresses hims as 'Stranger'). In answer to her questions Demeas
says that he has come from Cyprus and is searching for his
daughter. He learns from her that a girl called Krateia is living
next door to Kleinias.

The following lines (supplemented) survive from this scene:

DEMEAS(?). . . . I cannot say.   430
SYRA.   Where do you come from, stranger?
DEMEAS. From Cyprus.
SYRA.   So you've come to ransom slaves?
DEMEAS. Good heavens, no; I have not come for that,
  But for a girl who has become . . .
  But where she is . . .
SYRA.   What's that you say?
DEMEAS. . . . Help me in this . . .
SYRA.   Others, *I think*, old man,
  *Should deal w*ith that.
DEMEAS.   Searching *for her* again
  If . . .
SYRA.   .   .   .   .
DEMEAS. *If you will help me find her,* you'll be called   440
  My saviour . . .
SYRA.   What's her name?
DEMEAS. *She's called* Krateia . . .
SYRA. There is *a girl in there who has that name* . . .
  For this man . . .
DEMEAS. O Zeus, giver of victory, . . .
  What unexpected news!

The remaining forty-six lines of the act, of which only isolated
words and phrases survive, give no consecutive sense. Possibly
Demeas asks Syra to bring Krateia out ('Bring *her* out into the
street for me'), so that he can see whether the girl really is his
daughter, but she refuses ('Do your own business first').

ACT 3

The opening thirty lines of the act are damaged beyond repair. We then have a few lines which give some sense. There are two speakers, perhaps Syra and Krateia's nurse; a third, probably Getas, is eavesdropping. The nurse is carrying a suppliant branch and may be going to pray for a reconciliation between Krateia and Thrasonides; she recounts a conversation she has had with Getas. The text is doubtful and the meaning obscure. Getas had apparently tried to stop the nurse going on her mission of supplication. He makes occasional asides until he is detected by Syra.

SYRA. A suppliant branch?* What did you say?   532
NURSE.   'You'll fight
 With me? oh dear!' 'Not you,' he says, 'but him;
 He lives a life of misery.'
GETAS [*aside*].   That's true.
NURSE. When he was happy and envied *by all*—
GETAS [*aside*]. Yes, so he was.
NURSE.   — why *did she put a stop*
 To this?
SYRA. She knows her own position best . . .
[Two lines too mutilated to give sense.]
GETAS [*aside*]. What's that?
SYRA [*hearing* GETAS' *aside*]. Whatever's that? Who have we here?
NURSE. This whispering comes from someone, I am sure. 540
             [*She discovers* GETAS
 Be off with you!

There follow eighteen lines of which only isolated words survive. It seems that Getas withdraws and the Nurse and Syra continue talking. The passage ends with the words: 'Let's go, Syra.'

 Getas re-enters and gives a puzzling account of a scene he has just witnessed; he saw two men drinking and singing; he thinks one of whom was behaving suspiciously but keeps changing his mind about this. We have no clue as to who the fat-faced man and his companion were; they belong to a sub-plot which is entirely lost. Arnott speculates that the fat-faced man may have been a brothel-keeper who had invited Thrasonides to dinner.

GETAS.   comes back.   559
  I left. A fat-faced man sang songs; he was
  A perfect pig; *he went to try* and watch
  The women from outside. Is he a slave . . .?
  One of the two sang clearer *than the first* . . .
  The man . . . Heavens above, it's really fair enough,
  Men say, to sing a chorus when you drink.
  You've brought us a good concert! But why
  Do you turn back and come again and give
  These signs, unless you mean to do us harm?   570
  Nonsense! Am I to tell him to come back
  To dinner, since he asked my master first?
  It's clear *that he's a villain.* I'll go in
  And try to hide myself and keep a watch
  On anything they do or say inside.

                              [*Exit to* THRASONIDES' *house*

                    Enter SYRA *from* KLEINIAS' *house.*

SYRA. Great gods, I've never seen an odder guest
  Than this. Oh dear! What ever does he want?
  When he had seen our neighbours' swords in here,
  He wanted me to bring them out *for him*
  And then examined them for ages . . .   580

There follow ten lines in which only isolated words and phrases
survive; Demeas seems to have followed Syra out of Kleinias'
house; he may have questioned her about the swords and then
asks her to knock on Thrasonides' door for him; perhaps he has
by now identified his son's sword amongst the others.

DEMEAS.   knock on the door for me.
SYRA. You knock yourself. Why bother me? Oh dear!
[One line spoken by Demeas missing and half a line of Syra's
reply.]   590
  I'm trotting off. I've shown *the house* to you.
  Now call them out *yourself* and talk to them . . .
DEMEAS. I am *confounded . . . when* I see this *sword* of mine.
SYRA [*aside*]. He will knock on the door; and when he's knocked
  He'll still . . .

[Eleven lines too mutilated to give sense.]

DEMEAS. Now this has just begun to worry me.   605

Perhaps he is worried by having found his son's sword in the possession of Thrasonides. Two more unintelligible lines follow, after which Syra goes into Kleinias' house, leaving Demeas alone; he knocks on Thrasonides' door but draws back when he hears the door being opened from inside.

DEMEAS [*knocking on the door*] . . . Boy! Boys! But I'll withdraw.
    The door is creaking; someone's coming out.

> DEMEAS *withdraws.* KRATEIA *and her* NURSE *come out, talking to each other.*

KRATEIA. I could not endure . . . Why these?   610
DEMEAS [*aside*]. Good god, what do I see? A sight beyond
    All I could even dream.
KRATEIA.   Nurse, what do you mean?
    What are you telling me? My father? Where?
DEMEAS [*comes forward*]. My child, Krateia.
KRATEIA.   Who is calling me?
                                    [*She turns and sees* DEMEAS
    Oh Father! Blessings on you, dearest one.
                                            [*They embrace*
DEMEAS. I hold you in my arms.
KRATEIA.   I longed for you
    And now you've come. I feast my eyes on you
    I thought that I would never see again.

> *Enter* GETAS *from* THRASONIDES' *house.*

GETAS. She came out here. [*Aside*] Good heavens, what is this?
    Hey, what has she to do with you, my man?
    What are you doing, you? Did I not say so?
    I've caught the man we're looking for, yes, caught
    Him in the act. He seems an old grey beard,   620
    Sixty at least, but still he'll pay for this.
                                    [*He shouts to* DEMEAS
    Hey, you, who do you think you're cuddling there
    And kissing?

KRATEIA.   Getas, look, my father's here.

GETAS. My, what a story, quite ridiculous! . . .
Who *are* you? Where've you come from? *What do you want?*

DEMEAS. I've travelled *here* alone *from far*. And I
Am *father* of this girl.

GETAS.   What? Is this old man
Your father? Is this true, Krateia?

KRATEIA.   Yes.

[*Pointing to the* NURSE

Take her as witness that it's true.

GETAS.   What's that?
Old woman, do you call *this man your master?*

[*She nods assent;* GETAS *turns to* DEMEAS

Good sir, where *have you come* from? From your home?   630

DEMEAS. I wish I had.*

GETAS.   But are you really far
From home?

DEMEAS.   I'm here from Cyprus, and this is
The first one of my family I've seen.
It's plain that war, man's common enemy,
Has scattered others of my house this way
And that.

GETAS.   That's true. That's how this girl
Was captured and so came to us. But I
Will run and call my master . . .

DEMEAS. You do that.   639

[*Exit* GETAS *to fetch* THRASONIDES

There follow seven (?) lines damaged beyond repair, in which
Demeas and Krateia converse. When the text again becomes
intelligible, Demeas is asking Krateia about her brother's death.

DEMEAS. He's not alive? Who gave you this report?   647

KRATEIA. I'm sure of it.

DEMEAS.   Then that's the end for me.

KRATEIA. Oh, my unhappy fate! What miseries
We've suffered, dearest father.   650

DEMEAS.   He is dead?

KRATEIA. Yes, killed by him who least of all men should

Have done this deed.

DEMEAS. You know the man?

KRATEIA. I do

And taken prisoner . . .

DEMEAS. But why, Krateia, *are you carrying*
*These suppliant branches?**

KRATEIA. The man who did this *wants to marry me*.
But, father, *let's go in* . . .
All . . .
We must consider now *what we should do*.
I lived *the way I had to. How can it*
Be right for me *to live on now like this?*

DEMEAS. How strange life is and how unhappy too!

[*Exeunt* DEMEAS, KRATEIA *and the* NURSE *into* THRASONIDES' *house*

Enter THRASONIDES *and* GETAS *from the city.*

THRASONIDES. You say Krateia's father's just arrived? 660
Now you* will either make me blessed or else
The most unhappy of all men alive.
If he does not approve of me and give
Her to me as my wife, Thrasonides
Is finished. God forbid! Let us go in.
No more of this conjecture; we must know.
I shrink and go in trembling. My soul
Portends disaster, Getas. I'm afraid.
But anything at all is better than
Vague guesses. I'm amazed by these events. 670

[*Exeunt* THRASONIDES *and* GETAS *into the house*

Enter from the city KLEINIAS *with a cook.*

In an earlier scene, which is lost, Kleinias must have planned a
party; the guests are to be Demeas and a girl, whom he refers to as
'my girl'.

KLEINIAS. There is my guest for one; then me, and third
My girl, if she indeed is coming; I'm
In agony myself as well; if not,
My guest alone. Now I'll be running round

The city everywhere to find the girl.   675
Go in and, cook, for heaven's sake be quick.
> [*Exeunt,* KLEINIAS *to the city, the* COOK *into his house*

CHORAL INTERLUDE

ACT 4

> *Enter* KLEINIAS *from his house, talking back to the* OLD WOMAN.

KLEINIAS. What's that you say? He recognized the sword
  Lying inside our house and off he rushed
  To see our neighbours when he heard that it
  Belonged to them? When did they put it here,   680
  And why, old woman, did they bring the thing
  To us? It's obvious that you . . .
[one and a half lines unintelligible.]
                              But one of them
  Is at the door, it seems, and coming out,
  So I shall hear the whole thing properly.

> *Enter* GETAS *from* THRASONIDES' *house, talking to himself. He does
> not see* KLEINIAS *and walks up and down in high indignation.*

GETAS. Great gods, what quite extraordinary,
  Inhuman savagery they both* have shown!
KLEINIAS. Getas, a stranger has just called on you?
GETAS [*disregarding* KLEINIAS]. Good god, what surliness! Surely a
    man
  May ask to take *a girl as wife?* . . .   689
[Seven lines mutilated.]
KLEINIAS.   What can
  I make of this? . . .
GETAS. .   .   .
KLEINIAS. . . . Demeas . . .
GETAS.   *My master begged,* but not a squeak
  From Demeas *in answer. Then master cried,*

'I love Krateia, Demeas, as you can see;
You are her father and her guardian.'
All this he said with tears and prayers.
You might as well play music to an ass!
KLEINIAS [*to himself*]. I think I'll walk around with him myself
[*He falls in step with* GETAS

GETAS. His only answer: 'I demand my daughter back
From you; I've come to ransom her; I am
Her father.' And *he* says, 'Now I have met
You, Demeas, I ask your daughter's hand.' 700
KLEINIAS [*aside*]. My guest has gone inside; he's in the house.
This fellow's naming him as Demeas.
GETAS. Good lord, could he not treat what's happened like
A rational man? A wild mountain boar,
As people say! But still, that's not the worst.
She looked away from him while master said,
'Krateia, don't desert me, please, I beg;
You were a virgin when I captured you,
I first was called your man; yes, I adored
You and adore you still; I am in love
With you, Krateia darling. What do you find
In me that you dislike? If you desert 710
Me now, you will soon learn that I am dead.'
She answered not a word.
KLEINIAS.   What *is* all this?
GETAS. The girl's a savage, she's a lioness.
KLEINIAS [*facing* GETAS]. You wretched man, you've seen me right
enough.
GETAS [*still ignoring* KLEINIAS]. So unexpected.
KLEINIAS.   He's quite off his head.
GETAS. My goodness, I would not have let her go.
It is an old Greek custom, everywhere
Observed, I know. It's right to pity one
Who shows some pity in return, but when
You have no thought for me, I have no care
And no regard for you. That can't be done? 720
Why not? I think there's nothing strange in that.
But he will shout and plan to kill himself

He stands there, while his eyes are blazing fire . . .
                    and tears his hair.
KLEINIAS. Man, you'll do for me!
GETAS.   Why, hello, Kleinias.
Where's he popped up from then?
KLEINIAS.   It looks as if
My guest's arrival's causing chaos . . .

Thirty-four verses unintelligible; surviving words suggest that
Getas and Kleinias converse for some seventeen lines and that
then Kleinias returns to his house ('I'm going in') and Thrasonides
enters. After a short exchange between him and Getas, the latter
leaves. When the text again makes sense, Thrasonides is alone and
has a long monologue which continues until the end of the act.
The first four lines are mutilated and obscure and the supplements guesswork.

THRASONIDES. Someone perhaps may've said I'm spiritless   757
If I should let her go, ignoring many things.
But if in public *I can* bear *my grief without*
Revealing it, this is the other *way;*   760
Provided I can keep a heart of stone
And bear it, I'll be able to conceal
My wound from those I'm with. *But* how shall I
Then master my distress and bear the pain
More easily? For drunkenness one day
Will rip apart the plaster covering
My wound though I may wish to keep it dark.

Of the next twenty-three lines only fragments survive; these
suggest that Thrasonides is thinking over his relationship with
Krateia and wondering where he went wrong. We then have
eighteen difficult lines in which Thrasonides argues with
himself—shall he ransom Krateia or keep her by force? He
decides that he must give her up and live in misery. (I follow
Handley's interpretation of this passage in a seminar paper
entitled 'A Bow at a Venture' (July 1996).)

THRASONIDES. *If she is* angry, *you become* pathetic.   790
If Simiche's come out, you say, 'How is she?'

All that you say's concerned with her. My care
For her is selfish? Don't say that. Is this
Misfortune all my fault? Don't I blame him?
Well then, there's one thing you can do, stop him
From taking her away. But it's the same
In everything; the past upsets the life
We live. You'll let her go? 'But then,' you'll say,
'By pity you will draw all hatred on
Yourself and suffer pain.' What life is left
For you? Where's glory in survival now?
If one should let one's angry passions rip,   800
Would that be selfishness? But when you look
As if you'll seize her, perhaps you're too headstrong!
And so be logical, be brave. Live on
In helplessness, in pain and feebleness.
To her you must bequeath this deathless shame:
'She was well treated but took vengeance on
The man who did her good.' But surely I
Can *punish her by* feigning *suicide?* . . .

The rest of the act, about nine lines, is too mutilated to give sense.
His threat to feign suicide probably anticipates events of Act 5, in
which it seems that Thrasonides took a drug to make it seem that
he was dead.

CHORAL INTERLUDE

ACT 5

Of the opening of the fifth act a few words survive in the first five
lines, including the word 'drug', which suggests that Getas may be
saying that Thrasonides has taken a drug to feign suicide. A
mosaic from the 'House of Menander' at Mytilene in Lesbos (3rd
century AD) entitled 'Misoumenos Act 5' would help here if we
could interpret it with confidence. There are three figures: on the
right stands a woman with right arm raised (Krateia?); in the

centre a man (Demeas?) whose gesture is uncertain; on the left a man in a white tunic, facing them and apparently tightening the two ends of a scarf wrapped round his neck; this may be Getas mimimg Thrasonides' threat or attempt to commit suicide.

There follow a lacuna of about ninety-nine lines, fourteen lines in which only odd letters survive, and another lacuna of about fifteen lines. Then it seems that Krateia's brother enters and has a monologue (twelve lines), of which only isolated words survive. As this ends, Getas comes out of Kleinias' house and is met by Thrasonides. Getas, not knowing who Krateia's brother is, tells him to get out. He has learnt that Krateia and her father have agreed that she should marry Thrasonides, now that it is known that he did not kill her brother.

GETAS. Get out, man, from the door.

                       [*Exit* KRATEIA'S BROTHER *to the city*

THRASONIDES [*to* GETAS].   What's this then, boy?

You seem to bring good news. *Tell me at once.*   960

GETAS. They're giving you Krateia as your wife.

THRASONIDES. That's what I prayed for, *but it can't be true.*

GETAS. As I have hopes of happiness, *it really is.*

THRASONIDES. You're not deceiving me?

GETAS.   *I swear I'm not.*

THRASONIDES. How did he say this?

GETAS.   Heavens, *what do you mean?*

THRASONIDES. *Tell me* the actual words *her father spoke.*

And hurry up, if . . . .

GETAS. He said, 'Dear daughter, *will you have this man?*'

'Yes, father,' she replied, 'I will.' I heard

These words, and what I heard *I tell you true.*   970

She *gently* laughed; her heart was filled with joy.

THRASONIDES. What splendid news.

GETAS.   And I'm delighted too.

But one of them is coming to the door.

          Enter DEMEAS *from* KLEINIAS' *house.*

DEMEAS. I've come to see you.

THRASONIDES.   That's most kind of you.

DEMEAS. I give my daughter to you as your wife
  To bear a crop of lawful children* and
  I give with her a dowry of two talents.
THRASONIDES. *I gladly take her.* Demeas, you only have
  To give me back your daughter . . .   977

The rest of the play is too fragmentary for translation but surviving words show that Thrasonides proposes to hold a party in
celebration now and the wedding tomorrow. He calls for torches
and garlands. The play ends with the customary appeal for the
spectators' applause and victory in the dramatic contest.

DEMEAS.   .   .   .   .   .   .
  Slave, light the torches and distribute them
  To us. With garlands *on our heads* . . .   990
  And don't let's have the dinner yet
  But wait . . .
  You . . . [*to the audience*] Now youths and pretty boys
  And men, all give us the applause we've earned.
  And may that noble laughter-loving maid,
  Victory, attend us always as our friend.

Fragments quoted by ancient authors (Loeb numbers):

5. Scholiast on Homer, *Odyssey* 17. 442
  I've/He's come from Cyprus where I/he did
  Great deeds; for there I/he served one of their kings.

This might be either from the Prologue or a boast of Thrasonides
in any part of the play.

7. [Justinus], *de monarchia* 5
  If only I could see this and get back
  My spirits once again; for now—but where
  Can one, Getas, find gods so just to us?

Thrasonides, in despair at Krateia's rejection of him, speaks these
lines, perhaps towards the end of Act 4.

8. Scholiast on Aristophanes, *Thesmophoriazousai* 423
  I've got to carry round a Spartan key,
  It seems.

Spartan keys were supposed to be exceptionally secure. Is Thrasonides at some point in the play, reduced to trying to lock Krateia in?

9. Photius a 2534
    Father, Thrasonides(?)—they have not killed him.

Krateia, perhaps, is telling Demeas that her brother is not dead, presumably at some point in the fifth act when her brother has turned up.

12. Hermeias, Commentary on Plato *Phaedrus,* p. 33, 16 Couv.
    THRASONIDES(?). You never were in love, Getas?
    GETAS. Not me, I never had my belly full enough.

This might equally well come from *Heros* (see p. 212, fr. 10). If this does come from from this play, it is impossible to place it. A full belly was supposed to provoke desire.

The Man from Sikyon (Sikyonios)

The papyri on which parts of this play are preserved were recovered from three separate mummy cases; all are badly damaged and the first three acts so mutilated that it is impossible to reconstruct the plot with confidence; acts 4 and 5 are better preserved.

Characters

DEMETER(?), speaker of the Prologue
STRATOPHANES, a captain of mercenaries, in love with Philoumene
SMIKRINES,* an Athenian who turns out to be Stratophanes' father
MOSCHION, Smikrines' son, also in love with Philoumene
THERON, a hanger-on of Stratophanes
PYRRHIAS, Stratophanes' servant
MALTHAKE, Stratophanes' mistress?
KICHESIAS, an old man who turns out to be Philoumene's father
DROMON, Kichesias' servant, kidnapped with Philoumene
AN UNNAMED DEMOCRAT
ELEUSINIOS, an Athenian democrat
SMIKRINES' WIFE
DONAX, a slave (mute)
(Philoumene does not appear in any of the extant fragments)

The scene is a street in Eleusis with two houses, one that of Smikrines, the other of Stratophanes.

Stratophanes' supposed father was a citizen of Sikyon, a small state west of Corinth. When the play opens, he has just returned from a campaign in Karia (southern Asia Minor) to Eleusis, the deme (parish) of Attica where the sacred mysteries of Demeter were celebrated. Many years earlier he had acquired a 4-year-old girl, Philoumene, with whom he later fell in love. When he went

off on campaign, he had left her with her loyal servant Dromon in
Eleusis at his supposed mother's house.

ACT I

Prologue: Our text begins in the middle of the Prologue. A
divinity (Demeter?) describes how Philoumene and Dromon were
captured by pirates, taken to Karia, and sold to an army officer.

DEMETER(?).　　.　　.　　.　　.　　.　　.

   I say the daughter of this man* is *there.*
   When they had got possession of the three,*
   They thought it would not pay to carry off
   The nurse, but took the servant and the child
   To Mylasa in Karia and made
   Use of the market there. The servant sat
   Holding his mistress on one arm. Then, while
   They were for sale, an officer came near
   And asked, 'How much for these?' He heard the price,
   Agreed, and bought them. Then another man,　　　10
   A local who was up for sale with them,
   And who was sitting near the servant, said,
   'Cheer up, my friend, the Sikyonian
   Who's bought you is a gallant captain and
   He's rich . . .

There follow four fragmentary lines which give no sense. Then a
lacuna of unknown length, followed by four more fragmentary
lines: finally two lines which look like the formula completing the
Prologue (compare *Dyskolos*, lines 42–3):

   These are the main points, and the rest you'll see,
   If you are willing, and willing you must be.

Following the Prologue there are eleven fragmentary lines, a
lacuna of five lines, and sixteen more broken fragments. From
these fragments we can deduce that two female characters enter
(Malthake and another?), who are discussing a parasite (Theron?)

with an insatiable appetite, whom Malthake will have to feed if
they marry. There follows a lacuna of unknown length.

In the next fragment, badly mutilated, two men are discussing a
plan to get a witness to say at a meeting of the Eleusinians that a
girl is a freeborn Athenian. The girl concerned must be Philoumene. Who the men are, is disputed, probably Stratophanes and
Theron, who now know that Moschion is in love with Philoumene
and may attempt to rescue her.

The first three lines of this scene, spoken by Stratophanes, are
too mutilated to give sense. The following ten lines, with supplementation, may be translated:

THERON(?). *What is the difficulty?* One could find
   A witness who would testify to this
   In many places in the town; *we're in*
   Eleusis; and a public meeting's on,
   I think. For heavens' sake, who'll notice it?
   If all the people *gather*, then one man*
   Could scarcely drag the girl off for himself.   60
   But if I hang around *here*, evening
   Will come while you're still nattering.
[Lacuna of twelve lines.]

The next fragment, thirty-seven part-lines, begins with Stratophanes and Theron conversing. It seems that by now Philoumene
and Dromon have run away and taken refuge at the altar where
they are found in a later scene; a fragment quoted by an ancient
grammarian may belong somewhere in this scene, if we assume
that Theron is reporting to Stratophanes what he had heard from
slaves:

   She left you and went off, gnashing her teeth
   In anger, so they say.

Stratophanes blames Theron for this. He sends him off to try to
get her back.

After five fragmentary lines, Stratophanes curses Theron (l. 80):

     May god destroy you! You've not got   80
   A straight or healthy notion in your head
          and now you've ruined me

I learnt that . . .
[Eight fragmentary lines.]
    You would have given twice; . . .
    Now run and *fetch* the girl

.   .   .   .

THERON. You won't let me put in *a word* to you.   95
STRATOPHANES. *Who* will not let you? I have given you
    The chance to speak and you've received it. Now
    Off you go!

                    [*Exit* THERON *to the city; exit* STRATOPHANES *to his house*

There follows what appears to be a monologue in which the
speaker is Moschion(?); he is in love with Philoumene and wishes
to rescue her from the clutches of Stratophanes. He quotes words
spoken by Stratophanes which he had overheard:

MOSCHION. She is afraid, he says, of one who is
    At once her master and a foreigner
    And in love with her. *I heard* him* say
    These words near by, 'What's that to me and him?'   100
    Nothing? Don't talk to us like this.
    For I must take the risk. But if there's truth
    In what the servant *said*, my god, the girl
    Is the concern of all the citizens. First her

.   .   .   .

    I don't know what to say. For me and for
    The servant . . .
    Young man . . . prostitute.

Moschion says he must risk trying to rescue Philoumene from
Stratophanes, but hesitates because he had heard Theron say she
is an Athenian citizen and, if this is true, the whole citizen body is
involved in her fate.

    After a lacuna of unknown length we have a longer fragment,
perhaps at the end of Act 2. Stratophanes and Theron are talking.
Theron appears to be making suggestions with which Stratophanes agrees.

    Theron seems to be proposing a plan to save Stratophanes'
property falling into the hands of a creditor (presumably the
Boeotian who had won a law case brought against Stratophanes'

supposed father—see below, lines 135–6). This dialogue is inter-
rupted by the appearance of Pyrrhias, whom Stratophanes has
sent on home to announce his return from abroad.

The first line, spoken by Theron(?) is too fragmentary to give
sense. In the second Theron says:

'An opportunity will come for this some time'.   111
To which Stratophanes replies: 'That's good, by god.'
THERON continues:

For . . . him; he* will be yet more enraged.
Whether they . . . in this way or not,
All will *by now* have been achieved; and so
Let us agree on this.
STRATOPHANES.   By god, yes, now
I do agree.
THERON.   You were *not* here and *made*
No reckoning of anything. *It would*
Have been more sensible *to do this* first.
STRATOPHANES. Good god, you're right.
THERON.   *I want to see* that none
Makes profit from your property but you.
STRATOPHANES. I said . . . and I did not foresee who—
   [*seeing* PYRRHIAS *approaching*] *Surely that's not him approaching over*
      there?*
THERON.   Who do you mean?
STRATOPHANES. Pyrrhias, whom *I sent* home to tell them we were
   safe and soon   120
   We'd be with them.
THERON.   Yes, I know. *You sent him on* to tell your mother.
STRATOPHANES. What's he learnt to bring him back here? Why's
   he walking here so fast?
THERON. And he's looking very gloomy.
STRATOPHANES [*shouts to* PYRRHIAS]. Pyrrhias, has some misfortune
   Struck us? Can it be my mother—
PYRRHIAS.   Yes, your mother died last year.
STRATOPHANES. How distressing!
PYRRHIAS.   She was old, extremely old
STRATOPHANES.   *But dearly loved.*

So she's gone.

PYRRHIAS.   Stratophanes, sir, you will find that things have
     changed

In a way quite unexpected. You were not, it seems, her son.

STRATOPHANES. Not her son? Then whose son am I?   129

PYRRHIAS.   When her end was imminent,

Anxious for you, she wrote down here all the history of your
     birth.

                                             [*He hands over a packet*

THERON. No one near to death begrudges happiness to those
     alive.

She had no desire to leave you ignorant of your own kin.

PYRRHIAS. Wait, that's not the only thing. Your father, when he
     was alive,

Lost a case apparently to some Boeotian—

STRATOPHANES.   That I heard.

PYRRHIAS. And according to the treaty,* he was liable to pay
     Many talents.

STRATOPHANES.   Yes, a letter came to me in Karia

Straightaway about all this and told me of my father's death.

PYRRHIAS. When she learnt from lawyers here that you and all
     your property

Might be seized on, she took thought for you and on her
     death-bed tried

To restore you to your kindred, which was very sensible.   140

STRATOPHANES. Hand the letter over.

                              [STRATOPHANES *receives the letter and reads it*

PYRRHIAS.   Master, quite apart from what they wrote,

I have here some tokens also, proofs of your identity,

So the men who gave them told me she had said when still
     alive.

THERON [*aside*]. Great Athene, make this man here one of your
     own people, so

He may wed the girl he loves and I may marry Malthake.

STRATOPHANES. Theron, come this way. Get cracking.

THERON.   Aren't you going to tell me what—

STRATOPHANES. On you go, and no more talking.

THERON.   All the same—all right I'm coming.

STRATOPHANES. Pyrrhias, you too come with me. You will bring
> the evidence   148
To support my words and show it anyone who wants to see.

> *[Exeunt to the city*

CHORAL INTERLUDE

ACT 4

Act 4 is relatively well preserved. Smikrines enters with a
character who is a rabid democrat. He seems to have told
Smikrines about a scene in which someone wept and asked for
help; this must be Stratophanes at the meeting described in detail
by Eleusinios below. They quarrel, and Smikrines sends him off
with a flea in his ear.

The democrat's withdrawal is immediately followed by the
entrance of Eleusinios,* who proceeds to give a long account of
the incident to which the first had referred. This is a sort of
messenger's speech, a common feature of tragedy. He describes
how a girl had taken refuge at an altar together with her servant.
A crowd gathers and shouts that she is an Athenian citizen.
Stratophanes intervenes and says that he is her protector; he
claims that he has just discovered that he himself is an Athenian
citizen and asks that she should be given refuge with the priestess
of Eleusis. Moschion then jumps up and disputes his claim but the
crowd shouts him down and tells her to go to the priestess.

Enter SMIKRINES *and a* DEMOCRAT.

SMIKRINES. You are a nuisance, just a bag of wind;   150
> Poor wretch, if you suppose a man who weeps
> And begs for help has justice on his side;
> These days it's proof the man is up to tricks.
> That's not the way to judge the truth; a small
> Committee's much more likely to do that.
DEMOCRAT. Good heavens, Smikrines, you really are
> A blasted oligarch.

SMIKRINES.   *Who cares?* Not I.
Good god, you'll do for me, you and your gang
Of toughs. Why this abuse, you blabber mouth?
DEMOCRAT. I hate you and your supercilious friends,   160
All of you. I'm a nuisance, I admit,
But can be trusted.
SMIKRINES.   That could never be.
DEMOCRAT. *Then* I *denounce* you; you are rich but steal
These people's property* and cash.
Maybe you're not *removing* from the house
Some of the *slaves* who're being taken there? . . .
SMIKRINES. Oh, go to hell.
DEMOCRAT.   The same to you.   [*He moves off*
SMIKRINES [*shouts after him*]. You're wise
To flee. I would have made you button up
Your lips more tight than any immigrant.*
                                        [*He moves towards his house*

    Enter ELEUSINIOS *from the city, who calls to him.*

ELEUSINIOS. Good sir, just wait a minute by your door.
SMIKRINES. I'm waiting. What're you shouting for?   170
[The following eleven lines are badly mutilated; supplements
speculative.]
ELEUSINIOS.   So you
*M*ay learn about a wisp of smoke* *I saw.*
SMIKRINES. *No smoke without a fire.* I want to hear
The facts about . . . and . . .
ELEUSINIOS. I knew of your inquiries *and I heard*—
SMIKRINES. Tell me the whole *thing then from first to last.*
ELEUSINIOS. I happened to be on my way,* *not from*
The country to the city gates, indeed,
Nor *from my home, when someone told* me this—
Most kindly; *so I stopped and clearly learnt*
Of others' troubles—I'm a terror for   180
The details. *On I went,* shouting to all
I met impartially, a democrat,
And they're the only saviours of our land.*
I'd come from town to meet one of my deme*

Who was to portion out a skinny ox
And to be cursed as he deserved by those
Who got a bit—and I was one of them—
The goddess' deme gives me my name—look here
At me—I'm Eleusinios. I stopped
When I beheld a crowd before the gates
And saying 'Let me through', I saw a girl,
A suppliant, sitting there and those who stood   190
Around forming a meeting; *and they asked*
Who was the guardian of the suppliant girl.

[Lacuna of seven or eight lines; the following supplements speculative.]

A man who stood beside her intervened
And said, 'This girl is an Athenian,
Captured by pirates as a child and sold
Far from her home; I am her faithful servant,
Who've kept her from all harm; I hope to find
Her father; where he is I've not yet learnt.
But she's afraid her present guardian means
To do her ill. I too now sit as suppliant
Among you.' So he did, and we all roared,
'The girl's a citizen'. The flare of noisy shouts
Which rang around was quenched at last. And when
The crowd was silent, a young man, pale-faced,   200
Smooth-chinned—no beard—went up and stood beside
The servant, wanting to whisper something. We
Would not allow him to do this. At once
Someone cried out, 'Speak up. What does he want?
Who is this man? What are you whispering?'
And he replied, 'This servant knows me well.
In fact I've helped him for some time. And I
Am asking if there's anything he needs.
Most of the facts I heard just now when he
Was talking to his master.' Blushing red,
He then fell back a little. He was not
Completely loathsome, but we did not like
The boy at all. He had a lustful look.   210
We cried aloud *in anger, telling him*

To go to hell, then let him be. He joined
The crowd, stared at the girl, and talked to those
Near him at length. I *heard him say* the girl
Had run away *in fear.* And next a chap
Who looked a proper man *came up and* stood
Beside her, with another man, and third
A slave of theirs. He looked at her close to,
And suddenly let fall a flood of tears;   220
He clutched his hair and gave an anguished cry.
Those who stood by were *quite amazed; they cried,*
'What is the matter? Tell us what you want.'
'*The girl is mine,*' he said, 'I swear, so may
The goddess grant you blessings, gentlemen,
For ever. I have brought her up from when
She was a little child . . .   226
[Eight lines too mutilated to give sense.]
The servant was her father's; now he's mine—
I give him to the girl. And I remit
The cost I've had in rearing her; I ask
For nothing in return. Just let her find
Her father and her family. I won't object.'
'Well said,' we cried. 'Then listen, gentlemen,
To what I now propose. You are her guardians;   240
As far as I'm concerned she need not fear;
Install her with the priestess* and let her
Care for the girl on your behalf.' This won
Him strong support, deservedly. All cried
Again, 'Quite right', then shouted, 'Tell us more.'
'I too once thought I was a Sikyonian,
But now my servant here has brought to me
My mother's will and tokens of my birth;
I think, if I should trust the evidence   250
Provided by these documents, I am
Like her a fellow citizen of yours.
Don't take this hope from me; if I am proved
A fellow citizen of her whom I
Have rescued for her father, let me ask
Him for her hand and take her as my wife.

And don't let any of the men who rival me
Have charge of her before her father's found.'
'That's right and fair,' we cried. He said,
'Now take her to the priestess. Take her, go.'
Then suddenly the pale-faced boy jumps up
Again and says, 'You really believe this tale,   260
That he has suddenly received a will
From somewhere and is proved a citizen?
You think, relying on this melodrama,
He'll take the girl away, then let her go?'
Then someone shouted,* 'Kill the smoothy!' 'No'
He shouted back, 'You won't but, as for you,
Whoever you may be—' 'Oh, won't I then?
Get out, you pathic!' 'Bless you', he replied.
And then the soldier said to her, 'Come on,
Stand up and go.' The servant said, 'At your
Command, she'll go. Command her, gentlemen.'
'Yes, go,' we shouted. Up she stood and went.
I stayed till then; what happened after that   270
I cannot tell you; I went on my way.

       [*Exeunt,* SMIKRINES *into his house,* ELEUSINIOS *to the city*

Enter STRATOPHANES *and* THERON *from the city, pursued by*
          MOSCHION.

MOSCHION. Kidnappers, I arrest you—
STRATOPHANES.   You're arresting us?
MOSCHION. I am, by god.
STRATOPHANES.   You're raving mad, young man
MOSCHION. How suddenly *you've proved to be* a citizen!
   Good work! But you can't *get away with this.*   275
STRATOPHANES. What's that? I don't know *what on earth you mean.*
MOSCHION. You see? Come on, and put your case before
   The court. . . .
   From the priestess . . .

A lacuna follows of about twenty lines; perhaps Stratophanes says
he is looking for Smikrines, who he now believes to be his father
(from evidence provided by the 'tokens' his 'mother' had left him).
Moschion may have answered 'Why, he's *my* father', and agreed

to fetch him. Smikrines then comes out together with his wife.
When the text resumes, much damaged, Smikrines' wife (?) is
describing how they gave their baby to a foreign woman and how
the baby was clothed at the time:

SMIKRINES' WIFE(?).   .   .   .   .

> Half of a woman's dress was folded round   280
> And covered up your body when we sent
> You to the foreigner who asked us for
> A child* . . .

The following twenty five lines are too damaged to provide continuous sense but it seems that a description of the dress in which
the baby was wrapped confirms that the baby was indeed
Stratophanes ('dyed', 'it had a border green in colour, and in the
middle purple'). Smikrines' wife greets him: 'I look on you, my
child' 'how contrary to all hopes . . .'. Stratophanes addresses her
as 'Mother'. Smikrines says, 'Let us go in'. The last three lines of
the act may be supplemented to give:

STRATOPHANES. So, father, Moschion's my brother then?
SMIKRINES. He is your brother. Come into the house;   310
> *We'll find him waiting for us there* inside .

CHORAL INTERLUDE

ACT 5

At the beginning of the act Kichesias and Theron enter. Kichesias
is Philoumene's father. He is poor and old. Theron does not know
who he is and has picked him out of the crowd with the intention
of bribing him to say that he knows Kichesias is Philoumene's
father; if he succeeds, Philoumene will be accepted as a freeborn
Athenian and the way will be open for Stratophanes, now that he
has proved to be an Athenian by birth, to marry her.

The opening lines are fragmentary and their sense doubtful; the
following is based on Arnott's ingenious supplements:

KICHESIAS. What is this serious business *you have*   312
   With me, *my friend*, which may turn out to make
   The walk on which you've taken me worth while,
   Always insisting earnestly that we
   Should go a little *further on*? But now
   I must insist *on learning who you are.*
THERON. Who am I? *That you shall not learn*, by god . . .

There follow six lines too mutilated to give sense, in which
Kichesias, now extremely angry, may have abused Theron as a
'beast' and a 'stony-hearted tax collector'; of the next twenty-
seven lines only a few letters survive. In the course of these
Theron, not knowing who he is talking to, must have tried to
bribe him to say that Philoumene was Kichesias' daughter.

   After this there are sixty comparatively well-preserved lines.

KICHESIAS. Oh, go to hell.
THERON.   You really are a pain.
KICHESIAS. Leave me, get lost! You thought Kichesias
   Would do a thing like that or take a bribe   345
   From anyone—
THERON [*ironically*]. What wickedness!
KICHESIAS.   When he's
   Kichesias Skambonides.*
THERON.   That's right.
   Well done! You've understood? Then take
   Your pay for this and not for what I said
   To you just now.*
KICHESIAS. Pay me for what?
THERON.   To be
   Kichesias Skambonides. Your scheme
   Is much superior to mine. You seem   350
   To grasp the outline of the business.
   You become him! You're luckily snubnosed
   And small like him the servant then described.
KICHESIAS. I have become the old man that I am.
THERON. Then add you lost your daughter, only four
   Years old, from Halai.*
KICHESIAS.   And I lost Dromon

My servant too.

THERON.   Well done! That's excellent—
Kidnapped by pirates.

KICHESIAS.   You've reminded me
Of my past suffering and my sad loss.

THERON. Well done! Just keep it up like this and shed
Some tears as well. [*Aside*] The fellow's really pretty good.   360

Enter DROMON *from the city, talking to himself.*

DROMON. Young mistress is now safe and guarded well,
  Now I must find her father—
[Lacuna of four lines; supplements speculative.]

KICHESIAS [*seeing* DROMON].   *Who is here?*
  I cannot believe my eyes. It can't be him.
  Dromon! How've you got here? Where is my girl?

DROMON. She's living and she's here.   [KICHESIAS *faints*
                    Don't faint. Stand up,
  Kichesias. Theron, fetch water, quick.

THERON. All right, I'll run and fetch it and I'll send
  You out Stratophanes.

DROMON.   We shall not need
  The water now.

THERON.   In any case I'll call
  Him.

DROMON. There, he's coming round. Kichesias!

KICHESIAS. What's happening? Where am I? And what did I
  Hear someone say?

DROMON.   Your daughter is alive   370
  And safe.

KICHESIAS.   She's really safe, Dromon,
  Or simply still alive?

DROMON.   She is a virgin still,
  Untouched by man.

KICHESIAS.   Thank god.

DROMON.   And you, sir, how
  Are you?

KICHESIAS.   I am alive, Dromon, that I
  Can say, but, that apart, when you behold

A man who's old and poor and lonely, then
He must be in a thoroughly bad way.

Enter STRATOPHANES *from* SMIKRINES' *house, talking back
to his* MOTHER.

STRATOPHANES. I'll see what's up here, mother, and be back.

[DROMON *leads* KICHESIAS *to* STRATOPHANES *and introduces him*

DROMON. Stratophanes, the father of Philoumene!

STRATOPHANES. Who is?

DROMON.   This man here.

STRATOPHANES.   Greetings to you, sir.

DROMON [*to* KICHESIAS]. This is the man who kept your daughter
 safe.

KICHESIAS. All happiness to him!

STRATOPHANES.   If you consent, I shall
 Be happy, father, yes, and truly blessed.   380

DROMON. Stratophanes, for heaven's sake, let's *go*
 At once *to find Philoumene.*

STRATOPHANES.   Take him
 Ahead, and I'll be on your heels, when I
 Have said a few things to my folk inside.

DROMON. Let us be on our way, Kichesias.

[*Exeunt* DROMON *and* KICHESIAS *to fetch* PHILOUMENE.
       STRATOPHANES *shouts into the house*

STRATOPHANES. Donax, Boy! boy!

Enter Donax.

       Donax, go in and say
To Malthake she must *remove* all of
My stuff here to my neighbour's house, the trunks,
The knapsacks, all the baskets, all the chests;
And *after this* she's not to find them there.   390
Tell her to come away herself to join
My mother here with you, but of my stuff
I want to leave behind the foreign slaves,
And Theron and the donkey drivers and
The donkeys too. You tell her that; and I'll
Soon meet with her myself *to fix* the rest.

[*Exit to follow* DROMON *and* KICHESIAS *to the priestess*

Enter MOSCHION *from* SMIKRINES' *house.*

MOSCHION. Now, Moschion, you must not even look
 At her again. *Be steadfast*, Moschion—
 She is so pale,* she has such lovely eyes—
 You're *talking* nonsense; it's your brother now   400
 She'll marry; *he shall be called* a blessed man.
 What joy *he'll have*! Still rambling on, you fool!
 I'll have a job to praise him *to his face*
 And *show him* kindness—but I'll not say that;
 No, don't! But when I ride upon the cart*—
 Clearly I must—as their best man with them,
 Then, gentlemen, I'll not be able *to*
 Conceal my agony . . .

Five lines mutilated beyond repair then a lacuna of uncertain
length. There follow fourteen lines, mutilated and obscure, which
conclude the play. They form a dialogue between a man
(Theron?) and a woman (Malthake?). Theron is pressing his suit
with Malthake and she rejects him. In the first two surviving lines
Malthake seems to be talking about the past, when together they
fed the donkeys while they were on campaign. Theron disregards
this and asserts his long devotion to her. Malthake replies that
both he and Stratophanes are wronging her (Stratophanes has not
fulfilled a promise—to give her money as a dowry?). There follow
three lines which give no sense. Then Theron suddenly calls for
torches and garlands, the symbols of a wedding celebration and a
common motif at the end of a comedy; she at last consents.

MALTHAKE.   .   .   .   .   .
 Carrying barley for the donkeys *then*
 On our long marches, how completely . . .
THERON. I always prayed that I would *have* such *luck*.
MALTHAKE. You prayed for this? Why do you both wrong *me*?
 This villain here's not stuck to *what he swore*.
THERON. . . . . a man who hoped . . .
MALTHAKE. It's possible to . . . your request. How would you
 break down his defences?
THERON. *Give me* a torch, *someone*—

MALTHAKE.   Before I've answered 'Yes'?
THERON. And garlands. Please do as I say.
MALTHAKE.   I will.
THERON. Then nod your head. [*To the audience*] Youths, *men and*
    boys stretch out
  Your hands to clap and give us your applause.
  And may that noble, laughter-loving maid,
  Victory remain with us for ever, as our friend.

Fragments quoted by ancient authors:

1. Photius α 50
  Buying instead a lady's maid for this
  Woman, he did not give *Philoumene*
  To her to have, but brought her up apart,
  Like a free girl.

This fragment may come from the Prologue. It might mean that
Stratophanes intended to give Philoumene to Malthake as a lady's
maid, but later, falling in love with her, decided to bring her up as
a free girl until she was old enough to marry.

2. Stobaeus, *Eclogae* 4. 12. 4
  The soldier's bearing, and the foreigner's,
  Prove easy to abuse apparently.

This might be Stratophanes defending himself when he is still
thought to be a foreigner (a Sikyonian).

3. Photius p. 542 s.u. Stratophanes
                        Stratophanes,
  Time was you had a simple soldier's cloak and
  But one slave to serve you.

This cannot be placed.

4. Photius α 95
  A sailor comes ashore; he's judged an enemy.
  If he has anything worth taking(?), he's forced
  To do hard labour.

This cannot be placed; it appears to be a piece of moralizing on
the injustice of the world.

5. Photius κ 81, *Suda* κ 149
His looks are poor, his wits within are weak.

This cannot be placed.

6. Stobaeus, *Eclogae* 2. 33. 4
Choice of like-minded friends most makes, I believe,
For harmony in life.

This cannot be placed and may not be from this play.

7. Photius ε 770
She went off leaving you, gnashing her teeth in anger.

See p. 183.

9. Pollux 55. 119
'In comedies young men wear purple clothing, parasites black or grey, except in *The Sikyonian* where the parasite wears white when he is about to marry.'

10. Eustathius 998. 31
I know how to cheat

Aelian, *NA* 9. 7: 'And Menander's Theron is proud because by cheating men he made them his source of plenty.'

11. A papyrus fragment (Papyrus Oxyrinchica 1238) of nine lines which contains the names Theron, Malth(ake), and P(yrrhias) but which is unintelligible, and another of about 25 fragmentary lines which contain the name Malthake (see OCT p. 346).

Twice a Swindler (Dis Exapaton)

Some hundred lines of this play survive in a papyrus roll put together from thirteen fragments. Menander's play was adapted for the Roman stage by Plautus in the *Bacchis Sisters*; the papyrus fragments which correspond to lines 496–560 give us a unique opportunity to study how Plautus adapted a play of Menander.

Characters

MOSCHOS, a young man
PHILOXENOS†, Moschos' father
LYDOS, Moschos' tutor
SOSTRATOS, a friend of Moschos
NIKOBOULOS†, Sostratos' father
SYROS, a slave of Sostratos

Characters who do not appear in surviving fragments:

BACCHIS† OF ATHENS, a courtesan
BACCHIS† OF SAMOS, her sister

 † These are the names in Plautus' play; we do not know what Menander called them but we use these names for convenience.

The scene: a street in Athens; two houses, one belonging to Sostratos' father, the other to the Bacchis who lives in Athens.

The following summary of the plot is based on Plautus' *Bacchides*:

A young man called Sostratos was sent to Ephesus with a slave, Syros, to collect some money owed to his father. On his journey, in Samos, he met and fell in love with a courtesan called Bacchis.

She had been hired by a solider for a year, who took her to Athens. Sostratos wrote to his friend Moschos, asking him to find her. Moschos discovered that she had arrived in Athens with the soldier and had gone to visit her sister, another courtesan, also called Bacchis.

The play may have opened with a conversation between Moschos and Bacchis of Athens. A papyrus fragment claiming to be the beginning of the play reads, 'By heavens, young man . . .'. This may be Bacchis of Athens asking Moschos why he has accosted her or telling him to go away. No doubt he soon learnt that he was talking to the sister of the girl he was looking for and that she was to arrive at any minute. This opening scene may have been followed by a 'prologue speech' in which Moschos explained the circumstances outlined above. By now he was already falling in love with Bacchis of Athens.

In a second visit Moschos meets Bacchis of Samos and is persuaded to organize a welcome-home party for her.

In the second act, probably, Moschos is returning from the market with provisions for the party when he meets his old tutor, Lydos. Lydos scolds him for getting involved with a courtesan; he accompanies him to Bacchis' house to keep an eye on him.

At this point Syros enters; he has returned from Ephesus with Sostratos after successfully recovering the money owed to Sostratos' father. He meets Moschos, who tells him that he has found Sostratos' Bacchis but that money is needed to secure her release from her contract with the soldier. Syros says that he will pay for this from the money he has recovered in Ephesus. Syros then meets Sostratos' father Nikoboulos and pretends that they have recovered the money but that it is deposited for safety in Epheseus with the priest of Artemis, Theotimos, because he and Sostratos had been threatened by pirates after they had recovered the money. This is the first deception practised by Syros.

Sostratos enters and overhears Lydos telling Philoxenos of Moschos' behaviour at the party. He comes forward and greets them. Lydos tells him that Moschos is in the arms of a courtesan. Sostratos naturally assumes that this is his Bacchis and is furiously indignant at his friend's disloyalty.

Philoxenos supposes that Sostratos' indignation is caused by

Moschos' ill behaviour and asks him to take on the rescue mission. It is at this point that our first fragment begins, at the end of the second act; Philoxenos, accompanied by Lydos, is addressing Sostratos:

PHILOXENOS. *Tell him* to leave the house, It's perfectly   10
    Appropriate *for you.* You call him out
    From this whore house; upraid him face to face
    And save him and your friend's whole family.
    Lydos, let us be off.
LYDOS.   But if you left
    Me here as well—
PHILOXENOS.   Let's go. He'll be enough
    To cope with him.
LYDOS.   Go for him, Sostratos;
    Keep on at him. He has no self-control
    And brings disgrace on all of us, his friends.
                        [*Exeunt* PHILOXENOS *and* LYDOS *to the city*
SOSTRATOS. He's done for now. One single blow and she
    Will make a slave of him. Yes, Sostratos
    Was your first catch, my girl. She will deny   20
    It all, that's plain—for she's a ruthless girl;
    She'll summon all the gods as witnesses:
    'Then may I never thrive, *if I*—' God, yes!
    'May I be damned—.' But hold on, Sostratos!
    Perhaps she will persuade you: '*You have come*
    As father's slave then?' Yes, indeed I have.
    But let her try to win her way when I
    Have nothing but an empty purse. I'll give
    Back all the gold to father. Then she'll soon
    Stop wheedling when she sees she's talking to
    A corpse,* as people say. Now I must go
    And find my father. Wait, I see him here . . .   30

Nikoboulos enters to greet Sostratos for the first time since he has returned from Ephesus. Of the next sixteen lines only a few letters survive. Nikoboulos must have complained about his son's failure to bring back the money from Ephesus. When the text becomes

intelligible, Sostratos has told his father that he has the money—
Syros was lying.

NIKOBOULOS. *He* had the money* and he gave it you　　　　47
　　And added all the interest *that was due?*
SOSTRATOS. *He did indeed.* I saw *myself. So* don't
　　Get bothered and accuse an honest friend.　　　　50
　　Keep calm. I'm back and bring it here for you.
NIKOBOULOS. *That's good.* Give me the money quickly, son.
SOSTRATOS. *You'll get it* from us soon. So pay no heed
　　To empty lies.
NIKOBOULOS.　　　　So no one anchored near
　　Or made a plot?
SOSTRATOS.　　　　　No one.
NIKOBOULOS.　　　　　　　　The gold was not
　　Deposited with Theotimos?*
SOSTRATOS.　　　　　　　　　What
　　Do you mean 'with Theotimos'? No, he* took
　　The cash himself and kept it safe and made
　　It pay twice over.
NIKOBOULOS.　　　　There's an honest man;
　　He used his brains. But what did Syros mean?
SOSTRATOS. Oh, let it be. Come on with me and get
　　The money.
NIKOBOULOS.　　You're not playing games with me?
SOSTRATOS. Come on and get it.　　　　　　　　60
NIKOBOULOS.　　　　　　　Right, I'll come with you.
　　Just give it me and you'll have treated me
　　Quite fairly, as you should. Why needle you
　　Before I get it? That's the vital thing.

　　　　　　　　　　　　　　[*Exeunt to get the money*

CHORAL INTERLUDE

ACT 3(?)

Enter SOSTRATOS *and* NIKOBOULOS *in mid-conversation.* SOSTRATOS *is
pleading on behalf of* SYROS, *who has evidently been forgiven for telling lies,
but* NIKOBOULOS *still considers him a rogue.*

SOSTRATOS. What are you saying? That because he got   64
  The money from your friend he has become
  Quite blameless in your eyes?
NIKOBOULOS.   Indeed he has.
SOSTRATOS. And even pleases you still more?
NIKOBOULOS.   Still more,
  Yes Sostratos.
[Lacuna of ten lines.]
SOSTRATOS. So he's not guilty of what has been done?   77
[Three lines indecipherable; then one legible word—'under my
control'; the following supplements speculative.]
NIKOBOULOS. *But don't forget that he is still a rogue . . .*
SOSTRATOS. *Maybe, but I have got him* under my
  Control . . .
NIKOBOULOS. But all the same, *though* you did get *the cash,*   82
  Don't trust him, as I said before.
SOSTRATOS.   *Why not?*
NIKOBOULOS. If Syros stood beside me now and said
  The sun was shining, I should think that it
  Was dark and night had come. A rampant cheat!
SOSTRATOS. Does this then, father, not apply to me:
  'If you are good, your father will deny
  You nothing.' *So please grant me what I ask*.
NIKOBOULOS. I'll go to town and do this business.   90
  That other job is given you to do.
                          [*Exit to the city;* SOSTRATOS *is left alone on the stage*
SOSTRATOS. I think I'd really love to see my fine
  And lady-like mistress start wheedling me
  Now that my purse is empty; she'll expect
  To lay her hands 'at once' (she'll tell herself)
  On all the cash I bring. 'He's bringing it

For certain, and, good lord, he's generous
—None more so—and it's just what I deserve.'
She's fully proved to be the sort of girl
I thought her once, and that just serves her right.
But silly Moschos, I do pity him;
I'm partly angry with him, but again
I don't consider him to blame for what   100
Has happened but blame her, the boldest tart
Of all the lot.

Enter MOSCHOS *from Bacchis' house, speaking back over his shoulder.*

MOSCHOS.   Then if he's heard I'm here,
    Wherever is he? [*He sees* SOSTRATOS] Hello, Sostratos.
SOSTRATOS. Hello.
MOSCHOS.   Downcast and glum? Do tell me why.
    And why these hidden tears? Surely you've not
    Received some new blow here?
SOSTRATOS.   Yes.
MOSCHOS.   Won't you tell
    Me then?
SOSTRATOS.   In there,* Moschos, of course.
MOSCHOS.   How so?
SOSTRATOS. *I've found* the man who always was so fond
    Of me before *a double-crosser;* that's
    The first way you have wronged me *terribly.*
MOSCHOS. I've wronged you? Sostratos, no, god forbid!   110
SOSTRATOS. I never thought it possible myself.
MOSCHOS. What *do* you mean?
SOSTRATOS. You've wronged me and my love;
    The rest* pained me too much.

What follows may be reconstructed from Plautus' adaptation.
Sostratos is soon convinced that there are two Bacchises and that
Moschos has not been disloyal to him. Syros embarks on a second
scheme to cheat Nikoboulos out of his money, so that Sostratos
can pay off the soldier and secure his Bacchis. Eventually the truth
comes out and the play concludes with the usual happy ending
when both the friends get their girls.

Fragments quoted by ancient authors:

1. P. IFAO 337 (*ZPE* vi. 5), *Twice a Swindler*, which begins:
   For heavens' sake, young man . . .

See p. 200.

2. Fulgentius, *Mythol.* 3. 1, p. 199
   As far as counsel goes,
   You have anticipated, Demeas,
   Our own view.

Context and speaker unknown; perhaps wrongly attributed to this play.

3. *Suda* α 3545
   Stand by me. I will knock and call out one
   Of them.

Speaker and context unknown.

4. Stobaeus, *Eclogae* 4. 52b. 27
He whom the gods love dies while he is young.

A much-quoted line to which Plautus' adaptation gives the context. Syros is being offensive to Sostratos' father about his senile stupidity when he his about to cheat him out of his money for the second time.

Compare Plautus, *Bacchides* 816–17: 'He whom the gods love dies when he is young | And still has strength, sound judgement, and good sense.'

5. Photius ζ 7; Suda ζ 9
   Whoever was custodian of the shrine,
   It was not Megabyzos.

Arnott suggests that Nikoboulos is here speaking to Syros; Syros has been telling his story about depositing the money with Theotimos, the priest of Artemis, and adds that Megabyzos is custodian of the temple. Nikoboulos, doubting the truth of Syros' tale, interrupts to say that Megabyzos is not the custodian.

The Hero (Heros)

Of this play about fifty lines survive from the opening scene, another fifty lines, badly damaged, from later in the play, and some quoted fragments. There is also a synopsis of the play and a cast list.

The play is entitled *The Hero*; a hero was 'a being intermediate between god and man' (Sandbach, p. 386); some were the children of unions between god and man, such as Herakles; others were wholly human, raised to the status of hero after death for the benefits they had conferred on their people; founders of cities and colonies belonged to this class. The hero of our play, who spoke the Prologue, was presumably the guardian spirit either of Laches' family or, perhaps, of the deme of Ptelea.

Cast in order of appearance (according to the cast list):

GETAS, a slave of Pheidias
DAOS, a slave of Laches
[THE HERO (the speaker of the Prologue)]
MYRRHINE, wife of Laches, mother of the twins
[PHEIDIAS, a young man, a neighbour]
[SOPHRONE, a nurse]
[SANGARIOS, a slave]
[GORGIAS, a young man (one of the twins)]
LACHES, an old man

(Those in square brackets do not appear in our surviving fragments)

The scene is set in Ptelea, an unidentified village in Attica, perhaps two miles or so north-west of Athens. Two houses are visible, one belonging to Laches, the other to the family of Pheidias.

The plot cannot be fully recovered from the existing fragments; the following account is based on the surviving 'synopsis'. The play opens with a conversation between two slaves, Daos, a slave of Laches, and Getas, a slave of Laches' neighbour, Pheidias. Daos says that he has fallen in love with Plangon, the supposed daughter of an old shepherd, now dead; she works for Laches' wife, Myrrhine, while her twin brother works as shepherd to Laches. Laches has promised to let Daos set up house with her and is now abroad on business in Lemnos.

There must have followed a postponed Prologue in which the Hero, after whom the play is named, explains that the twins are in fact the children of Myrrhine, who was raped eighteen years before by an unknown assailant, Laches himself, as it turns out, who later married her; neither of them knows the true situation.

The second, third, and fourth acts are completely missing. In these, according to the 'synopsis', it emerges that Plangon has been raped by Pheidias and is pregnant. Daos, in his eagerness to marry Plangon, claims that he is the culprit. Myrrhine has discovered she is the mother of the twins and is distraught.

In the last act, from which scattered fragments survive, Laches has returned from his visit to Lemnos; it opens with an agitated conversation between him and Myrrhine, in the course of which he learns that he is the father of Myrrhine's twins. Plangon is therefore worthy of Pheidias' hand and the play ends with their marriage.

The play opens with a conversation between the two slaves, Getas and Daos.

GETAS. You look to me, Daos, as if you've done
    Some shocking crime, and you're in agony,
    Expecting you'll be in the treadmill* soon
    With shackles on your legs. It's obvious
    You're in a fix. Why else continually
    Keep beating your own head? Why do you stand
    There tearing out your hair? Why groan?
DAOS.   O my!
GETAS. That's it, you poor old thing! Well, if *you chance*
    To have a bit of cash saved up, should you

Not give it me to keep it for a while,
Until you put your situation *straight?*
I like you, Daos, and I sympathize   10
With you *if you're expecting trouble soon.*
DAOS. You're talking rubbish. No, I've had a blow
Which is quite unexpected, and I am
Confounded, Getas.
GETAS.   *How, you blasted fool?*
DAOS. For heaven's sake, don't curse *a lover, friend.*
GETAS. What's that? Are you in love?
DAOS.   I am in love.
GETAS. Your master's giving you a double share
Of grain. That's bad; perhaps you eat too much.
DAOS. It's in my heart I suffer when I see the girl;
She was brought up with me, she's innocent,
She's of my class, Getas.
GETAS.   Then she's a slave?
DAOS. Yes, partly, more or less. There was a man,   20
A shepherd, called Tibeios, living here
In Ptelea who'd been a slave when young.
He had these twins, he said, Plangon, with whom
I am in love—
GETAS.   Ah, now I understand.
DAOS. And the boy Gorgias.
GETAS.   The one who works
Here with you looking after sheep?
DAOS.   Yes, him.
Their father, this Tibeios, growing old,
To feed them, borrowed money from my master,
And once again, in time of famine, had
To borrow more, and then he starved to death.   30
GETAS. Starved, when, maybe, your master would not give
Him a third loan.
DAOS.   Perhaps. And Gorgias,
When he had died, borrowed a little cash
Again for funeral expenses and performed
The usual rites;* then he came here to us
And brought his sister; here he stays while he

Is working off the debt.

GETAS.   And what of Plangon?

DAOS. She's working with my mistress, spinning wool
And serving all her needs.

GETAS.   Serves you?*—

DAOS.   That's right—
You're laughing at me, Getas.

GETAS.   I swear I'm not.

DAOS. She's quite a lady, Getas, in her ways
And well behaved.

GETAS.   And you? What are you doing   40
To help yourself?

DAOS.   I've not tried anything
That's underhand, oh no. I've had a word
With master, and he promised he would speak
To Gorgias and let her live with me.

GETAS. You're doing brilliantly.

DAOS.   How, brilliantly?
He's been away three months in Lemnos on
Some private business. And so we both
Now hope the same: we *only* pray that he
May come back safely.

GETAS.   He's a decent chap.

DAOS. *But as for travelling abroad*—I hope
He gets some good from it.

GETAS.   Much . . .
You're sensible. For I . . .
Would sacrifice in vain . . .   50
For whom I carry wood . . .

[The end of this scene, a few lines, is too fragmentary to yield sense.]

This scene must have been followed by a postponed Prologue in which the Hero told the audience the facts they needed to know, above all that Laches is the father and Myrrhine the mother of the twins.

The remaining fragments of the play probably come from the fifth act. In the first of these, which begins a new act, Laches, who has returned from Lemnos, is talking to his wife Myrrhine; he proposes to give Plangon to Daos, as he had promised. Myrrhine knows that Plangon is her daughter, born after she had been raped eighteen years earlier, but cannot tell Laches this. She is appalled by his plan to give her daughter to a slave.

LACHES. Good heavens, let me be. *You think I'm wrong*   55
   If I give Plangon to a husband now?
[A lacuna of unknown length, then four lines of which only odd words survive.]

In the next fragment Laches seems to have discovered that Plangon is pregnant and intends to throw her out; Myrrhine is distraught. Laches seems to know that Tibeios was not the father of the twins.

MYRRHINE. Poor you! [MYRRHINE *refers to* PLANGON]
LACHES.   What's that? it's obvious, good wife—
Oh, let them go to hell!
MYRRHINE.   You must be mad.
   What a thing to say!
LACHES. I'm going to do what I
   Decided long ago—[*aside*] She's sweating now,
   She's in confusion—Myrrhine, my god,
   I did do well to take a shepherd on
   Who brought with him a bleating *lamb* . . .

Laches' last remark is obscure; Arnott suggests that it is a bitter joke; 'bleating' is used of the sounds made by both lambs and babies; by the 'bleating lamb' he means the baby Plangon.

   There follows a lacuna of about twenty lines, then a fragment which leads to the revelation that Myrrhine was raped eighteen years earlier by an unknown assailant. This starts with a broken line in which Laches may be saying of Myrrhine: '*She stands there* like a statue', petrified by the knowledge that she will have to confess that Plangon is her daughter.

LACHES [*aside*]. . . . like a statue . . .
MYRRHINE. How sad, that I alone endure a fate   75
   Far worse than any man could well believe.

LACHES. Reason *will surely comfort* your distress.
Did someone once *abuse* you forcibly?
MYRRHINE. Yes, *he was drunk*.
LACHES.   Do you suspect who *may*
Have been the man? . . . .

[Lacuna of about twenty-one lines and three line-endings of which only odd words survive.]

In the next fragment Laches is questioning Myrrhine about the rape.

LACHES.   First tell me this:
It happened eighteen years ago?
MYRRHINE.   I'm not
The only one *to have suffered this*. But yes,
Let's say it's true, if that is what you want.
LACHES. The facts are getting *more obscure*. How did
The man who raped you stay unknown? How did
He get away? When . . .?

Two other papyrus fragments may belong to this play, including one printed at the top of page 139 of OCT, but they cannot be placed and and are too mutilated to give any sense.

The remainder of the play is entirely lost. Laches' cross-examination of Myrrhine must have led to the revelation that he was the rapist and so the father of the twins. The way is then clear for Plangon to marry Pheidias, by whom she is pregnant, and no doubt the act ended with a wedding celebration.

Fragments quoted by ancient authors:

1. Photius a 3453
   But now I'll lead the huntsmen who have come
   Here from the city round the wild pears.

There is no clue as to the speaker. Arnott suggests that the lines introduce the Chorus at the end of the first act, in this play huntsmen, instead of the usual tipsy youths.

2. Stobaeus, *Eclogae* 4. 20a. 21
   Mistress, there is no power greater than love,

Not even Zeus, who rules the gods in heaven;
In all his acts he is compelled by love.

A slave is speaking to his or her mistress. Perhaps Daos is defending to Myrrhine his love for Plangon.

3. Stobaeus, *Eclogae* 4.29d.60
    Virtue should be the noblest of things,
    And the free man should everywhere be proud.

There is no clue as to the speaker or context.

4. Athenaeus 10. 426c
    A beaker of diluted wine. Take it and drink it up.

This could possibly come in celebrations at the end of the play.

5. Photius α 1548
    You have been drugged, my dearest, and you've just
    Been purged of it.

Obscure. Arnott suggests that Myrrhine is speaking metaphori-
cally to Laches, who may have collapsed into a faint on learning
that he was the father of the twins.

6. Ammonius, *de differentia* 249 Nickau
   You may be sure, I too will grant you this.

10. Hermeias on Plato's *Phaedrus*, p. 33, 16 Couv. (= K–A vi. 2.
490)
DAOS(?). . . . . You never were in love. Getas?
GETAS(?). No, for I never ate my fill.

Hermeias does not name the author or play from which this
comes but it might belong to the opening scene (it might equally
well come from *Misoumenos*).

The Lyre-Player (Kitharistes)

Parts of this play survive in three papyrus fragments, all mutilated, and in quotations from ancient authors.

Characters (as far as is known)

MOSCHION, a young Athenian in love with Phanias' daughter
PHANIAS, a wealthy lyre player
LACHES, Moschion's father
MOSCHION'S MOTHER (or NURSE)?
An UNNAMED COMPANION of Phanias (Anon.)

The scene is a street in Athens, with two houses, one belonging to Phanias, the other to Moschion's father.

The following reconstruction is speculative. There was, no doubt, a Prologue in which some deity explained the facts the audience needed to know if they were to understand the complex situation. When Phanias was a young man, he went to Ephesus and there fell in love with a woman whom he raped and then deserted. She became pregnant and had a daughter. Many years later Phanias returned to Ephesus, met her again, and resumed his relationship with her; as an Athenian he could not contract a marriage with a foreigner; possibly he had contracted a marriage with her which was recognized at Ephesus, but not at Athens. Laches' son Moschion also went to Ephesus and met and fell for the woman's daughter; he raped her and she became pregnant. He loved her but deserted her; he could not marry her because she was a foreigner.

What happened in the first act and a half we cannot tell. The first and most substantial fragment seems to come from the end of the second act. It is too fragmentary for translation but surviving words and phrases show that a man and a woman are discussing marriage, desertion, and rape. The man must be Moschion; the woman to whom he is confessing, addressed as 'Dearest', may be his old nurse or his mother.

In a new scene, perhaps from the beginning of Act 3, two men enter, probably Phanias and an unidentified poor man; they are discussing a misfortune Phanias has suffered. Phanias has returned from Ephesus, leaving his mistress/Ephesian wife to follow with her daughter, but she has not arrived.

ACT 3(?)

Enter PHANIAS, *who has just returned from Ephesus, and a* COMPANION *(Anon.) from the direction of the harbour, followed by* SLAVES *carrying a mass of luggage.*

The first four lines are too mutilated to give sense and the meaning of the next lines, translated below, is obscure, since we do not know the context.

ANON.   You are envious *of her position?*   35
    You've married *Kleo's** daughter and come here
    And think that only she is rich, not you.
PHANIAS. I reckon all belongs to her alone
    And . . . She was freeborn
    And came from a Greek city, and I have
    Acquired all this.   [*He points to the baggage*
ANON.   Good luck to you!   40
PHANIAS.   No need
    For me to get a woman from some pimp.
ANON. Then what's your trouble? *Why did you not*
    Bring back your woman *with her property?*
PHANIAS. I don't know where on earth she is.
ANON: She's not
    Arrived?
PHANIAS.   Not yet, and it's a long time now
    Since she's been missing. There is nothing I

Don't think of—has there been some accident
At sea? Or have *some pirates captured her?*
ANON. Don't *say* that.
PHANIAS.   I don't know. I'm in despair
And terribly afraid,
ANON.   It's no surprise
That you should feel like this.
PHANIAS.   So if you come
Along with me towards the market-place,
You'll hear the rest, and give me your advice.   50
ANON: There's nothing to prevent me.
PHANIAS [*to the* SLAVES].   One of you
Take all this in at once out of the way.

> [*The* SLAVES *take the luggage into* PHANIAS' *house*
> [*Exeunt* PHANIAS *and* Anon *towards the city*

In the next scene Moschion's father appears, followed by
Moschion, who tells his father that while he was in Ephesus he fell
in love with Phanias' daughter. Here the papyrus breaks off and
we can only speculate about the denouement.

> MOSCHION'S FATHER *hurries in from his farm in the country.*

FATHER. Whatever can this mean? He's acting quite
Unlike himself. He's called me from the farm.
Before this, if I happened to be here,
Then Moschion would run off to the farm;
If I went there, he'd come back here—and drink.
That's no surprise; he had no father there
Rebuking him. I was not angry. I
Myself was one of those who knew the way   60
To waste their fortune. So my wife was not
To blame for this; it came from me. The boy's
No good. I must go in. And if he's not
At home, I'll go straight to the market place;
I'll see him there, beside the Herms* no doubt.

> *Enter* MOSCHION *from the city; he does not at first see his* FATHER, *who
> pauses and watches him.*

MOSCHION. Well, has my father come? or must I go

And look for him? The business will not
Admit delay, not even for a minute.
I think I'll wait *for him beside the door.*

> [MOSCHION *moves towards the door of his* FATHER'*s house*
[Twenty-two lines follow of which only the first words survive,
heavily supplemented below.]

FATHER [*aside*]. He means to ask *for something.* I suppose   70
   I ought to stay. *But* let him wait *until*
   He sees me.
MOSCHION.   *Where's he got to? I'm concerned*
   For him.
FATHER [*aside*]. *And I'm concerned* for you.
MOSCHION [*seeing* LACHES].   Hello!
FATHER. Hello to you, *my son.*
MOSCHION.   I did not tell
   You straightaway, but now I must be brave
   And tell you—
FATHER.   Tell me what? *You* always *have*
   A lot to say on lots of things.
MOSCHION.   You want
   Me to get married *and I've often put*
   My mind to this; for it needs careful thought.   80
FATHER. Well, Moschion, I'm quite prepared *to let*
   You take another bride if you refuse
   To have the one you should. *Then choose a girl*
   Who is freeborn; that *is what matters* most,
   The only reasonable choice. And if
   She can't be faulted on her birth, *make sure*
   That she's a virgin. But if you ask *me*
   For advice when you've decided on your own
   The girl you want to wed, I'll say no more.
   What you have given me . . . No one should *ask*   90
   Advice unless he means it.
MOSCHION.   You must hear
   The rest. *I went* to Ephesus and there
   I fell *in love.* A great parade took place
   Of girls who brought a feast to Artemis
   Of Ephesus; and there I saw a girl,

The daughter of one Phanias Euonymeus*—
FATHER. Are there Euonymeans in Ephesus
  As well as here?
MOSCHION.   No, he had come from here
  To collect some debts.
FATHER.   Are you then serious
  And want to wed the child of Phanias,   100
  The lyre-player, who's now our neighbour here?

The papyrus breaks off here and what follows can only be
guessed; perhaps Moschion confessed that he had made the girl
pregnant and Laches objected that by Athenian law he could not
marry a foreigner. No doubt eventually all misunderstandings are
cleared up; Phanias' woman proves to be Athenian by birth and
Moschion is able to marry the girl he loves.

Quotations by ancient authors:

3. Stobaeus, *Eclogae* 3.9.17
MOSCHION. If we avoid all those who have been wronged,
  What others, father, can we easily help?

Moschion is, perhaps, trying to persuade his father that he ought
to help the girl he raped (by marrying her); perhaps Laches had
said, 'You should have nothing more to do with her.'

4. Stobaeus, *Eclogae* 3. 9. 18
  To learn to do no wrong, in my opinion,
  Laches, is a fine enterprise for life.

5. Athenaeus, 12. 511 a
  He's fond of music and enjoys a song
  And always schools himself in luxury.

Arnott suggests that Laches is trying to dissuade Moschion from
marrying Phanias' daughter by saying that he pursues a useless
and extravagant way of life.

6. Athenaeus 6. 247 f.
  The audience *you* get don't pay a fee.

Someone (Laches?) tells Phanias he has to bribe his audience to
listen to him.

7. Stobaeus, *Eclogae* 4. 46. 9
　　How wearisome it is to have to wait!

Could this be Moschion, waiting for his wedding to Phanias'
daughter?

8. Stobaeus, *Eclogae* 1. 7. 1
　　How fickle fortune is and changeable!

10. Papyrus Vindobonensis 19999 A
　　Don't pay attention pointlessly to scandal, Phanias

From a collection of single lines—perhaps a schoolboy's exercise.

11. Papyrus Vindobonensis 19999A
　　If you're lazy, Phanias, then you'll be poor.

From the same collection of single lines.

12. Strabo 10. 5. 6
Strabo introduces this quotation: 'Amongst them [the people of
Ceos] a law seems to have once been passed which Menander
recalls':

　　The Ceans' custom's splendid, Phanias,
　　The man who can't live well shall not live ill.

When the Athenians were besieging Ceos after the battle of
Marathon(?) and provisions were short, tradition says that all men
over 60 were ordered to take hemlock.

The Farmer (Georgos)

Of this play about eighty-seven lines from the end of the first act survive on a papyrus together with twenty-eight half-lines or single words from Act 2 on another papyrus. Apart from this we have seven isolated fragments quoted by ancient authors and six small fragments of papyrus containing the middle of lines which cannot be placed in context. Consequently a full reconstruction of the plot is impossible.

Characters

A RICH YOUNG MAN (unnamed in our text, perhaps called
   MOSCHION)
MYRRHINE, a poor widow
PHILINNA, an old woman, perhaps a nurse
DAOS, a slave to Moschion's father
GORGIAS, son of Myrrhine
KLEAINETOS, a farmer, for whom Gorgias works
SYROS, a slave (mute)

The scene: a street in Athens with two adjoining houses; one belongs to Moschion's father, the other to Myrrhine, who has a daughter besides her son Gorgias.

From the surviving lines of Act 1 it emerges that Moschion has got Myrrhine's daughter pregnant and that she is about to have the child. He wants to marry her, but, on his return from a business trip to Corinth, he finds his father proposing to marry him to his daughter by his second wife, the young man's stepsister; in fact the wedding preparations are already under way.

Our text begins with a monologue, in which Moschion laments the dilemma in which he finds himself. He is in mid-speech; the first four surviving lines are deficient.

MOSCHION. *Hearing that she was pregnant, I at once*
  Approached *her mother*, acting *as I should,*
  To ask to have her hand; I had *no* fears;
  I was no rogue and no one thought that I
  Did wrong. But while the boy* was staying on
  The farm, disaster struck, that's done for me;
  I had gone off on business abroad
  To Corinth; I have just got back at dusk
  To find another wedding is in train
  For me; the gods are being garlanded,
  My father's making sacrifice inside—
  It's he himself who gives away the bride,   10
  My own half-sister, who's the daughter of
  His present wife. I don't know how I am
  To cope with this disaster—I see no
  Way out. But this is how I stand: *I've slipped*
  Out from the house without a word to them,
  Abandoning the wedding there. I never would
  Injure my dearest girl—it would be wrong.
  I've long been meaning to knock on their door*
  But shrink from doing so; for I don't know
  Whether her brother's back yet from the farm.
  I must make plans for everything. I'll go   20
  And think how to escape the wedding here.

                                          [*Exit to his house*

            Enter MYRRHINE *and* PHILINNA *from the city.*

MYRRHINE. I'm talking to you as a friend, Philinna,
  And tell you all my cares. That's how things stand
  At present.
PHILINNA.   When I heard your words, I swear
  By both the goddesses,* I nearly went
  Up to his door, my child, and called the cheat
  To tell him what I think of him.
                    [*She starts to move towards the door of* MOSCHION'*s house*
                                      but is restrained by MYRRHINE
MYRRHINE.   No. don't,
  Philinna. Let him be.

PHILINNA.   Why 'Let him be'?
Must he not pay for being such a rogue?   30
He's to be married when he's wronged your girl,
The scum?
                    [DAOS *appears in the distance, returning from the country; he is*
                         accompanied by SYROS *and both carry masses of greenery*
MYRRHINE.   *He is; why else is* Daos here,
His servant, on his way back from the farm
With all the greenery* he's cut. Let's move
Out of the way a bit, my dear.
PHILINNA.   Why should
We care for him?
MYRRHINE.   We'd really best step back.

    Enter DAOS *followed by* SYROS; *he does not at first see* MYRRHINE
                         and PHILINNA.

DAOS. I don't think anyone at all farms land
More pious* than this is! Myrtle it bears,
And splendid *ivy* and so many flowers,
And if it's sown with other crops, it gives
A true and fair return—not in excess,
But just the right amount. But, Syros, you
Must take inside all that we're carrying,   40
All's for the wedding.
                    [SYROS *carries the greenery in;* DAOS *notices* MYRRHINE
                         Myrrhine, good day.
MYRRHINE. Good day to you.
DAOS.   I didn't see you, lady, good
And honest soul. How are you? I should like
To give you a foretaste of some good news
Or rather, if god wills it, of some good
To come; I want to be the very first
To tell you. Well, Kleainetos, for whom
Your boy is working, just the other day
Was digging in his vineyard when he well
And truly slashed his leg.
MYRRHINE.   Oh dear, poor man.
DAOS. Cheer up! and hear the rest. After three days   50

The old man's groin was swollen from the wound;
He had a fever and was in an awful state.
PHILINNA. May you be swept away like dirt! Is that
    The happy news you've brought?
DAOS.   Be quiet, old lady!
    He needed someone to look after him;
    The servants in whose care he was were all
    Just foreigners and told him he could go
    To hell, but your good son behaved to him
    As if he were his father, and did all
    That needed to be done—put ointment on
    His leg, massaged him, washed him, brought him food   60
    To eat, and cheered him up, and though the man
    Appeared to be a hopeless case, he got
    Him on his feet through his good care.
PHILINNA. Dear boy!
DAOS.   God, yes, he certainly did well.
    For while the old man was recovering
    Indoors and had some leisure, freed from
    His mattock and his cares—his life is hard
    You know—he started questioning the boy
    About his situation; something he knew
    Before, perhaps. But when the youth confided
    In him and told about his sister and   70
    Yourself and said *how difficult things were,*
    He felt as you'd expect and thought he should
    In any case make some return for all
    The care your son had given him, and so,
    As he was old and lonely, he now showed
    Good sense; he promised he would wed your girl.
    That's all I have to say. They'll soon be here,
    And he will take the girl back to his farm.
    You'll cease your struggle against poverty,
    That stubborn and ill-natured beast, that's worse
    In town; one must, I think, either be rich,
    Or live so you don't have a crowd of men   80
    To witness your misfortune. And for this
    The country's solitude is what you need.

I wished to bring this happy news to you.
And so, goodbye.
MYRRHINE.   Goodbye to you.

> [*Exit* DAOS *to* MOSCHION'*s house. When he is gone,* MYRRHINE
> *walks round in distress, wringing her hands*

PHILINNA.   My child,
What ever is the matter? Why do you walk
Around wringing your hands?
MYRRHINE.   You ask me why?
I don't know what to do.
PHILINNA.   Do about what?
MYRRHINE. Dear friend, my daughter's just about to bear
A child . . .

The act ends with eight fragmentary lines in which no doubt
Myrrhine put Philinna in the picture.

At the beginning of the second(?) act there is a lacuna of about
twenty-five lines; the text resumes with broken fragments which
defy interpretation. We find that Gorgias is speaking; perhaps the
act opens with a monologue from him and he seems to be in some
dilemma ('What am I to do?'); he may be worried about how to
break the news that Kleainetos is on his way to claim his sister as
bride. Philinna then enters and a dialogue ensues. She asks,
'What's the matter?', to which Gorgias replies 'Nothing' but adds,
'Philinna, call my mother.' Philinna refuses to do this: 'No, by the
two goddesses'. In the middle of this someone calls on Artemis,
the goddess of childbirth, and it has been suggested that the cry
comes from Gorgias' sister in labour off stage. Someone (Gorgias?,
who did not know about his sister's pregnancy?) says 'Now what
must we do?'

Nothing can be made of the remaining papyrus fragments and
all that we have of the rest of the play are some isolated quotations
from ancient authors:

1. Stobaeus, *Eclogae* 4. 32b. 24
   It's easy to despise a man who's poor,
   However good his case is, Gorgias;
   Men think he's arguing for just one end—
   To make a bit. You wear a workman's cloak,

> Well then, you're called a twister straightaway,
> Even if it's you who's really being wronged.

It looks as if Kleainetos is addressing Gorgias, who perhaps had told him that Moschion had raped his sister; he will be telling Gorgias of the difficulties of making Moschion pay for this.

2. Stobaeus, *Eclogae* 4. 41. 28

> The man who's wronged you in your poverty,
> Whoever he may be, is cursed, for he
> Has wronged those in a state which he may share;
> Though he be very rich, his luxury
> Is insecure; the tide of fortune can
> Reverse its course, and quickly too.

These words may perhaps be part of the same speech of advice from Kleainetos to Gorgias.

3. Stobaeus, *Eclogae* 3. 1. 62 and 3. 20. 22

> He is the strongest, Gorgias, who best
> Can keep his self-control when he is wronged;
> This temper and excessive bitterness
> Is proof to all of petty-mindedness.

This may also be part of Kleainetos' advice to Gorgias.

4. Maximus Planudes (*Rhetores Graeci* v. 525 Walz)

> Are you mad? it's quite absurd that when you've fallen for a
>   girl
> Who's freeborn, you still say nothing but just watch the
>   preparations
> For your wedding helplessly.

It seems that someone (Daos? or an unknown friend of Moschion's?) is urging Moschion to pull himself together and put a stop to his father's wedding plans. The metre is trochaic, which Menander often uses in passages of high excitement or farce.

5. Orion, *Anthologia* 1. 19

> I am a country man, I don't deny,
> And I'm not quite au fait with city ways,
> But length of years increases what I know.

Clearly Kleainetos is speaking but on what occasion and to whom we cannot tell.

We can only guess how the plot developed, but we may be sure that it had a happy ending. It has been suggested that Kleainetos is found to be the long-lost husband of Myrrhine and father of Myrrhine's children; then he could not marry the daughter; Myrrhine, reunited with her husband, would no longer be a pauper, and the way would be clear for Moschion to marry her daughter.

The Apparition (Phasma)

Some hundred lines of this play survive, many of which are mutilated. The first fifty-six come from Act 1; the remainder are so fragmentary that they cannot be placed.

Characters

A GOD (Prologue)
PHEIDIAS, a young man, betrothed to his neighbours' daughter
PHEIDIAS' TUTOR*
COOK
SYROS, a slave of Pheidias
CHAIREAS(?), stepbrother of Pheidias' betrothed.
A SLAVE OF CHAIREAS(?)
? THE NEIGHBOURS, husband and wife

Characters not appearing in our fragments:

PHEIDIAS' STEPMOTHER
HER DAUGHTER, the 'Apparition'
HER HUSBAND, Pheidias' father
THE NEIGHBOUR'S DAUGHTER, betrothed to Pheidias

The scene is a street in Athens, two houses adjoining, one that of Pheidias' father, the other the house in which live the 'Apparition' and Pheidias' betrothed.

The general outline of the plot is given us by an ancient commentator (Donatus) writing on Terence's play *The Eunuch*. A woman had a daughter, probably as the result of rape. She later married a widower who had a grown-up son. She put her daughter out to foster parents who lived in the house next door and made a hole in the party wall so that she could talk to her daughter through it, decking it out to look like a shrine. Her stepson, Pheidias, seeing that she often appeared to worship at this shrine, became curious and decided to have a look himself. Seeing a beautiful girl through the hole, he took it for a divine apparition. When the truth emerged, he fell passionately in love with the girl. Eventually the father consented to his marriage to her and the play ended with the wedding celebrations.

But Donatus omits complications in the plot; it appears from the papyrus text that Pheidias was already betrothed to the neighbours' daughter and the wedding was about to take place.

The first eight surviving lines are fragmentary and their interpretation is disputed. I follow Arnott in supposing that they form the conclusion of a dialogue between Pheidias and Syros, which forms the opening of the play. We may guess that before our fragment begins, Pheidias tells Syros that he has seen the Apparition and has since then suffered from depression and insomnia. Syros then advises Pheidias on how he must behave; although he has fallen in love with the 'Apparition', he must carry on as if he intended to marry his betrothed.

SYROS(?): . . . you help to celebrate (?) . . . You
　　Must think yourself a bridegroom; *don't alarm*
　　The mother of the girl; *explain* this* to
　　Her step-brother some other *way;* and don't,
　　For heaven's sake, give *anyone suspicions*
　　Of yourself. That's what you must do.
PHEIDIAS.　　　　　　　　　　　　　*All right.*
　　I will do so. What else is one to do?

　　　　　　　　　　　　　　　　[*Exeunt into their house*

　　　　　　　Enter a GOD *(Prologue).*

　　It's *not a phantom*, but a real girl,
　　Who's hidden in the house where the bride* lives.　　　　10
　　Her mother bore the girl before she came here;
　　And *when she was sixteen* she put her out

To foster parents to bring up; she lives
Here in the house next door, close guarded when
The husband's here but otherwise, when he's
Gone to the farm and there's less need to guard her,
She often leaves the house which is her home.
How does the vision *then* appear? Perhaps you want
To have a clearer view of this. The wife   20
Has made an opening, breaking through the wall,
To keep an eye on all *that goes on there;*
She's covered it with garlands *and green leaves*
So that no *busybody* coming near may know
The truth . . . inside . . . of the goddess . . .

The conclusion of the Prologue is missing.

When the text resumes, Pheidias and another (his old tutor?)
are having a conversation; Pheidias may be returning from the
market where he has bought provisions for the wedding feast. He
is complaining that he is unwell and cannot sleep.

TUTOR. What are they asking in the market now
    For wheat?
PHEIDIAS.   What's that to me?
TUTOR.   Nothing. But still,
    Perhaps I may speak out and tell the truth;
    If it's expensive, that should worry you
    For my sake; I am poor. Think, Pheidias,
    You're human; but a poor man's human too.
    You must not set your sights on what's beyond
    Your powers. And when you say you cannot sleep,
    You will find out the cause if you just think
    What your own life is like. You stroll around
    At leisure; when your legs are tired, at once
    You go back home. You bath luxuriously;
    Then up you get and *stroll around* again
    To please yourself. Your very life is just
    A sleep! In short, you have no illness; no,
    Your sickness is what you have just described—
    A rather coarse expression comes to mind;
    Forgive my cheek, sir; as the saying goes,

You are so chock-a-block with luxuries,
You can't find room to have a shit, I tell
You that.
PHEIDIAS.   Damn you!
TUTOR.   By god, I speak the truth.
That's what your illness is.
PHEIDIAS.   But still, it's strange—
I can't control myself; I'm very down.
TUTOR. Your foolishness is weak; *stand up to it.*
PHEIDIAS. Oh well, your words are logical enough.
Then what do you advise?
TUTOR.   You ask me for
Advice? Well, if you really suffered from   50
Some illness, you should now be looking for
The proper cure for that. But you have none.
So for a fancied illness you must find
A fancied cure and then imagine that
It does some good. Let women circle you
And purify you with a ritual bath;
Take water from three springs and add some salt
And lentils; sprinkle this all over you . . .

Donatus' incomplete summary does not help us to tell how the plot developed, but a mosaic from the House of Menander in Lesbos, clearly entitled 'Phasma act 2', gives a hint of what happened: there are three figures; a girl stands at an open door, her right arm raised; in the centre an old man steps towards her, his right arm raised and his left holding a stick; the figure on his right, a woman, lifts her right arm in a gesture to restrain him. Arnott interprets the scene as follows: the girl is the 'Apparition', the man and woman are Pheidias' father and stepmother. The former has learnt that the 'Apparition' is his wife's illegitimate daughter and threatens her while his wife tries to protect her.

Another papyrus fragment gives thirty-five mutilated lines of which the first twenty two are too fragmentary to give sense; they are part of a conversation between Syros and a cook. Syros says, 'The marriage is on again'; this suggests that Pheidias' betrothal to his neighbour's daughter was broken off when he had seen the

Apparition and went melancholy-mad, but on the advice of Syros
he was again prepared to go through with the marriage. In lines
73–4 the Cook says: 'Tell me whether the menu is to be simple or
sophisticated.' The cook must have been hired to prepare the
wedding feast.

The next fourteen lines give enough sense to make translation
possible (with supplements). They are part of a new scene which
follows immediately on the departure of the cook. There are two
speakers, a slave and a young man who must be the stepbrother of
Pheidias' betrothed, Chaireas, who is himself in love with the
'Apparition'. The slave has been telling of Pheidias' behaviour
when he was mad, or shamming mad. The metre has changed to
trochaic tetrameters.

CHAIREAS. Then I'm done for.   79
SLAVE.   He himself *is mad about* the girl, *I'm sure.*
  He is off his head, and, rightly, I suspected this at once.
  Then he had no *shame in saying* lots of different things . . .
[Two lines unintelligible.]
SLAVE. Then he rushed at her again, *sir.*
CHAIREAS.   I've no luck at all in love.
SLAVE. You are one of those, my master, who give food to
    prisoners.*
  If the fit once more attacks him, in his sickness he *maybe*
  Will bite off the maiden's *nostrils.*
CHAIREAS.   God forbid!
SLAVE.   He will by god,
  Or her lips, while he is giving her a kiss. And that will be
  Best perhaps; you'll cease to love her if you see her after that.
CHAIREAS. Now you're mocking me?   89
SLAVE.   I mock you? Never, on my life, I swear.
CHAIREAS. I shall go in to my sister and hear clearly what is up.
  I suspect she's not too happy at the prospect of this match.

A third fragment consists of thirteen half lines for which we have
no context and which give no consecutive sense. Two speakers, a
husband and wife are talking about the rape of a girl at a religious
festival (the Brauronia). Arnott suggests that the speakers are the

husband and wife living next door to Pheidias, discussing the rape
of the Apparition's mother:

WIFE: Who is it? Who dishonours . . .   93
HUSBAND. . . . I do not know; for she being . . . when
  There was a festival at night and dances . . .
  Surely you understand? You'll question her
  And she will say 'At the Brauronia',
  And you say 'When?' . . . Wandering alone,
  Poor girl . . . You will ask . . .   100

The remaining seven lines give no sense except for the third line
in which the wife says, 'Dear husband . . .'

The Flatterer (Kolax)

About 140 lines of this play survive, fifty complete, ninety incomplete; they are not consecutive and appear to be extracts, intended, perhaps, for recitation at a dinner party. The supplements which have been made to fill the gaps are often highly speculative.

Characters (as far as is known)

PHEIDIAS, a young man in love with a courtesan
BIAS, a wealthy soldier in love with the same courtesan
GNATHON, the hanger-on of Bias, alias Strouthias (see below)
DAOS, the slave of Pheidias
A BROTHEL-KEEPER, owner of the courtesan
COOK

The plot centres round the rivalry of two young men, Pheidias and Bias, for the favours of the same courtesan. Each, perhaps, is accompanied by a hanger-on, Pheidias by Gnathon, Bias by Strouthias, but it is, perhaps, more likely that Strouthias and Gnathon were different names borne by a single character, 'who adopted Strouthias as an alias when associating with the soldier, but used his real name when associating with other characters such as Pheidias and Daos' (Arnott, Loeb vol. ii, p. 158). In my translation I have assumed that Strouthias and Gnathon are the same person.

Terence wrote a play called *The Eunuch*, based on Menander's play of the same name, in the Prologue of which (lines 30–2), he says that he has transferred to it two characters from Menander's *Flatterer*, namely a fawning flatterer and a boastful soldier. In the last scene of Terence's play the flatterer persuades the free young man (Phaedria) and the soldier (Thraso) to share the favours of the courtesan; if, as many believe, Terence adapted this scene from

Menander's *Flatterer*, this play will have ended with Gnathon
persuading Pheidias and Bias to share the girl they loved.

THE FIRST EXTRACT

Of the first extract of thirteen lines, only the second half of each
line survives. It appears to be from an opening monologue in
which Pheidias explains his situation to the audience. All we can
gather from these half-lines is that Pheidias' father has gone
abroad on business, leaving him alone, that he is miserable, and
that he has to receive a party in his house (the reference to a child
entrusted to guardians is obscure; the girl(?) concerned must
belong to a sub-plot):

PHEIDIAS(?).   .   .   .   .   .

> *For nothing is* incredible in my present life.
> Born of . . . parents . . .
>   son, as all believe.
> *My father's sailed off* on some business
> *And has left* an empty house to me.
> . . . the child; he himself *left* its upbringing
> . . . to certain guardians;
> Oh, unhappy that I am, perhaps
> . . . in such misery;
> . . . I must do this.   10
> . . . We have a party* on
> *when I must be* the host and master *of the house.*
> . . . told me to receive them.

THE SECOND EXTRACT

Pheidias and Gnathon enter, followed by a boy carrying wine jars,
presumably for the party he has to give; they are in mid-
conversation. The extract opens with five unintelligible line-
endings; the reference to someone 'brilliant or great in reputation'
might be to his rival Bias.

PHEIDIAS. . . . must . . .
   . . .brilliant or great in reputation
   . . . if not, a third . . .
   . . .; bring a wild . . .

. . . . .

[Of the following seventeen lines only the second half of each line survives. There follow nine lines slightly less deficient, then twelve pretty well complete.]

Accepting that Gnathon and Strouthias are identical, we find that Gnathon in this scene is acting the part of Pheidias' ally; he makes a virulent attack on Bias' character.

   The first five lines, heavily supplemented, may be rendered:

GNATHON.   Now I'm
   Advising you to cheer up, Pheidias.   20
PHEIDIAS. Cheer up? *When* I'm so worried for this girl
   Of mine. *Don't* talk such nonsense.
   . . . Lady Athene, save me.

Gnathon seems to reply with some high-faluting explanation of Pheidias' situation, referring to 'ancestral customs' and 'cities'.

GNATHON. *Those who observe* with care the customs of
   Our ancestors *do no good to themselves,*
   . . . the same men, they . . . cities.
   PHEIDIAS. What do you mean, you miserable man?
   GNATHON. The wicked *get more help than us* from god;
   For if we're good, we don't do well at all.
   This chap on double pay,* who used to hump . . .
   His own . . . bag, helmet, haversack,   30
   His pair of spears and rug, *a burden more*
   Than any wretched ass can bear, . . .
   . . . has suddenly *become*—Bias,
   Because the gods have made him rich.
PHEIDIAS.   *If you*
   Are talking of the man who just last year
   Was so unhappy here and kept us so
   Amused, the butt *of all our* jokes, *and now*
   Has fifty servants following on his heels,

Then I am done for.

GNATHON.   *Well*, he's landed here   40
From somewhere after he's betrayed some city,
Or some governor, or an army camp.
He's clearly *made his pile dishonestly*.

PHEIDIAS. How so?

GNATHON.   No one who's honest gets rich fast.
The honest man is thrifty, stores his gains,
The other lays a trap for him who's saved
So long and takes the lot.

PHEIDIAS.   How monstrously unfair!

GNATHON. I swear to god, that if this boy* were not
Here walking just behind me with these jars
Of Thasian wine, and so men might suppose
That I am drunk, I'd now be following him
And in the market place I'd shout, 'Last year
You were a beggar, a mere skeleton,   50
And now you're rich. So tell me, what's your trade?
Answer me this: Where have you got your wealth?
Out of my way! Why teach us what is wrong?
Why demonstrate to us that evil pays?
. . . me?

PHEIDIAS. . . . Yes . . .

There follow about thirty lines of which only line-endings survive.
In the course of these Daos enters (unless he has been in the
background throughout this scene). There is a reference to a
brothel-keeper.

THE THIRD EXTRACT

In this it seems that Daos is warning Pheidias of Gnathon's
duplicity.

DAOS. There is one man, one only, master, who   85
Has brought disaster on all your affairs.
In short I tell you; all the cities you

Have seen laid waste have been destroyed by this
Alone, as I've discovered now through him.
All the dictators there have ever been,
All mighty leaders, every governor
And garrison commander, founders of cities,
And generals—I mean, that is, those who
Have been completely ruined—all have been   90
Destroyed by this alone—by flatterers;
And these it is that cause their misery.

THE FOURTH EXTRACT

Someone (Gnathon again?) is advising Pheidias on how to overcome his enemy, Bias; as we don't know the context, the passage
is obscure.

PHEIDIAS. Your words are quite impressive but I don't
   See what it's all about.
GNATHON.   Well, anyone
   Whose judgement was unsound might think the man
   Who's hatching plots against you was your friend.
PHEIDIAS. And if the plotter doesn't have the power?
GNATHON. But anyone can harm a stronger man
   If he's not on his guard . . .
   Suppose Astyanax* were lying here   100
   Flat on his back, why, I could *take* a pestle
   And smash in his nose . . .
   But the hit-man, hired for fifty pounds,
   Who's come expressly just to *beat you up,*
   Would not have done the job so easily.
   His victim's on his guard; . . . he looks him in
   The face and knows that he is *dangerous* . . .
   . . . He will beware of you likewise . . .
   . . . door . . .
   You'll say that *you will send for* your own friends,
   Since he is acting violently . . .
   He'll come at once and send for other troops.

But possibly he'll not be on his guard
Against you after all. Boys!

> [*The speaker knocks on some door, summoning the servants*

                Either you
Or he will be wiped out. But if you're trusted
And seem to do nothing that's different
From what you usually do, you'll have the man
Quite off his guard, away from his own house
And all his business. The rest of it
You will arrange however you may wish.

THE FIFTH EXTRACT

The brothel-keeper is speaking; he owns the girl for whom Bias
and Pheidias are competing.

BROTHEL-KEEPER. The man's *a braggart*; that is plain enough.   120
   They're hungry beggars, aren't they, who arrive
   With nothing in their hands but *cudgels?* and
   My neighbour's* one of them. But all the same
   If he hears this, he'll come with sixty friends
   (The number that Odysseus* took with him
   To Troy), and shout with threats, 'I'll do for you,
   You villain—have you sold my girl to one
   Who has more money?' Why should I sell her?
   Heavens above, I won't, . . . because of him.
   The girl earns practically as much as ten,
   Three hundred drachmas every day, from him,
   The foreigner;* I'm afraid to take so much.   130
   Given the chance they'll seize her in the road
   Then I shall have much trouble, go to law,
   Call witnesses *to get her back again.*

There follow eighteen half lines which give no sense.

Quotations from ancient authors:

1. Athenaeus 14. 659d

A cook is instructing a slave while making a sacrifice; the victim has been killed; three libations of wine are then poured; next the heart, lungs, liver, and kidneys will be eaten by the participants; here the cook reserves the tongue for himself.

Athenaeus introduces his quotation as follows: 'Menander in *Kolax* makes the cook who is serving the fourth-day celebrants in the festival of Aphrodite Pandemos utter these words':

COOK. Pour a libation! Follow me and give
   The offal here. Where are you looking? Pour
   Again. Come on, boy, Sosias. Now pour
   Once more. That's good! Now let us pray to all
   The Olympian gods and goddesses at once—
   You take the tongue meanwhile—to grant us health,
   Protection, many blessings, and that all
   Enjoy the good things now before them. Let
   That be our prayer.

In the first papyrus extract (ll. 11–13) Pheidias says he has to organize a party; perhaps this party, celebrated in honour of Aphrodite, goddess of love, on the fourth day of the month, formed the conclusion of the play. And possibly it is the prospect of this party which has put the wind up the brothel-keeper, who is afraid that Pheidias and his mates will forcibly abduct the girl he is in love with.

2. Athenaeus 10. 434c

Bias is boasting to Strouthias (= Gnathon)

BIAS. In Cappadocia I three times drained
   A golden beaker, Strouthias, brimful,
   Which held five pints.
STROUTHIAS.   You've put away more than
   King Alexander.
BIAS.   Quite as much, I swear.
STROUTHIAS. That is a lot!

3. Plutarch, *Moralia* 57a

Plutarch introduces his quotation: '. . . just as Strouthias, walking around with Bias and exulting in his stupidity by praising him, says: "You've drunk more than King Alexander" and':

> I'm laughing when I think about that joke
> You made against the Cypriot.

Plutarch quotes fragment 2 inaccurately and then quotes Strouthias again, referring to some wisecrack of Bias, probably about a Cypriot bullock; these were said to eat dung and so the term was used as an insult ('you're a Cypriot bullock' = 'you eat shit').

(Terence, *Eunuch* 497–8 seems to echo this:

> GNATHO. Ha, ha, ha!
> THRASO. What are you laughing at?
> GNATHO. At what you said just now and when your joke about
> the Rhodian occurred to me.)

4. Athenaeus 13. 587d

In these lines Strouthias again seems to be flattering Bias by listing the famous coutesans who have been his mistresses:

> STROUTHIAS(?). You had them all   Chrysis and Antikura,
> Korone, Ischas, and the beautiful
> Nannarion.

5. Erotian, *Glossary on Hippocratic Terms* (p. 116 Nachmanson) (doubtful; Erotian ascribes it, probably wrongly, to the comic writer Philemon)

> But I can't find a single relative,
> Although I have so many, but I'm cut
> Off on my own.

Terence seems to adapt these lines in *The Eunuch* 238, where the Fawner says: 'See what I'm reduced to; all my acquaintances and friends desert me.'

6. Plutarch, *Moralia* 57a

Plutarch introduces this quotation: 'The flatterer does not introduce his praise with a frontal attack but leads (his victim) off in a circle':

'And approaches him in silence, like a beast,

'touching him lightly to try his temper'.

7, 8, 9 of OCT omitted, but add (see Loeb vol. ii, pp. 192–5)

7. Plutarch, *Moralia* 547c (not specifically attributed to *The Flatterer*)
Plutarch introduces this quotation as follows: 'Some people tickle up their victims by flattering, others continually ask questions, as is done to the soldier in Menander, to get a laugh'.

'How did you get this wound?' 'I got it from
A javelin.' 'Do tell us how?' 'Climbing
A scaling ladder.' I then demonstrate,
Quite serious, while they choked back their mirth.

Gnathon seems to be describing how he mocked Bias by asking him how he was wounded and then miming his reply.

8. Plutarch, *Moralia* 547de
GNATHON(?). He slaughters me, his entertainment makes
Me thin. What clever jokes, quite worthy of
A general! The devil really is
A charlatan.

If these two quotations are rightly ascribed to this play, they show how two-faced Gnathon is.

The Girl Possessed (Theophoroumene)

Of this play there survive only two papyrus fragments, both much damaged, which probably come from the second act, and a book fragment.

It is impossible to reconstruct the plot. In the first fragment a slave, Parmenon, is telling two young men, Lysias and Kleinias, about a girl who is, or claims to be, demoniacally possessed. Parmenon considers her an impostor; Kleinias, who is perhaps in love with her, believes that she is genuinely possessed. Lysias suggests that they put her to the test. He tells the piper to play music associated with the worship of Kybele, mother of the gods and mistress of all nature, whose cult was accompanied by ecstatic states and wild dances performed to the drums and cymbals.

Characters

Besides PARMENON, KLEINIAS, LYSIAS, and the GIRL, there was an old man called KRATON, whose part in the play is unknown.

The scene is perhaps a street in Athens, showing the house where the girl lives and an inn.

The first fragment begins in the middle of a speech by Parmenon, who is telling Kleinias and Lysias of the girl's behaviour.

The words 'I filled *their cups*' are obscure; perhaps Parmenon was watching the girl at some kind of party. Nor can we explain the reference to the 'gifts' which the girl says were taken from her.

PARMENON. She's an impostor, Kleinias, . . .but knew
   Her part full well . . .
   Rivers of tears ran swiftly down *her cheeks*
   And more sprang from her eyes. I filled *their cups*.
   'My gifts—you hear—' the girl exclaimed, 'They took

My gifts from me.' He said, 'What did you get,
You greedy whore? And how do you know the man   20
Who gave them to you? What? A lad *gives gifts*
To you, a girl? And why the garland? Why
Do you walk around outdoors?* Are you deranged?
Why don't you rave away shut up indoors?'
KLEINIAS. You're talking nonsense. Lysias, she's not
    Pretending this.
LYSIAS.   We can lay on a test.
    If she's in truth possessed by god, she'll come
    Leaping out here in front. [*To the piper*] You, play the tune
    'The Mother of the gods', or better still
    A Korybantic hymn.* [*To* KLEINIAS] Stand here by me
    Beside the inn's front door.
            [*The piper plays and* KLEINIAS *and* LYSIAS *retire to the door*
KLEINIAS. That's fine; god, Lysias, it's excellent   30
    That's what I want. It'll be a lovely sight.

The papyrus breaks off here. A mosaic from the House of
Menander (Mytilene, 3rd cent. AD) is an illustration of what
followed next; it is entitled 'Second Act of Theophoroumene
(= The Girl possessed)'. On the left a young man, named Lysias,
stands garlanded and wearing a long cloak; he seems to be playing
the cymbals, his right foot raised as if he is beating time. In the
centre stands a slave, named Parmenon. On the right another
young man, named Kleinias, also garlanded and wearing a purple
cloak, holds an object which may be a tambourine or cymbals. In
front stands a boy carrying what appears to be a pipe.

Some lines must be missing in which the girl enters; then
another papyrus fragment which probably belongs here shows the
girl speaking ecstatically. This fragment contains twenty seven
half lines. She speaks the first five, ending with an appeal to those
present to raise their voices with her.

. . . and the gold
. . . pouring into the sea
. . . the beloved
. . . And I bid those present
. . . you must all raise your voices with me.

Then for six lines she bursts into lyric hexameters, singing a Korybantic hymn in honour of Kybele; the following, based on surviving phrases, may give some idea of what stood here:

> Mightiest queen, *Kybele, appear* to me, *come with your train*
> *Of eunuchs* tossing their heads and your sweet-faced
> Korybantes.
> *Come and receive* sacrifice, a great hecatomb *in your honour,*
> Goddess, Phrygian queen. *And worshippers, clash on the cymbals,*
> *Beat on* the drums, *your music,* mountain mother *of all things.*

Eight lines follow in the normal metre of dialogue, probably addressed to Kleinias and Lysias:

> Now raise your voices; you must make yourself
> *A garland; take* your place and *lift your torch*
> *To* light *the incense.* For I want *to call*
> The goddess *to our rites.* [*To the piper*] You, play for me.
> *Great queen,* may you be kind *to us* and stay
> *Our friend* for ever.

The fragment concludes with eight further half-lines probably in lyric metre:

> . . . Hail, queen of Agdos,* *we worship you with drums* and cymbals
> . . . and with shouts of joy; queen of Agdos, the mother of the gods, of Phrygia and Crete, come hither, mistress, . . . queen of the woodland glade . . . Lydians.

One other substantial fragment survives, quoted by Stobaeus (*Eclogae* 4. 42. 3) as coming from *The Girl Possessed.* In it an old man called Kraton speaks; he was probably the father of Kleinias or Lysias. We cannot guess the context of this outburst:

KRATON. Suppose one of the gods came up to me
And said, 'When you depart this life, Kraton,
You'll start again from the beginning. You
Shall be whatever you may like—a dog,
A sheep, a goat, a man, a horse. You've got
To live two lives; that's the decree of fate;
Choose what you want.' I think I'd say at once,

'Then make me anything except a man,
The only creature that has good luck or bad
All contrary to deserts. The champion horse
Receives more careful grooming than the rest;
If you're a well-bred dog, you will be much   10
More valued than a cur; a noble cock
Has better food, and the low-bred's afraid
Of his superior. But if a man is good,
Well born, and noble-hearted, this does him
No good these days; the flatterers do best
Of all, and then the blackmailers, the man
Of malice takes the third part in our play.*
It's better to be born an ass than see
Men worse than you living in brighter light.'

Several other isolated lines are quoted by ancient sources with no context.

2. Stobaeus, *Eclogae* 3. 3. 6
   The man who has most sense
   Is the best prophet and adviser, too.

3. Athenaeus 11. 504a
   He quickly whizzes round for them the first
   Beaker of undiluted wine.

Perhaps from a description of a drinking party at the inn (see line 29); a slave whizzes round a beaker from which all drink.

4. Athenaeus 11. 472b
   Half drunk he drained the Thericlean cup.

Thericles was a Corinthian potter of *c*.400 BC whose wares were very popular.

5. Scholiast on Plato's *Clitophon* 407a
   You have appeared just like a god on the machine.

The scholiast says this expression, taken from the *deus ex machina* of Greek tragedy, was used of someone turning up unexpectedly to help.

6. Scholiast on Plato, *Phaedo* 99c
   The second voyage

A proverbial expression for 'the next best way' (compare Menander fr. 205 (= K–A vi. 2. 183)—'this saying means | that if you've lost fair winds you use your oars'.)
(7, 8, 9—lexical entries on single words—omitted.)

The Girl from Leukas (Leukadia)

Ten lines are given by a papyrus fragment which seems to be the opening of the play. Lines 11–15 are quoted by Strabo 10. 2. 8, lines 15–16 by Hesychius on *Leukas*, quoting them as by 'Menander in the Leukadia'; they fit this point well but their positioning is speculative.

A second fragment of half-lines is tentatively attributed to this play. (These fragments have been published since the revision of the Oxford text; they appear in Loeb edition, vol.ii, pp. 226 ff.)

The scene is set at Cape Leukatas, the southern promontory of Leukas, an island off the north-west coast of Greece. On this promontory there was a temple of Apollo on a cliff which fell two thousand feet down to the sea. According to tradition Sappho, rejected by her lover Phaon, hurled herself over this cliff to her death.

The first fragment (lines 1–10) is probably the opening of the play. A girl, who has been shipwrecked on Leukas, comes with a jar to collect water and is greeted by the old custodian of Apollo's temple, who, after the opening dialogue, breaks into a chant in lyric metre (Menander very rarely uses lyric metres).

GIRL [*addressing the statue of Apollo at the temple doors*]. Apollo, what a
    place you've made your home!
  All cliffs, and down below there lies the sea,
  A fearful sight.
                         [*The* CUSTODIAN *comes forward*
CUSTODIAN.   Good day to you, my child.
GIRL. The same to you, whoever you may be.
CUSTODIAN. Whoever I may be? I am the god's
  Servant who keep his temple, child. You come
  For water?
GIRL.   Yes.

CUSTODIAN.   The spring's not far, just here;
    It's sacred to the god.
GIRL.   Dear mother, *listen*;
    Do you know if somewhere here there is a cliff,
    Please say, *from which there is* a sheer *drop dow*n,
    Where people—
CUSTODIAN.   Here, you see, a mighty rock.   10
    Yes, you must mean the towering crag up there.

    It was there, we are told, that first Sappho,
    As, spurred by desire, she followed her proud
    Lover Phaon, cast herself down from the rock
    Which shines from afar. But, master and lord,
    By your command not a word of ill luck
    Shall sound in your shrine by Leukas' shore.

A quotation from Choeroboscus' commentary on the grammarian Theodosius (1. 330. 32 Hilgard) is in the same metre as the
above and probably belongs to it:

    O my lyre of the hills, many toned . . .

In the second fragment (of half-lines), which is tentatively
attributed to this play, the Girl appears to be talking to the temple
custodian and explains that she was wrecked on the coast of
Leukas. It seems to be expository and so probably comes early in
the play.

GIRL. [three lines fragmentary]
    The ship sailed in . . .
    A wave following to drench me . . .   35
    The young man has a father of ripe years
    Who wants *me(?)* to become his wife . . .
    . . . a kinsman *gave* a fortune for
    The cost of travel
    But when he did *not* hear, he waited *there*
    No longer . . .
CUSTODIAN. Poor girl, how passionate *your words*! . . .   41
    The ship was carried by a wind *off course*
    *And driven o*nto this great rock.
    . . . the local custom . . .

. . . them to suffer . . .
. . . what he is to do. this . . .
. . . of the gods

.   .   .   .   .

GIRL.   he/she prayed, if Kleinias
. . . In vain and take
. . . may be unwilling, dearest friend,
. . . .excellence . . .   50

These broken lines might be interpreted as follows: first the girl describes how she was wrecked, then says that she was being pursued by an old man who wanted to marry her; when he did not hear what had happened to her, he waited no longer.
The Custodian tells her that his ship was wrecked.

Three quotations from ancient authors cannot be placed and throw no light on the play:

1. Stobaeus, *Eclogae* 3. 10. 20
   A man who holds his hand out to get cash
   Plans wickedness, deny it as he may.

2. Stobaeus, *Eclogae* 4. 32. 6
   Men always believe the gods protect the poor.

3. Photius ζ 7, *Suda* ζ 9
   A. Custodian, put fire *upon the altar.*
   CUSTODIAN. Like this?
   A. That's good.

The Girl from Perinthos (Perinthia)

Of this play twenty three lines survive on a papyrus fragment and ten small quotations from ancient authors. Terence says in the prologue to his *Andria* that he had used material from both the *Andria* and the *Perinthia* of Menander, their plots being similar. The papyrus fragment and the quotations from the *Perinthia* show that there are points of contact with Terence's comedy but not enough to recover the plot of Menander's play in detail.

Characters in the papyrus fragment

LACHES, an old man
DAOS, a slave of Laches
PYRRHIAS and SOSIAS, TIBEIOS and GETAS, slaves

The scene is a street in a city with two houses

Our fragment seems to come from late in the play. Daos, a scheming slave, is in trouble with his master Laches and has taken refuge at an altar. Laches may not drag him from the altar but may force him to leave it by burning him out. This he plans to do by lighting a fire all round the altar.

LACHES [*coming out of his house and speaking back to* PYRRHIAS]. You
    follow, *Pyrrhias.*
DAOS. He'll come out with a load of *brushwood now.*
LACHES [*to* PYRRHIAS]. *You've got* the fire?
DAOS.   Fire too? It's obvious;
    Tibeios and Getas, he's going to burn
    Me out. Then won't you free me, Getas, please,
    Your fellow slave, and rescue me? *That's fine.**
    You'll not free me but simply stand and watch

Me burning here? Is that the way we feel
Towards each other? Here comes Pyrrhias;
What a huge load he's carrying! I've had it.
And master's following behind and holds
A lighted torch.
LACHES.   Be quick and put them round.   10
Now, Daos, give us a demonstration
Of your knavish tricks; think up a scheme
To wriggle out of this.
DAOS.   Think up a scheme?
LACHES. Yes, Daos; it's a proper sinch to cheat
Your easygoing, empty-headed master.*
DAOS. Oh lord!
LACHES.   And if *one had* superlative
Intelligence*—that touched you to the quick?
DAOS. Master, that's not like you.
SOSIAS [*noticing that in his terror* DAOS *has fouled himself*].
                              This rogue who was
So bold just now *has fouled himself* all down
His legs—the legacy of dearest . . .
[The last seven lines of the fragment are broken and obscure.]

          .   .   .

Will be grateful . . . .
                    by us
LACHES. Light the fire.
SOSIAS. . . . he arrived
carried *there* and in the slave market

          .   .   .   .   .

Quotations from ancient authors:

2. Athenaeus 7. 301
The slave went in bringing some tiny fish.

Compare Terence, *Andria* 368 ff.

3. Photius α 36, Suda α 32
DAOS. Suppose a servant should take on and cheat
An easygoing, empty-headed master,
I don't know what great feat he has achieved

By fooling one who's always been a fool.

Daos' boast is thrown back at him by his master (see lines 13–15); either Laches had overheard him or it had been reported to him.

4. Athenaeus 11. 504a

> The old hag
> Never allowed the cup to pass her by
> At all but drank it as it circled round.

This might be a description of the drunken midwife, the Lesbia of Terence's *Andria* (228–32). Athenaeus introduces this quotation by explaining that on occasions all drank from one beaker passed round the whole party.

5. Stobaeus, *Eclogae* 4. 55. 2

> I've never envied an expensive corpse;
> It ends in the same bulk as the most cheap.

6. Pollux 10. 12

> Gather together all that you can move
> And quickly leave the town, my friend.

7. Photius α 1852, *Suda* α 2289

> The rest are slaves you may not take, they're not
> For seizing.

This may follow on the previous quotation.

8. Harpocration (π. 80 p. 217 Kerney), Photius (p. 442 Porson)

> There's some extremely rude abuse upon
> The wagons.

At a wedding when the bride was being driven by the bridegroom to his home, the guests heaped obscene abuse on them to avert the evil eye.

9. Maximus Planudes, Scholion on Hermogenes (*Rhetores Graeci* v. 486 Walz)

> And I'm not rotten underneath myself,
> I hope.

The Man from Carthage (Karchedonios)

Of this play about sixty lines or part lines survive on six papyrus fragments; they are badly mutilated and only lines 31–38 are complete.

Characters in our fragments

The CARTHAGINIAN, a young man who thinks he is Carthaginian
    by birth but perhaps turns out to be an Athenian
A SLAVE
A YOUNG MAN, probably a free Athenian

The scene is a street in Athens

When our fragment begins the Carthaginian is alone on the stage.

CARTHAGINIAN. *The door* has rattled; I'll get back *a bit.*
                                [*The* CARTHAGINIAN *withdraws*

      The SLAVE *and* YOUNG MAN *enter in mid-conversation.*

YOUNG MAN. *Don't* make him; nothing ever must . . .
    .   .   .   .
SLAVE. . . . He's not been badly buffeted . . .
    It's not an easy matter to put right
    A piece of folly that dates back so far
    In just one day.
CARTHAGINIAN [*aside*]. *What* is *the trouble here?*
    What is the *wretched fellow* drivelling
    About? The man's a slave . . .   10

Nineteen lines too fragmentary to give sense, in which the slave
and the young man seem to have continued their conversation
while the Carthaginian eavesdropped.

YOUNG MAN. Certainly not. The man's approaching us.

      [*The* CARTHAGINIAN *comes forward and is accosted by the slave*

SLAVE. My friend, *perhaps* you've come here ignorant   31
  Of who you are.

CARTHAGINIAN.   I don't think so.

SLAVE.   Then say,
  Who is your mother?

CARTHAGINIAN.   Who's my mother?

SLAVE.   Yes,
  And who's your father? Just imagine that
  The deme is making up the register.*

CARTHAGINIAN. My mother is the child of Hamilcar,
  The general of the Carthaginians,
  You scamp.* What is the meaning of that look?

SLAVE. So you, the grandson of that Hamilcar,
  Are plaguing us and think that you will have
  As wife a girl from Athens?

CARTHAGINIAN.   Yes, when I
  Am registered according to the laws.*   39

The remainder of this papyrus fragment and two other fragments tentatively assigned to this play are too damaged to give sense.

There are four quotations in ancient authors from this play which throw no light on the plot, and a fifth tentatively assigned to it.

1. Athenaeus 9. 385e
  I offered Boreas* some incense but I caught
  No fish; I'll boil myself some lentil soup.

2. Stobaeus, *Eclogae* 4. 24b. 27
  For no one knows who his own father was;
  We all just guess, or believe we know the truth.

3. Photius λ 363
  Singing the reaper's song from breakfast on.

4. Stobaeus, *Eclogae* 3. 9. 16
  Virtue no doubt is stronger than the law.

7. *Suda* χ 465
   Need teaches wisdom even to a clod
   Who comes from Carthage.

The Women drinking Hemlock
(Koneiazomenai)

Of this play two scraps of papyrus survive, the first contains the ends of
twenty lines, of which the last two can be completed by their quotation
by Stobaeus (*Eclogae* 4. 44–5); the second fragment gives only isolated
words. It is impossible to guess at the plot or know who are the women
who took, or threatened to take, hemlock to poison themselves.

The first fragment contains a conversation between two
characters, probably a slave and a young man. It may come from
the last act in which the Young Man, after various troubles, is to
be married to the girl he loves—he cannot believe it and thinks he
is dreaming, but her father, the slave says, is already offering a
dowry and preparing for the wedding.

YOUNG MAN.   *Is this a* dream?
SLAVE.   if we are sleeping.
   A dowry of two talents* and five *minae too*
   To deck *the bride.*
YOUNG MAN.   I'm not awake.
SLAVE. . . . He is already starting on the wedding.
   . . . fit as a flea*.
YOUNG MAN.   What's that you say?
SLAVE. *Fit as* a flea. I was there this evening.
YOUNG MAN. So what?
SLAVE.   . . . He sits and talks.
YOUNG MAN.   With whom?
SLAVE. With Chaireas.
YOUNG MAN.   Where? I want *to see him.*
SLAVE. . . . There is a bench just near . . . you know, I'm sure;
   It's on the right . . .
YOUNG MAN.   I'll go in and see.   [*Exit* SLAVE

I've been all wrong *in my abuse* of Luck;
I've spoken ill of her *as blind,* you know,
But now she's saved me—she can see all right.
I laboured hard; my labours were in vain.
I never would have met *with this success,*
Unless she'd helped me; so let no one be
Excessively downhearted if he fails;
This failure may perhaps result in good.*

Two further lines are quoted from this play with no context by
Stobaeus (*Eclogae* iii. 21. 2):

The saying 'Know thyself' means you must know
Your own position and what you should do.

Title Unknown

Five papyrus fragments, belonging to one codex, give us badly damaged extracts from this play, the title of which is unknown. Two further fragments are tentatively assigned to it.

Characters

MOSCHION, a young man
LACHES, an old man, father of Moschion
CHAIREAS, a friend of Moschion
KLEAINETOS, the father (or guardian) of Moschion's wife

As our fragments are disjointed and the plot complicated, it may be helpful to give a complete summary as far as it can be reconstructed.

While Laches was away, his son Moschion raped the daughter of Kleainetos and then agreed to marry her. He was afraid that his father would disapprove of this marriage, and so his friend Chaireas embarked on a trick to win his consent. He tells Laches that the girl had been promised in marriage to himself and that when Moschion failed to persuade him to give her up, he (Moschion) raped her; but he was caught in the act and imprisoned. To save his son, who was liable to the death penalty for raping a free girl, Laches presses Chaireas to accept Moschion's marriage to her and offers him his own daughter's hand. Although he is in fact in love with Laches' daughter, Chaireas pretends that his obligations to Kleainetos makes this impossible but is persuaded to agree.

When Kleainetos appears and Chaireas says that Moschion is legally married to his daughter, he pretends to be outraged by what has happened; it is clear from what follows that he too was in the plot to win Laches' agreement to the marriage. Laches accepts the situation, which, he supposes, frees his son from fears of execution.

When Kleainetos and Laches are left alone, Laches soon learns that the whole thing has been a trick to get him to agree to Moschion's marriage. He is very angry but can only howl with rage.

The next fragment is obscure since we do not know its context but we learn, if it is correctly placed here, that Laches has reneged on his promise to give Chaireas his daughter and is about to marry her to another man.

The last fragment, which seems to come from the end of the play, shows all problems resolved, as Laches betrothes his daughter to Chaireas and promises a dowry.

Of the first nine lines only isolated words and phrases survive. There are two speakers: Laches and Chaireas. The fifth line has been restored to mean:

LACHES. Save him, *I beg you, Chaireas.*

Other legible words: witnesses/ready for the neighbours/him locked up/Good heavens, Moschion/he is (?) an Areopagite/for . . . still your friend.

From these fragments we may deduce that Laches begs Chaireas to save Moschion, who, he believes, had been caught in the act of raping Kleainetos' daughter and had been arrested and locked up. The situation is complicated by the fact that Kleainetos (?) is an Areopagite, i.e. a member of the Council of the Areopagos who would hear Moschion's case.

When our text becomes intelligible, Chaireas may be replying to an appeal from Laches such as: *Help him, Chaireas*; for he still *thinks you* his friend.

CHAIREAS. He's wronging me, though I've done him no harm.   13
    He always loved the girl and gave me lots
    Of trouble, but when he got nowhere in
    His efforts to persuade me to give up
    The marriage in his favour, see, he raped
    The girl.
LACHES.   Well then, do you refuse to take

My daughter's hand?*

CHAIREAS.   But what am I to say
To those who have betrothed the other girl
To me, Laches?

LACHES.   Please, be—

CHAIREAS.   Oh, what am I
To do?

Enter KLEAINETOS *from his house.*

KLEAINETOS. Who's shouting here beside my doors?   20

CHAIREAS [*aside*]. Thank god, *he's come* at just the perfect time.
   [*To* LACHES]. O Laches, what am I to do?

LACHES.   We must
Persuade him*.

CHAIREAS. What a powerful force is rape!
I must persuade him to give away my girl
When I'm the one who's wronged?

LACHES.   Bear it, for me.

CHAIREAS. All right then, I defer to you, Laches.

LACHES [*aside*]. That's what we're striving for.

CHAIREAS [*to* KLEAINETOS].   Listen to me.
Kleainetos, Moschion's married to
Your daughter and posseses her—

KLEAINETOS [*shouts*].   We have
Been wronged!*

CHAIREAS.   Don't shout—in legal union.
Laches his father's here and will confirm   30
This. [*To* LACHES]. Do you not?

LACHES.   I do so, Chaireas.
For I don't want to . . .

Lacuna of five or six lines, in the course of which Laches may have
again promised Chaireas his daughter. Then nine fragmentary
lines which have been heavily supplemented to give the following.

LACHES. *All of the wounds his conduct's brought on you*
   I want to heal; he was a headstrong lad.

CHAIREAS. And I'll agree *to that; it's* right for me
   To give a friend a helping hand.

LACHES.   That's good.

KLEAINETOS. *Now everything is going to be* all right

CHAIREAS. *I'm off to deal with this;* it means *a lot*
   To me.

                                 [*Exit* CHAIREAS *to the city*

KLEAINETOS. What's happened *is amazing. I'm surprised*   40
   That you're so mild. I see you aren't the least
   Annoyed.

LACHES.   *How should I be annoyed* when I
   Have freed my son from those great fears he had?

KLEAINETOS. But still, we settled all this long ago.
   Your son is married to my girl, and took
   Her of his own free will, not forced. We thought
   You would be angry when you heard of this.
   But you've turned out to be a man of some
   Sophistication. We have had good luck.
   So why should we complain?

LACHES.   What do you mean?

KLEAINETOS. Just what I said   50

LACHES.   Did you not give your girl
   To Chaireas to start with?

KLEAINETOS.   I did not.

LACHES. What's that you say? Not Chaireas? To whom then?

KLEAINETOS. How ridiculous! You heard what I just said?
   To your own son.

LACHES.   What?

KLEAINETOS.   Yes, and she has had
   A child by him.

LACHES.   What's that? By Moschion?
   Good heavens, what a shocking business!

KLEAINETOS. Lord, are you mad? It looks as if I praised
   Your sense too soon.

LACHES.   And Chaireas has not
   Been wronged at all?

KLEAINETOS.   His dear friend Chaireas—
   What way has he been wronged?

LACHES.   Not wronged at all?   60
   Then why did he come here and make a fuss?

KLEAINETOS. Perhaps he wished—
LACHES.   He wished? You've all combined
    Against me then. Good god!
KLEAINETOS.   What are you doing?
LACHES. Nothing. But still for god's sake let me shout
    Aloud in two or three great howls of rage.

A new fragment (Papyrus Oxyrhinchica 4409), possibly from the
same play, is extremely difficult to place. (Handley and Arnott
place it early in the play before our main surviving fragment but it
might equally well come later, if Laches has changed his mind
about Chaireas marrying his daughter.)

    Laches and Chaireas(?) are in conversation. The first five frag-
mentary lines, spoken by Chaireas, make no consecutive sense
(Father . . . daughter, brother . . .; he will have his way by force
. . . justice; . . .) We do not know what he is talking about. The text
then becomes readable but impossible to interpret.

LACHES. That's how you feel? He'll never *bring himself*
    To come outside and punish you.
CHAIREAS.   That's so.
LACHES. Then you go in and sensibly discuss
    With him the fellow's ill behaviour.   10
CHAIREAS. *I've done so.*
LACHES.   *Perhaps* when he went out he was
    Upset and then this happened to him too.

Chaireas then objects that Laches is treating him as a son-in-law
when he has deprived him of his daughter. Laches replies that she
is already betrothed to someone else and he is about to hold the
wedding.

CHAIREAS. But, Laches, you expect to have me as
    Your son-in-law, when you have robbed me of
    Your daughter?
LACHES.   Why, am I expecting now
    Or saying anything?
CHAIREAS.   And what will be
    Your feelings then, when you, who've been so hard,
    See me approaching you? Shall I endure

To speak to you when I have been so much
Insulted and see her another's bride?
LACHES. I have already promised her and now
Things can't be changed. The wedding's on.   20
CHAIREAS. O Zeus, now may what must be come to pass
And may some kindly god be near to help.
But someone's at the door.

The last fragment,* if it is from the same play, may belong to
the conclusion when all troubles dissolve into a happy ending.
Chaireas has won the girl he loves and Laches announces the
official betrothal of his daughter to him.

CHAIREAS*. *Never, never must I be parted from*
The girl I've loved so long. My fears were vain.
LACHES. Yes, Chaireas, she's yours. So I betroth
To you this girl, my daughter here,
To bear a crop of lawful children; and
You know the dowry that I give with her.
CHAIREAS. Just now you offered me two talents.
LACHES.   And
The rest . . .

The fragment ends with six badly damaged lines which suggest
that there is to be a wedding celebration: . . . | now is the time . . .
| Moschion . . . | two for you . . . | the wedding hymn . . . | . . .

A Selection of Fragments Quoted by Other Authors

The selection is the same as that in the Oxford Classical Text and references in parentheses are to this text and to Kassel and Austin, *Poetae Comici Graeci*, vol. vi. 2.

A. Quotations from Named Plays

1 and 2. *The Flute-Girl* (*Auletris*)

1. Quoted by Athenaeus 559d (59 = K–A 64)

A. You will not marry, if you've any sense,
   And leave your present way of life. Myself,
   I'm married; that is why I tell you not to.
B. It's all decided. Let the die be cast.*
A. Go on then; and I hope that you'll survive.
   You'll throw yourself into a real sea
   Of troubles, not the Aegean sea, and not
   The Libyan, nor the *Sicilian* sea,
   On which not three of thirty ships are lost;
   Of married men not even one is saved.

2. Quoted by Stephanus of Byzantium under Dodona *(60 = K–A 65)*

If anyone stirs up this Myrtile,
Whom she calls 'nurse', to talk, he will produce
A perfect chatter-box. They say that if
A passer-by touches Dodona's bowl
Of bronze,* it sounds the whole day long, but he
Could stop it sooner than this chatterer,
Who keeps it up all night as well.

3. *The Superstitious Man* (*Deisidaimon*)

Quoted by Clement of Alexandria, Stromateis 7. 4. 24 (97 = K–A 106)

A. God bless me. Heavens above! I've broken off
   My right boot lace as I was tying it.
B. You silly ass, no wonder! It was rotten,
   And you, you fusspot, would not buy a new one.

4 and 5. *The Doorkeeper* (*Thyroros*)

Both are in trochaic metre and seem to come from the same
scene.
   A friend is encouraging a prospective bridegroom, saying how
lucky he is to be acquiring so few in-laws.

4. Quoted by Photius Berolinensis a. 1425 (208 = K–A 187)

Neither brother, nor a sister will annoy you, and she's not
Seen an aunt at all, and never heard about an uncle yet.
It's a godsend, really lucky, when one has so few relations.

5. Quoted by Athenaeus 71e (209 = K–A 186)

What a bore to be involved in dinner parties with in-laws,
Where the father takes the cup first and begins a lengthy
      speech,
Mixing his advice with wise-cracks, then the mother has her
      say,
Next some grandmother must chatter, then some gruff old
      man begins,
Father of an aunt, and lastly some old girl who calls you
      'darling',
While the father nods assent to all of these.

6. The Priestess (Hiereia)

Quoted by Justinus, de monarchia 5 (210 = K–A 188)

A papyrus fragment (Oxy. 1235) gives a summary of the plots of Menander's plays, including this one. The papyrus is mutilated, the plot complex. An elderly man came to find the beloved son whom the priestess had borne him long ago. But she had given him to neighbours to bring up as their own child; these neighbours had a son and a daughter of their own. The father, suspecting that something was up, sent a slave pretending to be possessed to the priestess to be exorcised. The slave detected the true situation. Meanwhile the real son of the neighbours wanted to marry the daughter of the priestess and sent his mother to discuss the proposition. The father overheard them talking and became suspicious and, told by his slave that the young men differed in appearance, thought that the younger boy was his son and addressed him as such. The boy realized his mistake and warned his 'brother', saying that the old man was mad and addressed all young men as his sons. The father then realized the truth and addressed the older boy as his son but he packed him off as a madman.

After the various confusions have been cleared up, the father gets back his son and marries the priestess, his son marries the daughter of the neighbours who had reared him, and their younger son marries the daughter of the priestess, with whom he had fallen in love.

'That is the summary; and the play is one of his best, containing a . . . elderly man, young men in love, and a faithful and unscrupulous servant . . .'.

It has been suggested that the surviving fragment comes from late in the play when the old man is explaining to the priestess, Rhode, why he left her. The reference to cymbals sugests that she was a devotee of Kybele, in whose worship, they were used; he could not stomach her outlandish religious practices:

God, lady, does not save one man because
Another intervenes. If man can draw

Some god to do his will by cymbals, then
The man who does so's greater than the god.
No, these are instruments of rash violence
Devised by shameless men, Rhode, and forged
To make *the gods* ridiculous.

7. *The Men of Imbros*

Papyrus Oxyrhinchica 1235

The Men of Imbros, which begins:

Good Demeas, what ages since *I saw* you . . .

He wrote this in 296/5 BC, his seventy-*first* play, and gave it for production at the Dionysia, but it was not performed because Lachares became tyrant. Later it was acted by the Athenian Kallippos.

The plot: two poor men who were friends of each other lived together and settled in Imbros. They married twin sisters and shared their whole substance in common. They worked industriously by land and sea . . .

8. *The Groom* (*Hippokomos*)

Quoted by Diogenes Laertius 6. 83 (215 = K–A 193)

A. There was a man called Monimos,* Philon;
    A wise man he, but not at all well known.
PHILON. The one who had a beggar's wallet?
A.   No,
    Not one wallet, but three. He spoke a saw
    That's quite unlike Apollo's 'Know thyself'
    Or other sayings which are highly praised;
    That filthy beggar did better than all those;
    He said that all assumptions were rubbish.

9 and 10. *The Helsmen* (*Kubernetai*)

9. Quoted by Stobaeus, Eclogae *3. 22. 19 (250 = K–A 218)*

Young man, you think that money can supply
The price not just of daily wants—like bread
And barley, vinegar and olive oil,
But something else more vital. But it can't
Supply the price of immortality,
Not if you should amass that fabled hoard
Of Tantalus. You'll die and leave all this
To someone else.

10. Quoted by Orion 8. 9 (151 = K–A 219)

What are we really like, who talk so big!
Unhappy men, all those who are puffed up
With pride! They do not know man's character.
This one is thought by all a blessed man
When in the market; but as soon as he
Has opened his front door, he's miserable.
His wife rules all and always tells him what
To do and fights with him. He's suffering
From lots of pains, but I from none.

The last six lines may not follow consecutively from the previous
lines.

11. *Drunkenness* (*Methe*)

Quoted by Athenaeus 364d (264 = K–A 224)

The speaker is complaining about the expenses of a sacrifice and
the accompanying feast. He may gain from the sacrifice but the
expenses of the feast will far outweigh this gain.

Then aren't our fortune and our sacrifice
Quite similar? I'm bringing to the gods
A nice enough small sheep for which I paid

Ten drachmas. But the pipers, harpists, scent,
Mendean wine and Thasian,* honey, eels
And cheese will cost almost a talent.* So
We get returns proportionate to this—
Ten drachmas' worth of good, provided that
The gods accept our sacrifice; deduct
Against this all the cost of those fine things.
Surely the evil which results from all   10
These offerings is double *any good?*
If I were god, I'd not have let a man
Put down the tail-end on the altar, if
He didn't sacrifice it with an eel,
So that Kallimedon,* its kin, might thus
Have met his death.

12 and 13. *The Misogynist* (*Misogynes*)

These are both, probably, from the same speech; 13 may follow
directly from 12.

12. Quoted by Clement of Alexandria, Stromateis 2. 23 (276 = K–A 236)

Clement introduces his quotation as follows: Menander runs
down the state of marriage but also argues its usefulness; he
answers a man who says, 'I can't abide the business', 'That's
because you take it stupidly';
then he continues:

You see in marriage what distresses you
And what will cause you pain, but don't look at
Its goods. You'll find there's no good in the world,
Simylos, to which there's not some bad attached.

13. Quoted by Stobaeus, Eclogae 4. 22. 71 (276=K–A 236)

A spendthrift wife is tiresome and does not
Allow her man to live the life he wants
But one good thing she does produce*—children.

When he falls sick she tends her man with care,   10
And when his luck is down, she sticks by him,
And when he dies, she duly lays him out
And buries him. Think of all this when you're
Annoyed by day-to-day upsets. So you
Will find the whole of marriage bearable.
But if you always single out what pains
You, never putting in the scales the goods
You can expect, you'll suffer to the end.

14 and 15. *The Ship's Captain* (*Naukleros*)

14. Quoted by Athenaeus 474b (286 = K–A 246)

A. Theophilos has left the salt Aegean deep*
   And has returned to us. How opportune,
   Straton, that I should be the first to tell
   You that your son is safe and well and that
   The golden vessel's* safe.
STRATON.   Vessel? You mean
   The ship?
A.   You don't know anything, poor man.
STRATON. You say the ship is safe?
A.   I do.
STRATON.   That ship
   Of mine once built by Kallikles which had
   As pilot Euphranor of Thurii?

15. Quoted by Athenaeus 166b (28 = K–A 247)

The traveller's return to home:

   O dearest mother Earth, how much revered
   You are and precious to all men of sense!
   So, if a man takes on his father's land
   And then devours his substance, he should have
   At once to start a voyage which has no end,
   And never set his foot on land, so that

He'd learn this way what a great blessing he'd
Inherited and how he'd squandered it.

16 and 17. *Anger* (*Orge*)

16. Quoted by Athenaeus 166a (303 = K–A 264)

A husband is complaining to his wife that she has forced him into
extravagant ways:

I too was young once, wife, but I did not
Then bath five times a day; I do so now.
I had no splendid cloak, but now I have.
I had no scent, but now I have. And I
Shall dye my hair and have my body-hair
Plucked out,* indeed I shall, and soon I shall
Become a Ktesippos* and not a man;
Like him, I shall devour my very stones,
Yes, every one of them, not just my land.

17. Quoted by Athenaeus 243a (304 = K–A 265)

The fellow, whoever he may be, is just
Like Chairephon,* who once, when he was asked
To join a dinner party at sunset
When shadows lengthen, saw the shadows cast
By moonlight and ran off at break of day;
He thought that he was late, and came at dawn.

Anger was Menander's first play, produced about 321 BC. Following the tradition of Old Comedy, he attacks contemporaries twice
in these lines, a practice he dropped in his later plays.

18, 19, 20, 21. *The Necklace* (*Plokion*)

The Roman dramatist Caecilius wrote an adaptation of this play,
which Aulus Gellius compares unfavourably with Menander's
original.

18. Quoted by Aulus Gellius 2. 23. 9 (333 = K–A 296)

Laches has married an heiress who is ugly but wears the trousers. She has made him dismiss a pretty young slave-girl of whom she was suspicious.

LACHES. Now my fine heiress is going to sleep
   Soundly on either side.* Great is the deed
   She's done, the talk of the whole town. She's thrown
   Out of the house the girl who troubled her,
   As she intended, so that all may look
   Upon the face of Krobyle and know
   The wife is mistress here. And what a face
   She's got herself! A donkey amongst apes,
   As people say. I'd rather not describe
   The night that started all my suffering.
   How I regret that I took Krobyle   10
   As wife; she brought ten talents* dowry, but
   She brought as well a nose a full arm's length.
   Then how can I endure her insolence?
   By all the gods in heaven, I'll not
   Put up with it. The girl was, sure enough,
   Ready to serve and a fast worker. But
   Away with her! There's nothing to be said.

19. Quoted by Aulus Gellius 2. 23.12 (334 = K–A 297)

LACHES. My wife's an heires and a true vampire.*
   I haven't told you that.
FRIEND.   No, you have not.
LACHES. She's mistress of the house and land and all
   I have from her.
FRIEND.   My god, that's difficult.
LACHES. Yes, very difficult. Hard lines for all,
   Not only me; far harder for our boy
   And girl.
FRIEND.   The situation you describe's
   Impossible.
LACHES.   I know that well enough.

20. Quoted by Aulus Gellius 2. 23.15 (335 = K–A 298)

Laches' neighbour is a poor man who has a daughter; she was raped at a night-festival and has just had a child; a loyal slave laments his master's misfortune:

LOYAL SLAVE. O thrice unhappy is the man who's poor
  And marries and has children. Thoughtless too
  The man who does not guard his family,
  And, when he has bad luck, can't hide it from
  The world by means of money, but buffeted
  By storms he lives a troubled life, exposed
  To public gaze, sharing in every sort
  Of misery but with no share of good.
  I grieve for one; my warning is for all.

21. Quoted by Stobaeus, Eclogae *4. 3242 (336 = K–A 299)*

LOYAL SLAVE. A man who's poor and wants to live in town
  Chooses to make himself more miserable.
  For when he looks on someone who enjoys
  All luxury and can be idle, then he sees
  How wretched is the life he leads and how
  Laborious. My master's got it wrong.
  When he lived in the country he was spared
  This test since he was one of those who have
  No station in the state and he could use
  His solitude to screen his poverty.

For the sentiment, compare *Georgos* 79 ff., p. 222.

22. *Trophonios*

Trophonios was the legendary builder of the first temple of Apollo at Delphi.

Quoted by Athenaeus 132e (397 = K–A 351)

A. The dinner's to receive a foreigner.

COOK. From where? This makes some difference to the cook.
   For instance, visitors who come here from
   The isles, brought up on every kind of fish
   That's fresh, are not much taken by salt fish;
   They taste it in a most disdainful way;
   They like it better stuffed and drenched in sauce.
   Arcadians* on the other hand who live
   Far from the sea, they fancy little stews.
   Ionian* plutocrats? I make thick soups
   For them, dishes to rouse their sexual itch.

23, 24, 25. *The Changeling (Hypobolimaios)*

23. Quoted by Stobaeus, Eclogae *4. 53. 6 (416a = K–A 373)*

   I say that he's most happy, Parmenon,
   Who, free from suffering, has gazed upon
   These holy sights and then goes quickly back
   To whence he came*—the sun which all men share,
   The stars, the rain, the clouds, and fire.
   All these you'll always see before your eyes,
   Whether you live a hundred years, or few.
   And nothing will you ever see holier than these.

24. Quoted by Stobaeus, Eclogae *4. 53. 7 (416b = K–A 871)*

   Think of this time I speak of as a festival,*
   A visit to the world above; crowds, thieves,
   The market place, dicing, and wasting time.
   If you leave early, you will lodge the better.
   You've left with money for your journey still,
   And no man's enemy. But he who hangs around
   Grows weary, losing all and growing old
   In misery, becoming poorer as
   He drifts around, he will find enemies,
   Suffer from treachery, and leave this world
   In an unhappy death when his time comes.

25. *Quoted by Stobaeus*, Eclogae *1. 6. 1a (417 = K–A 872)*

Stop reasoning; for human reason adds
Nothing to Luck, whether Luck is divine
Spirit or not. It's this that steers all things
And turns them upside down and puts them right,
While mortal forethought is just smoke and crap.
Believe me; don't criticize my words.
All that we think or say or do is luck;
We only write our signatures below..

26. *The False Hercules* (*Pseudherakles*)

Quoted by Athenaeus 172a (451 = K–A 409)

A. You seem to me extremely tiresome, Cook.
  'How many tables are we going to set?'
  That's the third time you've asked me this by now.
  We're sacrificing just one little pig
  To serve eight tables, two, or only one,
  What difference does it make to you?   [*Exit*
COOK [*to his* ASSISTANT].   Simias,
  Go in. [*Exit* SIMIAS] It is impossible to make
  A casserole now or the sort of sauce
  You used to make, mixing together eggs
  And honey and fine flour. All's upside down
  These days.* The cook makes fancy cakes, bakes buns,
  And boils some porridge, and he brings these in
  After the pickled fish, and next fig-leaves
  And grapes; the kitchen-maid who stands beside
  Him roasts the meat and thrushes—as desert.
  And when the diner's eaten the desert,
  He puts on scent and garlands and he starts
  Dinner again on thrush and honey cakes.

B. *Fragments from Unnamed Plays Attributed to Menander*

1. Quoted by Stobaeus, Eclogae *3. 38. 29 (538 = K–A 761)*

Young man, I think you do not understand
That everything is rotted by its own
Peculiar vice and that which does the harm
Lies all within. For instance, if you look,
Iron is destroyed by rust and clothes by moths
And wood by worms. And as for you, it's envy,
Worst of all vices, that's made you waste away,
And does so now and will do so again,
The godless failing of an evil soul.

2. Quoted by Plutarch, On Love, *fragment 134 (568 = K–A 791)*

What makes them slaves? A woman's face?
What nonsense! All would be in love with her;
For looking at her is the same for all.
Is it some pleasure in her company
That draws the lover on? How is it then
That one man who enjoys her company
Is quite untouched and goes off with a laugh,
Another's done for? No, the sickness of
The soul occurs just when the time is ripe,
And he who's struck is wounded to the quick.

3. Quoted by Stobaeus, Eclogae *4. 22. 119 (581 = K–A 804)*

We should all, god help us, choose our brides
The way we do our shopping, not ask a lot
Of useless questions, 'Who's the granddad of
The girl he's going to marry and who's
Her grandmother?', while asking nothing of
The habits of the very bride-to-be,
With whom he's going to live; but carry off
The dowry to the bank so that the clerk
Examine it to see if it's good coin,

Money which will not stay inside the house
Five months, while you make no examination
Of her who'll settle down inside your home   10
And stay throughout her life, but choose your bride
At random—she may be perhaps a fool,
Bad-tempered, difficult, a chatter-box.
My daughter I shall hawk all round the town,
And say to those who want to take her hand,
'You have a talk with her; find in good time
What sort of trouble you are taking on.'
A woman's trouble—no avoiding that;
But he is lucky who takes on the least.

4. *Quoted by Stobaeus*, Eclogae 4. 23. 11 (592 = K–A 815)

Wife, you exceed a married woman's bounds
Because you will talk so; a woman of
Free birth must think the yard door is the place
Where her home ends. To run into the street
And chase her husband, still abusing him,
That, Rhode, is the way a bitch behaves.

5. *Quoted by Stobaeus*, Eclogae 4. 29. 6a and 30 (612 = K–A 835)

SON. My family! It'll kill me. If you love
    Me, mother, don't keep saying 'family'
    The whole damned time. It's those who have no good
    In their own character that's theirs alone
    Who have recourse to them—memorials
    And family—and count the number of
    Their grandfathers. But could you see or tell
    Of anyone who has no grandfathers?
    How else could they've been born? But if they can't
    Say who these were because they've moved their home
    Or lost their friends, how are they less well born
    Than those who can? The man who's born with a
    Good character, he is the true 'well born',
    Though he may be an Ethiopian.

'A Scythian!' How ghastly!' Mother dear,
Was Anacharsis* not a Scythian?

6. *Quoted by Stobaeus,* Eclogae *4. 31. 30 (614 = K–A 838)*

Epicharmos* tells us that the gods are winds,
Sun, earth, and water, fire and stars, but I
Supposed silver and gold alone were gods
Which were some use to us. Set up these gods
Within your house and pray for what you want;
You'll get it all—land, houses, silver plate,
Servants, friends, juries, witnesses. Just give—
You'll have the very gods to serve your needs.*

7. *Quoted by Stobaeus,* Eclogae *4. 34. 7 (620 = K–A 844)*

All living animals are happier
And have more sense than man, far more.
Consider first this donkey here; he's an
Unhappy creature, all agree. But he
Brings none of his misfortunes on himself;
He only has the troubles nature gave.
But we, apart from those we can't avoid,
Provide ourselves with others self-imposed;
We're pained if someone sneezes,* angry if
Abused; we see a dream—we're terrified,   10
And if an owl shrieks loud, we shake with fear.
Our worries, fancies, our ambitions, laws,
These are all evils added to nature's gifts.

8. *Quoted by Alexander,* de figuris *11 (656 = K–A 420)*

No by Athene, gentlemen,* I can't invent
An image to describe what's happened, when
I ask myself what is it that destroyed
Me with such speed. A whirlwind? But the time
It takes to gather and draw near, strike and
Destroy, is an age. Well then, a wave that swamps

A ship at sea? This gives a breathing space
To say, 'God help us! Hold onto the stays!'
And to await another billow and
A third; and you might grasp some wreckage and
Survive. But once I held her in my arms
And kissed her, I was sunk for good and all.

9. *Quoted by Julian of Halicarnassus,* Commentary on Job *(714 = K–A 500)*

[For Fortune takes the side of him who's wise.]*
By every man the moment he is born
There stands a spirit who's his guide through life
For good; for we should not suppose that it's
An evil spirit who does harm to men
Who live a decent life, or that it's bad,
But believe that god is altogether good.
But those who have grown evil through their own
Bad ways and made their lives a tangled web,
Or frittered all away through foolishness,
These then declare their spirit is to blame
And say it's evil when it's they who are.

10. *Quoted by Ps.-Lucian,* Amores *43 (718 = K–A 508)*

Was it not right Prometheus* should be nailed
To the rocks, as painters show, and to him
No honour's given but the one torch-race?*
He fashioned women, that which all the gods
Abhor, I believe. O gods above, they are
A shocking crew! A man will marry, will he?
In future wicked lusts will always plague
Him, the adulterer revelling in
His marriage bed, and evil love potions
And, worst of all diseases, jealousy,
With which a woman lives throughout her life.

11. Papyrus Friburgensis 12 (722 = K–A 1027)

This may not be by Menander and really belongs to the following section containing papyrus fragments of uncertain authorship, where K–A place it in vol. viii.

LOYAL SERVANT. Why do you talk so sadly to yourself and seem
    To give the impression of a man in pain?
    Make me your confidant, let me advise
    You on your troubles. Don't despise advice
    A servant gives. Often a slave who has
    An honest character is wiser than
    His master. And if Fortune has enslaved
    His body, yet his mind still remains free.

12. Ps.-Plutarch, Consolatio ad Apollonium *103c (740 = K–A 602)*

EX-TUTOR. If you, young master, when your mother bore
    You, were the only one of all mankind
    Born on the understanding that you should
    Do what you wanted all your life, always
    Enjoying happiness, and one of the gods
    Had granted this to you, then you'd be right
    To be upset; for god has done you wrong,
    Deceiving you. But if you breathe the air
    That all men share, to quote a tragic phrase,
    On the same terms as all of us, then you
    Must bear these troubles better and be more
    Alive to reason. This is the real point:
    You are a man; no creature suffers change
    From pride to humbleness quicker than him.
    That's fair. By nature feeblest of all things,
    He manages the greatest of affairs.
    So when he fails, he shatters in his fall
    Much that is good. But you, young master, have
    Not lost outstanding goods; your present ills
    Are only moderate. And so you must endure
    What is, presumably, a middling pain.

13. Plutarch, de laude ipsius (on boasting) *547c (745 = K–A 607)*

See *The Flatterer*, fragment 7, p. 240.

14. Porphyry, de abstinentia *4. 15 (754 = K–A 631)*

Porphyry introduces the quotation as follows: 'Indeed, they say that the Syrians also abstained from living creatures in the past . . . . abstinence from fish lasted until the times of Menander the comic dramatist.'

> As an example take the Syrians.
> When they eat fish, because they can't control
> Their appetite, their feet and paunch swell up;
> So then they put on sack-cloth and sit down
> Upon the road amongst the dung; by such
> Great self-abasement they propitiate
> The goddess.

15. Strabo 7. 296 (794, 795 = K–A 877)

Strabo introduces the quotation: 'See what Menander says about them [sc. the Thracians], not making it up, probably, but taking it from historical sources.'

> All Thracians, and of them especially
> We Getans—I myself can claim to be
> One of their race—show little self-control.

And a little further on, he takes the example of their incontinence where women are concerned.

> Not one of us will marry less than ten
> Wives or eleven; and some twelve or more.
> And if a man should chance to die when he
> Has married only four or five, he's called
> A poor unwedded, brideless bachelor
> Amongst the people there.

Fragments of Doubtful Authorship

The following papyrus fragments are possibly by Menander (the references in parentheses are to Kassel and Austin, *Poetae Comici Graeci*, vol. viii (1995).

1. *Papyrus Antinoopolis 15 (K–A 1084)*

This fragment, which may come from a play called *The Ring*, is from the opening scene. A husband laments his fate; he has been deserted by his newly married wife.

HUSBAND. Has any of my fellow citizens
  Had sufferings more terrible than mine?
  By earth and heaven, no. Persuaded by
  My father, I've been married for four months;
  And from our wedding night—o Lady Night,
  I call on you as a true witness of
  The words I say—not for one night have I
  Yet slept apart from her
  [Four lines fragmentary.]
               should have had
  I have never been . . . and I've not
  . . . since my marriage . . .
  My love was real; and when . . .   10
  Drawn to her by her open character
  And by her unaffected way of life,
  I've come to love her just as she loves me.

        Enter SERVANT GIRL, *carrying a box.*

  Why bring me all this stuff and show it me,
  When I am sick at heart to look at it?
  Put it . . . and now . . .
SERVANT. So that it may be . . . before . . .
[Lacuna of ten or more lines; then four fragmentary lines.]

HUSBAND. My wife's . . .

SERVANT. Her mother's . . . And if she gave it to your wife   20
And through . . . it was thrown away . . .
Her ring . . . do you not see?

HUSBAND. Then open it, so we may see if it
Is keeping anything of use.

SERVANT.   Oh, look!

HUSBAND. What's there?

SERVANT.   There's half a cloak, all torn and old,
Eaten away by moths.

HUSBAND.   And nothing else?

SERVANT. A necklace and one anklet.

HUSBAND.   Bring the lamp
Close here and shine it on the box. Look, don't
You see some little figures there engraved
With writing? Quick! Open the lid.

SERVANT.   My word!
There's writing, yes, I see some letters here.   30

HUSBAND. What does it mean? . . . In here
There're recognition tokens of a child;
Its mother kept them safe. Put them all back
Just as they were before and I will seal
Them up. Now's not the time, by god it's not,
To look into such secrets. It's not our concern.
I only hope we can some time put straight
The muddle we're in now. If ever I'm
Myself once more, . . . I'll open it again.

[One more fragmentary line: '. . . nothing'.]

2. *Papyrus Didot 1 (K–A 1000)*

The following fragment shows a situation similar to that in the
Arbitration—a father wishes to remove his daughter from her
husband and she resists; but in this fragment the father is acting
simply because the daughter's husband has suffered financial ruin.

DAUGHTER. You, father, should have said the words
Which I now speak; it's more appropriate

For you to think it out than me and say
What needs be said. But since you've not done so,
It's left perhaps to me myself to say
What's right; I'm given no alternative.
If he's committed some appalling crime,
It's not for me to punish him for this;
If he'd done wrong to me, I should have known.
But I know none, perhaps because I am
A silly woman—that I'd not dispute—   10
But though a woman may not have the sense
To judge all else, yet on her own affairs
Maybe she can show sense. Suppose that you
Are right; then tell me how he does me wrong.
There is a rule laid down for man and wife,
That he should always love her to the end,
And she should do whatever pleases him.
He has behaved to me just as I wished
And all that pleases him pleases me too.
He is a husband, father, good to me,
Who's fallen on hard times, and now you want
To give my hand to some rich man, you say,   20
So I may not endure a life of poverty.
Where, father, will you find such wealth as will
Give me more comfort than my husband does?
And how's it fair or right for me to take
My share of those good things he had and not
To share his poverty? Suppose the man
Who's going to take me now—though God forbid—
It shall not be with my consent nor while
I can prevent it—but suppose this man
Should lose his wealth as well, then will you give   30
Me to another man? If he in turn should fail,
You'll give me to a fourth? How far will you
Experiment with fortune, father, in my life?
When I was still a child, that was the time
You had to find a man to take my hand
In marriage. Then it was for you to choose.
But once you've given me away, it is myself

Who must decide—and rightly too; for if
My judgement's wrong, it's my own life that I
Shall harm. That is the truth. So don't, I beg
You by the goddess of our hearth, deprive
Me of the man to whom you married me.   40
I ask this as a favour,* father, yes,
But one consistent with humanity
And fair. If you refuse, then you will do
What you intend by force, and I shall try
To bear my lot without incurring shame.*

3. Papyrus Didot II (K–A 1001)

Now I'm alone and no one's near to hear
The words I speak. Throughout the life I've lived
Till now, I was quite dead, you must believe
Me, gentlemen.* All was a shadow then,
The beautiful, the good, the holy and
The bad; such was the darkness that appeared
To enwrap my mind from long ago, which hid
All this from me and made me blind to it.
But now I have come here and, as it were,
Slept in the temple of Asklepios*
And have been cured—I've come to life again   10
For good; I walk around, I talk, I think;
I have discovered now this sun,* so great,
So splendid, gentlemen; I see you in
Today's clear light, I see the sky, I see
The theatre and the Akropolis.

4. Papyrus Ghoran II (K–A 1017)

This papyrus fragment contains about 120 lines of an unknown
play, possibly by Menander.

Characters

PHAIDIMOS, a young man in love with X's DAUGHTER
X, the FATHER of the girl
NIKERATOS and CHAIRESTRATOS, friends of Phaidimos
A SERVANT

Phaidimos is in love with a girl whose father opposes the marriage. While he was abroad, Nikeratos and Chairestratos looked after his interests. When he returns, he finds that the girl is living in Nikeratos' house and is convinced that he plans to marry her himself.

Our fragment begins when Phaidimos has just returned home. A slave has come out of the father's house and is speaking to his mistress over his shoulder. Phaidimos, who is either already on stage or enters at this moment, thinks that the slave is responsible for the supposed loss of his girl.

The first seven lines are fragmentary but with heavy supplementation may be translated:

SLAVE. For you *I feel* less *pity*, mistress, *at*
　All this than for her father here, who's
　Just arrived and hasn't learnt a thing, it seems,　　　　　75
　Of what has happened . . .

Enter PHAIDIMOS.

　　　　　　　　I see him here.
　Hello, and welcome, Phaidimos. *I came*
　Straight *out* when I had heard that you were here.
PHAIDIMOS. Don't you come near me.　　　　　　　　80
SLAVE. 　　　　　　　　　　　But why ever not?
PHAIDIMOS. You ask me this and *dare* to look me in
　The face?
SLAVE. 　　　I do . . .
[Four lines fragmentary.]
PHAIDIMOS. . . . . you saw yourself . . .
SLAVE. . . . . luck.
　But to the gods . . .
PHAIDIMOS. . . . . Understanding.

[Then a lacuna of about fourteen lines.]

In this lacuna the girl's father must have entered and Phaidimos must have told him that his daughter had run away to Nikeratos' house. When our text resumes, the girl's father is speaking:

FATHER. On whose instructions? . . .

PHAIDIMOS. Your own behaviour was responsible.*   100

FATHER. Good god, what have you done to me, my child?
  Now I begin to understand. She's in
  There now apparently?

PHAIDIMOS.   Yes, she's in there.*

FATHER. What a thing to have done, my child! I never would
  Have thought it. Why, my child? You cast me off?

                                              [*Exit into his house*

       Enter NIKERATOS *from the city; at first he does not see* PHAIDIMOS.

NIKERATOS. I could not anywhere find Phaidimos,
  So I've turned round and come back here. I hope
  I was not wrong to send Chairestratos
  Down to the harbour. [*He sees* PHAIDIMOS] There's our friend.
  There's no mistaking him.

PHAIDIMOS [*seeing* NIKERATOS; *aside*]. . . .
  . . . *He's back again* to find his friend . . .   110
  . . . and how should I *behave to him*?

NIKERATOS. Greetings, my dearest friend. Embrace me, please.

PHAIDIMOS [*aside*]. Oh, what should I do now? We have been
      friends
  So close, so long . . . He loved me and he was . . .

[Lacuna of two lines, then ten fragmentary lines in which occur the words 'honour', 'companionship', 'proof of friendship'.]

PHAIDIMOS [*ironically*]. You have outdone *all others* by your deeds.
  You really are a friend beyond compare.   126

NIKERATOS. What's that?

PHAIDIMOS.   You had my interests at heart?

NIKERATOS. I thought so, yes.

PHAIDIMOS.   God, I consider men
  Who wrong their friends and look them in the face
  Braver than those who fight the enemy.   130

The soldiers share a common fear; both sides
Suppose that they are acting gloriously.
But treacherous friends! I've often wondered how
Their conscience lets them be so confident.

NIKERATOS. What makes you talk like this?

PHAIDIMOS.   O misery,
How utterly I have missed out on life!
What greater good have we in life than friends?
If I've not learnt and do not understand
How to judge men, and am deceived by some
Who scheme against me, others who're no help   140
As friends, what use is there in living on?

NIKERATOS. What do you mean? What has upset you so?

PHAIDIMOS. You ask me that?

NIKERATOS.   I do, and I'm amazed
To see you ranting on at me like this.

PHAIDIMOS. Tell me, you know I love the girl and I
Confided all to you, and did not hide
A thing?

NIKERATOS. You told me everything; I don't
Dispute that; but hold on!

PHAIDIMOS.   Hold on, indeed!
Her father meant to take my girl from me,
So then you thought it fair to marry her
Yourself, I know.

NIKERATOS.   You're wrong.

PHAIDIMOS.   How? Didn't you mean
To take her as your wife?   150

NIKERATOS.   Listen to me,
My friend.

PHAIDIMOS.   Listen? I have.

NIKERATOS.   You do not know—

PHAIDIMOS. I know it all.

NIKERATOS.   Before you've learnt the truth?
How do you know?

PHAIDIMOS.   The facts convict you of
Your falsity to me.

NIKERATOS.   Friend Phaidimos,

You've turned things upside down. I pretty well
Now realize why you are suspecting me.
Since you're in love I can forgive you, though
You've got me wrong.
PHAIDIMOS.   Are you persuading me
To hear a paradox? [*Aside*] What will he say?

Enter CHAIRESTRATOS *from the direction of the harbour.*

CHAIRESTRATOS. I did not reach the harbour. For I met   160
A fellow passenger of his who turned me back
And said that he had long since gone off here.
NIKERATOS [*to* PHAIDIMOS]. I've saved you, so that you should not—
CHAIRESTRATOS.   Who's that?
Nikeratos and Phaidimos himself,
I think. [*He goes up to* PHAIDIMOS] Warm greetings to you,
    Phaidimos.
PHAIDIMOS. The same to you, Chairestratos, *if you*
Will help a friend.
NIKERATOS.   Our friend here's giving me
A roughish passage.
CHAIRESTRATOS.   What is it? He must
Surely know that you—
PHAIDIMOS.   I did not expect,
Chairestratos, a man who claims to be
A friend of mine—
CHAIRESTRATOS.   Be quiet! For heaven's sake,
Say nothing, Phaidimos.
PHAIDIMOS.   Why not?
CHAIRESTRATOS.   Because
You'll soon regret it.   170
PHAIDIMOS.   Certainly, I'd like
To do so. Yes, I'll easily change my mind
When I have learnt the facts. But this man here—
CHAIRESTRATOS. I'll not stay here and let you say a thing
That's out of place, when I know all about
Nikeratos' doings. If you had three
Such friends, there's nothing you'd not do as far
As loyalty goes. But go away from us,

Nikeratos, so I can talk with him
Without you here.
NIKERATOS.   I'll go. [*To a* SERVANT] You come with me
                              [*Exit into the house with the* SERVANT

Five more fragmentary lines bring the act to a close; Chairestratos
must have taken Phaidimos off to tell him how Nikeratos had
guarded his interests. Of the next act there are fourteen
fragmentary lines which give no sense.

5. Papyrus Hamburgensis 656 (K–A 1089)

Moschion is in love with a girl (Dorkion) but needs money (to buy
her freedom?). A woman friend of Dorkion offers him jewellery
and clothes which he can pawn.

Characters

MOSCHION, a young man
A WOMAN FRIEND of DORKION
PARMENON, a servant of Moschion.
DORIS, a servant of the Woman

The first eight lines are deficient; with supplements they may be
translated:

WOMAN.   But, Moschion,
    Look here at these, the clothes and jewels . . . I've got.
    Then take them all for Dorkion, and you
    Can use them as security; *if you*
    Can't get a thousand drachmas for them,
    May I be damned . . .
MOSCHION.   Good lord!
WOMAN.   *If you succeed*
    And all goes well, you'll give them back to me;
    But if you can't do so, then I make them
    A contribution to help rescue her.
MOSCHION. By god our saviour, noble lady, *that's*   10
    Excellent. What else is one to say?

Some god from the Machine as in a tragedy*
Has given you ten minae, Parmenon.*
Now man can do the rest without god's help.
WOMAN. I'm going inside here to Dorkion.
For that's what I agreed with her just now.
MOSCHION. Then carry all these things with you inside.
WOMAN [*to a* SERVANT]. You take them, Doris; come with me.
    Good luck!

               [*Exit* WOMAN *into the house with* DORIS
MOSCHION. I want to go and see her, Parmenon,
    Myself.
PARMENON. Go in and tell her to cheer up   20
And comfort her.
MOSCHION.   That's what I mean to do.
               [MOSCHION *follows* WOMAN *into the house*

6. *Papyrus Oxyrhynchica 10 (K–A 1006)*

A slave is speaking who has some news which he does not intend
to communicate to his young master.

. . . But all the same I have to disregard *this news.*
[One and a half lines deficient:]
    For we . . . of those who're wronged by . . .
    The young man is on heat, in love, and he
    Will throw me in the pit if he should have   10
    The tiniest excuse. To tell him this—
    Not likely—that's old-fashioned, out of date.
    So someone may speak well of me? That stirs
    My bile. Affection for my boss? Don't make
    Me sick. Riches are sweet, the rest *is crap.*
    From humble and unlikely starting points
    Can come a great excess *of wealth,* but first
    I must win freedom, and, by god, perhaps
    My present disregard of this may be
    The start. For first young master will at once
    Come here and learn of this, the girl . . .

7. Papyrus Heidelberg 184. 11 and Papyrus Hibeh 5, a (K–A 1093)

Four hundred lines of this play survive on two papyri but most are too damaged to make sense. The Oxford text prints two passages which are in fair condition.

In the first of these (Pap. Heidelberg) the cook, Libys, is complaining of how cooks are accused of petty theft in comedies:

LIBYS. When happening to watch a comedy
　In which there is a cook, I often think
　That we should feel sorry for us, the cooks,
　And our profession, if it's things like those
　We steal. Cooks are accused and blamed for this:
　They make two joints of meat from one;* they slice
　A sausage, steal the middle bit, and then
　They join it back together; they mop up
　The olive oil and *mead* with sponges and
　Make off with them [One and a half lines deficient and
　　obscure:]
　and . . . bad luck . . . of taking things of value
B. And what do you do then, by Hestia?*
LIBYS. Why, two for one, of course . . .

In Pap. Hibeh STROBILOS, a slave, encouraged by A, pretends to think that B is a god:
A. Imagine you are running in the Olympic games.
　If you escape, you are a lucky man.

[*Exit* A

Enter B.

B. Good god, whatever's happened here?

[STROBILOS *affects not to see* B
STROBILOS. I know for certain now why this one place
　In all the world is holy beyond doubt
　And all the gods have made their dwelling here,
　And here they still exist, here they were born.
B. Strobilos!
STROBILOS. Apollo, what a heavenly scent!*
B. Strobilos, you wretched boy!

STROBILOS.   Who's calling me?
B. I am.
STROBILOS. And who are you? O greatest of   10
  The gods, how glad I am I've seen you.

The Oxford Classical Text (pp. 354–6) adds two papyrus texts
which Sandbach considers are from plays of Menander.

1. Papyrus Antinoopolis 55 K–A 1096

This contains seventeen fragments of which the following are the
most complete.

  (*a*) A slave, Dromon, is left by another character to consider
how he should proceed now his young master is in love:

DROMON. This way I shall be no use to you . . .   10
A. But if you think that this will profit you,
  Go on and do it. Why should I oppose you?   [*Exit*
DROMON. Well then, now that you are alone, Dromon,
  You must think over the affairs which you
  Intend to manage—briefly, not at length.
  Master's in love—it makes no odds with whom.

  (*b*) Two characters are about to make a sacrifice when they find
that someone else has already burnt an offering on the altar and
left a message written on a tablet:

                         O lord
  Apollo! Grant us luck! [*He sees that there is fresh fire on the altar*] But
    help! What's this?   21
  Someone has put a challenge(?) on the altar;
  There's fresh fire there.
B.   Hold on a little. What
  On earth is this?
A.   I want to see what this
  Is first.
B.   A writing tablet. Oh, the gods
  Are making me go mad.
A.   It makes no odds.
  I still judge you the loyalest of friends.

(*c*) Perhaps he ordered you to find some scheme
For him; you promised this. For what? Well, first
He is your guardian; secondly he is   85
Reliable; and thirdly, he's in love

     .   .   .

Surely you're right to help the lovers and
Yourself at once?

2. *Papyrus Berolinensis 21445 (K–A 1128)*

See *The Shield*, p. 138.

Explanatory Notes

The Bad-Tempered Man (Dyskolos)

4 *the shrine*: the shrines of Pan were often caves and there was such a shrine not far from the village of Phyle, in which dedications to Pan and the Nymphs have been found. For the purposes of the play Menander has placed it near Knemon's house and has made it large enough to hold a considerable gathering.

5 *Cholargos*: this was a deme of the city of Athens, some twenty miles from Phyle.

5 *to the Nymphs*: the Nymphs, spirits of water and trees, were often associated with Pan. The girl was putting garlands on their statues.

6 *burn down the door*: by ancient convention excluded lovers sometimes burnt down the door to gain access to the girl they loved.

9 *Perseus*: when Perseus was sent to kill the Gorgon Medusa, Athene, to help him, gave him winged sandals. He killed the Gorgon and carried off her head which turned all who looked on it to stone.

10 *a park . . . a public meeting place*: 'park', literally 'a colonnade'; there were several colonnades in the Agora of Athens where people would meet and talk. 'Public meeting place', literally 'the shrine of Leos', a hero whose shrine was a common meeting place.

10 *heavenly Twins*: Castor and Pollux.

14 *Some credit*: a metaphor from finance.

14 *rouses pity*: juries in the Athenian courts were particularly sympathetic to poor litigants who would appear in rags etc. to rouse their pity.

15 *Two talents*: this was a considerable sum; Kallippides, a millionaire, gives three talents as the dowry for his daughter.

16 *The god*: i.e. the god of love, Eros.

18 *just like a ship*: ships were sometimes hauled on rollers across an isthmus to shorten a journey; this must have been a bumpy passage.

18 *Paiania*: Paiania was a deme about twenty miles from Phyle where there was a shrine of Pan.

20 *the basket*: the sacred basket contained items needed for a sacrifice—the sacrificial knife, barley grains for scattering on the victim's head, etc.

21 *the rest themselves*: when an animal sacrifice was made, only the inedible parts were burnt on the altar for the gods; the rest, as Knemon says, was divided up and eaten by the worshippers.

23 *put on gloves*: literally, 'engage in sparring practice'; in ancient boxing, gloves were worn for sparring, leather thongs for contests.

24 *pumping beam*: this was a pivoted beam used for drawing water from wells etc.; 'a rope carrying a bucket was attached to the longer arm, a counterweight to the shorter; hauling on the rope allowed the bucket to descend into the well; the rope was then released and the counterweight caused it to bring the full bucket to the surface' (Sandbach).

24 *the donkey at the festival*: an adaptation of the proverbial expression 'I'm the donkey celebrating the Mysteries'; the donkey carried a load of sacred utensils etc. while the humans enjoyed themselves.

25 *as I am*: i.e. without bothering to dress up in his fine cloak again.

25 *be generous*: i.e. he will give generous gifts to Pan.

27 *libations*: drink offerings made as a preliminary to a sacrifice.

28 *the dog | In the well*: in Aesop's fables when a gardener went down a well to rescue his dog, who had fallen in, the dog bit him.

31 *God help me, what*: the metre changes to trochaics for the remainder of this scene.

38 *By both the goddesses*: i.e. Demeter and Persephone, a common women's oath.

38 from this point the dialogue (in iambic tetrameters catalectic) seems to have been accompanied with music.

41 *He's coming round*: the Greek means literally: 'the man's soft'; on this interpretation Getas means Knemon is softening on his resolve not to join the party.

42 *pour water out into the sand*: i.e. women's thirst for wine can never be satisfied, an old canard.

42 *Donax*: a slave called in just to help carry off Knemon.

The Girl from Samos (Samia)

45 *Pontos*: this is the Black Sea; Demeas had probably gone there for trade.

45 *the register*: at the age of 18 all male children of Athenian parents were enrolled on the register of their deme (parish).

45 *choregus*: the choregoi were wealthy citizens chosen to organize and pay for the production of plays for the dramatic festivals. They rivalled each other in the splendour of their productions.

45 *I led my tribe*: the citizen body of Athens was divided into ten tribes for political and military purposes. Moschion had been elected to command the cavalry division of his tribe (as a phylarch), an honorary position.

46 *Samos*: a large island off the coast of Turkey, famous for its courtesans.

46 *Adonis' festival*. the festival of Adonis, an eastern fertility deity, was celebrated in Attica in midsummer; women sowed seeds in pots and carried them up to the roof tops; their quick germination symbolized the rebirth of Adonis.

48 *sacrifice . . . cake*: wedding ceremonies included preliminary sacrifice, a ritual bath, and a banquet at which guests were given cakes made from sesame seeds and honey.

48 *Foul tenement*: unwanted babies were either exposed to die or farmed out to poor foster parents.

49 *Byzantium! just wormwood*: merchants en route to or from the Black Sea had to stop at Byzantium (Istanbul) to pay tolls. Wormwood, an extremely bitter herb, flourished round Byzantium.

51 *lustral water*: see note on 'ritual water' on p. 298.

54 *seeds of sesame*: sesame seeds were needed for the ritual wedding cake.

56 *ritual basket*: this contained items needed for the sacrifice—the sacrificial knife, barley grains for scattering over the victim's head, etc.

59 *Apollo here*: Parmenon points to the statue of Apollo which stood by the house door.

60 *O citadel of Kekrops' land*: quoted from a lost play of Euripides. In his passion Demeas launches into the language of tragedy but quickly recalls himself (Kekrops was a mythical king of Athens; his citadel is the Akropolis, to which Demeas could gesture from the theatre).

60 *Helen*: Helen, who deserted her husband Menelaus and fled to Troy with Paris, was the archetype of the faithless woman.

63 *the accustomed | Offerings*: when an animal was sacrificed, the Olympian gods received the fat and bones and other inedible bits, burnt on the altar. The meat was divided amongst the participants and sometimes portions were sent to friends who had not been at the sacrifice.

64 *Wife . . . him*: the metre changes to trochaics, which continue for the whole of this act.

67 *Loxias*: a title of Apollo.

68 *Tereus, Oedipus, Thyestes*: these were the most famous incestuous characters in mythology. Tereus raped his sister-in-law, Philomela, and cut out her tongue to prevent her telling anyone; Oedipus married his own mother, Jocasta, unawares; Thyestes seduced Areope, the wife of his brother Atreus.

68 *Amyntor's rage on*: Amyntor's son, Phoenix, was said to have seduced his father's mistress; Amyntor, in his rage, blinded him. Phoenix, like Moschion, was innocent.

68 *absit omen*: literally, 'I spit (into my bosom), as men say and bow to Adrasteia'; saying that he would rather have the notorious Diomnestos as son-in-law than Moschion might result in this misfortune, so he takes ritual precautions. Spitting to avert evil was a common practice; Adrasteia was a goddess who punished presumptuous words. Nothing is known of Diomnestos; there may be a reference to some contemporary scandal.

69 *barber's shop . . . stoa*: barber's shops, where Athenians went for their daily shave, were venues where news and gossip were exchanged. Athens was liberally supplied with stoas (colonnades) where people could sit in the shade and gossip.

69 *Thracian*: the Thracians were notoriously savage.

73 *Zeus . . . gold*: Acrisios, king of Argos, received a prophecy that his daughter Danae would bear a son who would kill him; he imprisoned her in a tower of bronze, but Zeus visited her is a shower of gold and she bore a son, Perseus, who, when he was grown up, accidentally killed his grandfather with a discus.

73 *Chairephon*: a notorious parasite who attended parties unimvited.

74 *Androcles*: nothing is known about him.

75 *Baktra or for Karia*: Baktria, north of Afghanistan, was the remotest

area where a Greek mercenary might find employment at this time. Mercenaries were often employed in Karia (south-west Turkey).

76 *You're completely . . . I believe*: the metre changes to trochaics, which continue for the rest of the play.

77 *Hephaistos' flame*: Hephaistos was the god of fire.

79 *lawful children*: Nikeratos hands his daughter to Moschion with the customary betrothal formula, 'for a crop of legitimate children'.

80 *lustral water*: before a marriage, bride and bridegroom had a ritual bath in water brought from a sacred spring; the 'bathboy' was a young relative of the bridegroom who brought the water; the piper provided music to accompany the wedding procession.

80 *Bacchus*: Dionysos, patron god of drama, in whose theatre the plays were performed. These lines are a form of the conventional ending of all the plays, which conclude with a prayer for victory in the dramatic contest.

The Arbitration (Epitrepontes)

81 *Syros*: the name only occurs once in the play (line 269) where it is in the diminutive form 'Syriskos'. A mosaic from a house in Mytilene, portraying the arbiration scene names him as 'Syros'. The Oxford text prefers to call him Syriskos, but perhaps there were particular reasons for Smikrines' use of the diminutive—e.g. to mark his inferiority.

82 *dancing girl*: literally 'harp-girl'.

83 *I've sprinkled salt . . .*: this is probably a proverbial expression, meaning 'I've added fuel to the fire'.

84 *two obols a pint*: in normal years a pint of wine cost one-third of an obol (there were six obols to a drachma and 6,000 drachmas to a talent).

84 *Four talents*: this was a very large dowry; the millionaire Kallipides in the *Dyskolos* gives a dowry of three talents for his daughter.

85 *Yes, yours*: Habrotonon appears to mean that if she is to succeed in her profession, lots of houses neeed to be turned upside down with husbands being unfaithful to their wives.

86 *To arbitrate*: arbitration by a neutral party was commonly used in a dispute and the decisions of the arbiter were binding.

89 *Part of my find*: i.e. the baby.

90 *a Neleus and a Pelias*: in Sophocles' *Tyro* Neleus and Pelias, the children of Tyro and the god Poseidon, were exposed at birth and rescued by a goatherd, who brought them up until they were recognized by the tokens left with them; they were then able to save their mother from maltreatment by their stepmother.

94 *Act 3*: Sandbach and others think that Act 3 begins on the next day; in both tragedies and comedies the action is usually confined to one day but there are exceptions to this rule.

95 *Athene's basket*: the girls who carried baskets of offerings in the Panathenaic procession had to be virgins.

95 *the Tauropolia*: this was a night festival in honour of Artemis in which women took part.

96 *Aphrodite*: the goddess of love.

98 *By both the goddesses*: i.e. Demeter and Persephone, a common women's oath.

102 *some scheme*: Chairestratos perhaps suspects, as Karion supposes, that Habrotonon is scheming to become mistress of the house.

102 *not | Yet had a child*: divorce was easier if the wife had not had a child. The irony of Smikrines' remark is typical of Menander.

103 *one girl*: the meaning of these lines is disputed; Arnott thinks the same girl, i.e. Habrotonon, is referred to each time but Smikrines will not name her.

103 *The alien register*: resident aliens (metics) could not form a legal marriage with a citizen. Smikrines means that Charisios is behaving as if he was not legally married to Pamphile.

104 *Keep her*: i.e. keep Pamphile.

104 *my hopes*: later it appears that Chairestratos is himself in love with Habrotonon; he hoped to win possession of her. We do not know what task he had been assigned.

104 *flee a rogue*: this looks like a proverbial expression.

105 *the Skira ... the Thesmophoria*: these were women's festivals; Smikrines imagines Charisios having to pay for the expenses of both his women who took part in them.

105 *the docks*: i.e. the Piraeus, the port of Athens; Smikrines imagines that Charisios will have installed his mistress there.

105 *the Pythia*: the priestess of Apollo at Delphi, through whom Apollo made his unerring prophecies.

105 *Pamphile*: The text of Pamphile's reply to her father is mutilated and the sense is often obscure. She starts with an apology for arguing with her father, who is wiser than she and speaks out of love for her. She then takes up various points he has made, some of which may be lost in the lacunae; he had said perhaps that bad luck had landed her in a bad marriage and that she should not follow the example of fallen women(?). She dismisses these topics and, secondly, goes on to his attack on Charisios' behaviour (drunken orgies etc.?), saying that there is nothing wrong in his enjoying himself with a few friends. She then switches to what she ought to do if Charisios suffers ill luck. She married him to share his life (this is quoted by Charisios (line 920) and will not desert him even though he has stumbled and keeps his mistress in their house.

106 *No thanks*: the Greek is ambiguous; it either means this, or 'That's fine for me'.

106 *such a plight*: i.e. a second unhappy marriage (if she obeys her father's orders).

113 *our captain*: there was an ancient belief that every man was assigned a daimon or spirit which controlled his fate. But Onesimos has confused two ideas: (1) a man's character brings him good or ill fortune, (2) man has in him a guardian spirit which will reward good deeds, but punish offences. (See Sandbach, p. 378.)

115 *nature . . . this*: Onesimos quotes from Euripides' *Auge*. 'was born for this': i.e. for bearing children.

115 *your gesturing*: Sophrone is acknowledging the truth of what Onesimos says with wild gestures.

115 *with Charisios*: Smikrines has still not grasped what Onesimos is telling him.

The Shield (Aspis)

116 *tutor*: the Greek word means 'child-leader'; he was not a tutor in our sense but a loyal slave given the task of escorting the child and guarding him from moral and physical danger.

118 *the campaign*: Kleostratos had been campaigning as a mercenary in Lykia (southern Turkey) in order to make enough money to provide a dowry for his sister.

120 *forty minae*: 24 kilograms.

121 *Prologue*: Menander uses a postponed prologue in several plays to tell the audience facts they needed to know to appreciate the dramatic situation.

121 *it would not be right*: divinities avoided the pollution of death.

122 *his right*: by Attic law her eldest male relative might claim an heiress in marriage, if neither father nor brother was alive, in order to keep the family's property intact.

124 *Know yourself*: this was the famous maxim inscribed on the walls of Apollo's temple at Delphi, generally interpreted as meaning 'Remember that you are mortal'.

126 *empty flask*: the cook expected his assistant Spinther (= Spark) to steal a flask full of olive oil while the household was distraught.

126 *Aristeides*: this fifth-century statesman was so upright that he was known as 'Aristeides the just'.

126 *from Phrygia*: Phrygians were traditionally said to be effeminate. Thracians were notoriously randy and Getans, a Thracian tribe, were, according to the waiter, the manliest of all.

127 *the mills*: errant slaves were sent to the treadmills for punishment; Daos implies that the Getans' manliness took the form of criminal activity.

128 *restitution of his rights*: 'property that went with a woman was always regarded as being for the benefit of her children . . . Hence if Chairestratos' plan were carried through, a child born to the girl might argue that the arrangement had cheated him out of the property that was his by right' (Sandbach, p. 85).

133 *There is no man . . . all things*: the opening line of Euripides' *Stheneboia*. The following lines contain quotations from Aeschylus and other writers of tragedy.

134 *the 'doctor'*: Chaireas' friend disguised as a doctor speaks stage Doric, which is by tradition translated into pseudo-Scottish.

135 *I maunna . . . man*: this line, which could scarcely be bettered, is lifted from Norma Miller's Penguin translation of Menander.

136 *No doubt . . . drains*: the text of these lines is clear enough but their sense obscure. When a death occurred, the house was sealed up, so perhaps messages could only reach the outside world via the drains. There may be some contemporary allusion, now lost.

The Girl with the Shaven Head (Perikeiromene)

141 *the war began*: in the wars between the successors of Alexander the Great, Corinth was several times besieged by rivals between 315 and 304 BC.

143 *Boys!*: Doris calls on slaves in Myrrhine's house to open the door.

144 *master*: i.e. Moschion.

144 *Daos . . . no grain of truth*: the metre changes to trochaics, which continue for the rest of this scene.

145 *miller . . . treadmill*: errant slaves were sent to the mills to work the treadmill.

145 *farming contracts*: although the text is mutilated, the general sense is clear, that as Commander-in-Chief Daos would make a huge profit by farming out contracts.

145 *May no good old woman . . . honey*: this appears to be a proverb which suggests that all shop-keepers are dishonest.

146 *forgiveness | for this boasting*: literally, 'now is the time to pay respects to Adrasteia'; Adrasteia was the goddess who brought retribution on those who boasted.

149 *my master*: i.e. Myrrhine's husband.

149 *A prophet*: seers were regularly attached to army commanders. Daos ironically remarks that Sosias' grasp of the situation is as firm as that of a clairvoyant.

149 *Worth twopence*: literally, 'four obol men'; four obols a day was apparently the lowest pay for a mercenary soldier.

149 *tin-pot*: Arnott's translation of 'four drachma men'; four drachmas would have been very low pay for an officer.

150 *our doughty lads*: literally, 'light-shield boys', i.e. peltasts, the most formidable soldiers of the time.

151 *he's*: he is Pataikos.

152 *an erection*: this brilliant translation of Sosias' double entendre is taken from Arnott.

153 *lodge complaint*: a complainant might lodge a private law-suit if after discussion with the alleged wrongdoer he failed to reach agreement.

155 *His standing in society*: Moschion is, apparently, the child of wealthy parents, Glykera a poor foundling and a soldier's cast-off mistress.

157 *what members . . . survive*: Pataikos has recognized the tokens but cannot yet be sure that his children survive.

The following lines are tragic in tone and style; the alternation of single lines (stichomythia) is a common feature of tragedy and there is an echo of Euripides in line 788 (fr. 484. 3).

158 *to her*: i.e. Myrrhine. Glykera has sworn to Myrrhine that she will not reveal what she knows about Moschion's origins.

160 *the basket*: i.e. the ritual basket which contained the objects necessary for a proper sacrifice (the sacrificial knife etc.).

161 *lawful children*: the customary betrothal formula.

162 *Philinos*: perhaps a friend of Pataikos not mentioned elsewhere in our text, or possibly Myrrhine's husband.

The Man she Hated (Misoumenos)

NB Line numbers are those of the Loeb text, vol. ii.

164 *the proverbial dog*: e.g. 'It's not fit to let a dog out on a night like this'.

165 *you lucky man*: this is a literal translation of a phrase which is normally used as a polite greeting, e.g. 'My good sir', but Getas here takes it literally.

165 *Magnetic poles!*: it was known that opposite poles repelled each other.

166 *And so she is*: Thrasonides agrees with Getas that Krateia is spoiled.

169 *A suppliant branch*: suppliants, going to a shrine to ask the gods for help, carried branches of olive.

172 *I wish I had*: Demeas means he no longer has a home, since it has been destroyed by the war.

173 *are you carrying . . . suppliant branches*: this supplement, which assumes that Krateia was on her way to seek sanctuary, is highly speculative, as is Krateia's reply.

173 *Now you*: i.e. Krateia's father

174 *both*: i.e. Demeas and Krateia.

179 *a crop of lawful children*: this was the customary betrothal formula.

The Man from Sikyon (Sikyonios)

The play is entitled *The Man from Sikyon* in nine ancient references, *The Men from Sikyon* in three others. As Stratophanes, the chief character in the play, thinks he was born a Sikyonian and as there are no other Sikyonians in the play, the first is probably the correct title.

181 *Smikrines*: the name of Stratophanes' father occurs only once in the extant fragments, in the abbreviated form *Sm*, but as Menander uses this name for older men in other plays (e.g. *The Arbitration* and *The Shield*), we may fairly assume that this name is correct.

182 *the daughter of this man*: the Prologue deity must be referring to Philoumene and Kichesias but the context of this line is lost.

182 *they . . . the three*: i.e. the pirates . . . Philoumene, Dromon and Philoumene's nurse.

183 *one man*: i.e. Moschion.

184 him: Stratophanes; warned by Theron that Moschion is in love with Philoumene, he tells him not to mention it again.

185 *he*: presumably the Boeotian to whom Stratophanes owed many talents would be enraged by some scheme of Theron's to avoid payment.

185 *surely . . . over there*: the metre changes to trochaics.

186 *the treaty*: there were arrangements for the settlement of commercial disputes between parties of different states.

187 *Eleusinios*: I follow Arnott's view that the democrat who enters with Smikrines (unnamed) and the man who enters on his withdrawal are separate characters and that the name of the latter is Eleusinios, a common name in this period.

188 *These people's property*: obscure; the Democrat is perhaps accusing Smikrines of attempting to seize the property of Stratophanes on behalf of the Boeotian creditor. This may link up with an earlier scene which is lost.

188 *immigrant*: the word literally means 'a tray'; trays of offerings were carried in sacred processions by resident aliens (metics); the rights of metics did not include free speech.

188 *a wisp of smoke*: a proverbial expression for something unimportant. Eleusinios seems to know that Smikrines was making inquiries about Stratophanes and has seen something which he thinks may be relevant.

188 *I happened . . . way*: Eleusinios embarks on his long, rambling account with an allusion to the messenger's speech from Euripides' *Orestes*, which starts, 'I happened to be on my way from the country to the city gates . . .' (line 866).

188 *And they're . . . our land*: quoted from Euripides' *Orestes* 920.

188 *deme*: Attica was divided into 139 demes (parishes) for political purposes. Eleusinios' fellow demesman was going to make a sacrifice of an ox to which all members of the deme would be invited.

190 *the priestess*: i.e. the priestess of Demeter.

191 *someone shouted*: members of the crowd shout abuse at Moschion who answers back; his last reply, 'Bless you!' must be ironical.

192 *your body . . . child*: it seems that friends from Sikyon who were childless asked Stratophanes' Athenian parents to let them adopt one of their children.

193 *Kichesias Skambonides*: i.e. Kichesias from the deme of the Skambonidai. In his indignation Kichesias gives himself his official title—name and deme.

193 *just now*: Theron had first tried to bribe Kichesias to say that he knew Philoumene was the daughter of Kichesias, now he wanted Kichesias to impersonate himself.

193 *Halai*: there were two coastal demes called Halai.

196 *pale*: paleness was considered beautiful in women.

196 *ride upon the cart*: the bridegroom was accompanied on the cart which fetched the bride to her new home by a 'best man'.

Twice a Swindler (Dis Exapaton)

201 *talking to | A corpse*: a proverbial expression for speaking to people who are deaf to what is said to them.

202 *He*: i.e. Nikoboulos' friend in Ephesus who had borrowed the money.

202 *with Theotimos*: confused by Syros' story, Nikoboulos is checking out the details.

202 *he*: i.e. again, the man who originally borrowed the money.

203 *grant me what I ask*: Sostratos has been pleading on behalf of Syros and asking Nikoboulos to forgive him.

204 *In there*: he points to the house where the two Bacchises are living.

204 *The rest*: i.e. the fact that Moschos was a close friend and in a position of special trust.

The Hero (Heros)

207 *treadmill*: errant slaves were sent for punishment to work the tread-mill.

208 *The usual rites*: these might be either cremation and burial of the ashes in a tomb or inhumation. Both would no doubt cost more money than a poor man could easily afford.

209 *Serves you?*: this is Arnott's interpretation of the Greek which means literally: 'a girl/a prostitute?' Daos does not at first grasp Getas' double entendre and agrees.

The Lyre-Player (Kitharistes)

214 *Kleo's*: there is a gap in the papyrus here and this name is inserted *exempli gratia* as the name of the mother of the woman of Ephesus whom Phanias has 'married' and who turns out to be Athenian by birth; at this stage Phanias only knows that she came from a Greek city and is free.

215 *beside the Herms*: the statues of Hermes in the Agora were a meeting place for rich young men.

217 *Phanias Euonymeus*: the Athenian deme of Euonymon lay to the south of the city. Moschion's father assumes that the girl is an Ephesian but Moschion explains that her father came from Athens.

The Farmer (Georgos)

220 *the boy*: i.e. Gorgias, Myrrhine's son; as Myrrhine was a widow, Gorgias was head of the family and responsible for his sister.

220 *their door*: i.e. the door of Myrrhine's house.

220 *By both the goddesses*: Demeter and Persephone; a common women's oath.

221 *greenery*: the green branches were to deck out the house for the wedding ceremony.

221 *pious*: the fields were pious because they produced flowers sacred to the gods (myrtle for Aphrodite, ivy for Dionysos, etc.).

The Apparition (Phasma)

226 *tutor*: the Greek word means 'child-leader'; he was not a tutor in our sense but a loyal slave appointed to accompany a boy and guard him from physical and moral dangers.

227 *this*: perhaps his melancholy and sleeplessness.

227 *the bride* [*to be*]: i.e. Pheidias' betrothed.

230 *give food to prisoners*: obscure; Sandbach suggests that the prisoner is Pheidias, locked up because he is shammimg mad.

The Flatterer (Kolax)

233 *a party*: the party which Pheidias had to organize was probably in honour of Aphrodite Pandemos, held on the fourth day of each month, and this party may have formed the conclusion of the play (see fragment 1, p. 238).

234 *on double pay*: i.e. a soldier who received twice the basic wage; he was something like a corporal.

235 *this boy*: i.e. the slave who was carrying the wine jars.

236 *Astyanax*: a famous athlete who won the pancration at the Olympic Games three times running.

237 *My neighbour*: i.e. Pheidias.

237 *Odysseus*: in the *Iliad* (2. 637) Odysseus led twelve ships to Troy with several hundred men; the speaker is muddled, perhaps thinking of the one ship which survived the attack of the Laestrygonians on his return journey (*Odyssey* 10. 130 ff.).

237 *the foreigner*: i.e. Bias.

The Girl Possessed (Theophoroumene)

242 *outdoors*: women did not leave the house unaccompanied; the girl's behaviour was eccentric, if not mad.

242 *a Korybantic hymn*: the Korybantes were nature spirits associated with the cult of Kybele; their wild dances were accompanied by flutes, cymbals, and drums.

243 *Agdos*: Agdistis was an Asiatic goddess identified with Cybele, whose name comes from Mount Agdos in Phrygia.

244 *our play*: i.e. the play of life.

The Girl from Perinthos (Perinthia)

249 *That's fine*: if the supplements are here correct, this must be ironical.

250 *easygoing . . . master*: Laches is quoting words used earlier about him by Daos. See quotation 3 below.

250 *superlative | Intelligence*: obscure; perhaps Daos had earlier claimed to be superlatively intelligent.

The Man from Carthage (Karchedonios)

253 *the register*: all free Athenians at the age of 18 were registered on their deme roll and had to show that both their parents were Athenian.

253 *You scamp*: the Greek word means literally 'runaway slave'.

253 *registered according to the laws*: a foreigner could not legally marry an Athenian; it is hard to see how the Carthaginian could hope to be registered on the deme list and then contract a marriage with an Athenian girl.

253 *Boreas*: the god of the North wind.

The Women drinking Hemlock (Koneiazomenai)

255 *two talents*: two (or three) talents was the usual amount for a dowry in Menander's plays. The father of the bride in this case seems to have added five minae (= five hundred drachmas) for her trousseau.

255 *fit as a flea*: there was a Greek proverb 'healthier than a tick'; Arnott suggests this translation as the nearest English equivalent.

256 *so let no one . . . in good*: these two lines and a half are quoted by Stobaeus, *Eclogae* 4. 44–5 as coming from *The Women drinking Hemlock*.

Title unknown

259 *do you refuse . . . hand*: Laches offers Chaireas his daughter in marriage to compensate for his losing the girl to whom he claims to have been betrothed.

259 *Persuade him*: i.e. accept that his daughter is married to Moschion.

259 *We have | Been wronged*: Kleainetos, who we find is also in the plot to deceive Laches, pretends to be indignant on hearing that Moschion has married his daughter after he has raped her.

262 *The last fragment*: the distribution of parts and the meaning of these lines is disputed; Arnott's interpretation, which I follow, makes the best sense.

262 *Chaireas*:

A. Selection of Fragments Quoted by Other Authors

A. Quotations from Named Plays

263 *Let the die be cast*: these were the words spoken by Julius Caesar when he decided to lead his army over the Rubicon and so start a civil war. Caesar had a great admiration for Menander and he may have been quoting from this play.

263 *Dodona's bowl | Of bronze*: at the oracle of Zeus at Dodona a great bronze cauldron, set on a pillar, resounded long when struck with a whip; hence it became proverbial for long-winded speakers.

266 *Monimos*: a contemporary of Menander and a follower of the Cynic philosopher Krates; the Cynics rejected all the apparatus of civilization, never washed, and supported themselves by begging.

268 *Mendean . . . Thasian*: expensive wines.

268 *almost a talent*: this is a wild exaggeration of the cost.

268 *Kallimedon*: an unpopular politician who was exiled in 318 BC; the implication that he was still in Athens makes this one of Menander's earlier plays. Kallimedon was a glutton and the implication here is that he would have risked his life to save an eel, a favourite dish from the altar fire. The eel is 'his kin' because he was nicknamed 'langouste' on account of his squint(!).

Old Comedy was full of attacks on contemporary politicians;

Menander seldom attacks contemporaries, and here he attacks Kallimedon for his gluttony, not his politics.

268 *one good thing . . . produce*: there appears to be an hiatus in the text, since after saying a wife produces one good thing, three other benefits of marriage are listed.

269 *Theophilos . . . deep*: this line is adapted from the opening of Euripides' *Troiades*; hence its tragic tone.

269 *vessel*: the Greek word here (*kantharos*) can mean either a drinking cup or a boat. The speaker refers to a golden cup but Straton takes it to mean a boat.

270 *plucked out*: this practice was considered a sign of effeminacy.

270 *Ktesippos*: a spendthrift who even sold the stones of his father's tomb to pay for his pleasures.

270 *Chairephon*: a notorious parasite who never paid his contribution to a party (see *Samia* 603).

271 *sleep . . . either side*: literally: 'to sleep on either ear', a proverbial expression for tranquil sleep.

271 *ten talents*: this was a vast fortune; three talents is the usual dowry given by rich fathers in Menander.

271 *vampire*: literally, 'a Lamia', a monster who ate human flesh.

273 *Arcadians*: Arcadia, the central plateau of the Peloponnese, was entirely land-locked.

273 *Ionian*: Ionians were notorious both for their wealth and for their sexual proclivities.

273 *quickly back . . . came*: we have here a variation on the recurrent theme most famously expressed by Sophocles (*Oedipus at Kolonos* 1224–7): 'Not to be born is best, but second far, when a man is born, to return to where he came from as soon as possible.' But Menander combines with this the consolation of the joy which comes from contemplating nature.

273 *festival*: life is like a public festival to which all flock to waste their time in trivialities. If you leave early (die young), you will be better provided for the journey (to death—you will not have wasted your spiritual resources).

274 *These days*: the point of the cook's complaint is that in the old days the chef made elaborate dishes which were followed by cakes and desserts. Now the cook only makes the simple dishes (cakes and buns etc.) while some skivvy roasts the meat; and the courses are

now served in the wrong order. 'Scent and garlands' would not normally be put on until the main dinner was over and drinking was started.

B. *Fragments from Unnamed Plays Attributed to Menander*

277 *Anacharsis*: one of the Seven Wise Men, who according to tradition lived in the sixth century BC; he came from Scythia (south Russia).

277 *Epicharmos*: a Sicilian writer of comedies who lived in the early fifth century; but he was also, according to tradition, a philosopher and scientist.

277 *Just give . . . serve your needs*: i.e. even the traditional gods can be bribed.

277 *if someone sneezes*: sneezing was considered a bad omen.

277 *gentlemen*: the speaker is addressing the audience.

278 *For fortune . . . wise*: this line (Euripides, Fragment 598) seems to have got here by mistake

278 *Prometheus*: he fashioned human beings from clay. To help them, he stole fire from heaven and for this was punished by Zeus, who nailed him to the rocks in the Caucasus mountains. In the accepted tradition he was the champion of men against the gods. But the speaker here makes him the enemy of man, who created woman to plague him.

278 *torch-race*: there was at Athens a torch-race held in honour of Prometheus.

Fragments of Doubtful Authorship

284 *a favour*: it is uncertain whether a father could legally break up his daughter's marriage without her consent but in practice some fathers may have felt entitled to; if he agreed not to, it would be a favour.

284 *incurring shame*: i.e. if her father did break up the marriage, she would not incur the shame of resisting her father's decision.

284 *gentlemen*: he addresses the audience.

284 *slept in the temple of Asklepios*: the sick who slept in the temple of Asklepios, the god of healing, were cured by him in the night.

284 *sun*: the theatre was in the open; the speaker could point to the sun and the Akropolis which rose up immediately behind the theatre.

286 *Your own behaviour was responsible*: the girl's father asks who said she was to go to Nikeratos' house; Phaidimos answers that it was his (the father's) fault, presumably because he would not allow the girl to marry him and so he threw her into the arms of Nikeratos.

286 *in there*: i.e. in Nikeratos' house.

290 *god from the Machine*: when the plot of a tragedy was ending in an impasse, sometimes a god appeared on a platform (Machine) to resolve all difficulties (e.g. at the end of Euripides' *Electra*).

290 *given you ten minae, Parmenon*: evidently Parmenon had been given the job of raising the money to rescue Dorkion. Ten minae equal 1,000 drachmas.

291 *They make two joints of meat from one*: having divided the joint, they steal one half.

291 *Hestia*: the goddess of the hearth, at which the cook worked.

291 *what a heavenly scent*: a divine odour was thought to emanate from the gods.

The Oxford World's Classics Website

www.worldsclassics.co.uk

- Browse the full range of Oxford World's Classics online

- Sign up for our monthly e-alert to receive information on new titles

- Read extracts from the Introductions

- Listen to our editors and translators talk about the world's greatest literature with our Oxford World's Classics audio guides

- Join the conversation, follow us on Twitter at OWC_Oxford

- Teachers and lecturers can order inspection copies quickly and simply via our website

www.worldsclassics.co.uk

American Literature

British and Irish Literature

Children's Literature

Classics and Ancient Literature

Colonial Literature

Eastern Literature

European Literature

Gothic Literature

History

Medieval Literature

Oxford English Drama

Poetry

Philosophy

Politics

Religion

The Oxford Shakespeare

A complete list of Oxford World's Classics, including Authors in Context, Oxford English Drama, and the Oxford Shakespeare, is available in the UK from the Marketing Services Department, Oxford University Press, Great Clarendon Street, Oxford OX2 6DP, or visit the website at www.oup.com/uk/worldsclassics.

In the USA, visit www.oup.com/us/owc for a complete title list.

Oxford World's Classics are available from all good bookshops. In case of difficulty, customers in the UK should contact Oxford University Press Bookshop, 116 High Street, Oxford OX1 4BR.

	Classical Literary Criticism
	The First Philosophers: The Presocrates and the Sophists
	Greek Lyric Poetry
	Myths from Mesopotamia
APOLLODORUS	**The Library of Greek Mythology**
APOLLONIUS OF RHODES	**Jason and the Golden Fleece**
APULEIUS	**The Golden Ass**
ARISTOPHANES	**Birds and Other Plays**
ARISTOTLE	**The Nicomachean Ethics**
	Physics
	Politics
BOETHIUS	**The Consolation of Philosophy**
CAESAR	**The Civil War**
	The Gallic War
CATULLUS	**The Poems of Catullus**
CICERO	**Defence Speeches**
	The Nature of the Gods
	On Obligations
	Political Speeches
	The Republic and The Laws
EURIPIDES	**Bacchae and Other Plays**
	Heracles and Other Plays
	Medea and Other Plays
	Orestes and Other Plays
	The Trojan Women and Other Plays
HERODOTUS	**The Histories**
HOMER	**The Iliad**
	The Odyssey